P9-EEG-138

Interactive Homework Workbook

Grade 2

Scott Foresman • Addison Wesley

enVisionMATH™ California

Scott Foresman is an imprint of

PEARSON

pearsonschool.com

Glenview, Illinois • Boston, Massachusetts • Chandler, Arizona • Shoreview, Minnesota • Upper Saddle River, New Jersey

ISBN – 13: 978-0-328-38442-6

ISBN – 10: 0-328-38442-9

Copyright © Pearson Education, Inc. or its affiliate(s). All Rights Reserved. Printed in the United States of America. This publication is protected by copyright and permission should be obtained from the publisher prior to any prohibited reproduction, storage in a retrieval system, or transmission in any form or by any means, electronic, mechanical, photocopying, recording, or likewise. For information regarding permission(s), write to: Pearson School Rights and Permissions, One Lake Street, Upper Saddle River, New Jersey 07458.

11 V0N4 15 14 13

Pearson, Scott Foresman/Addison Wesley, and enVisionMath California are trademarks, in the U.S. and/or other coutries, of Pearson Education, Inc. or its affiliate(s).

Contents

Name ______________________________

Reteaching
1-1

Writing Addition Number Sentences

How many counters are there in all?
Add the parts.

2 + 4 = 6
is called an
addition sentence.

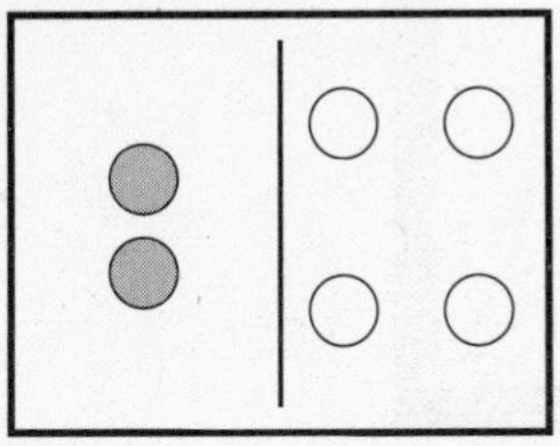

2 plus 4 equals 6.

2 and 4 is 6

Part Part Whole

2 + 4 = 6

Write the addition sentence for each problem.

1.

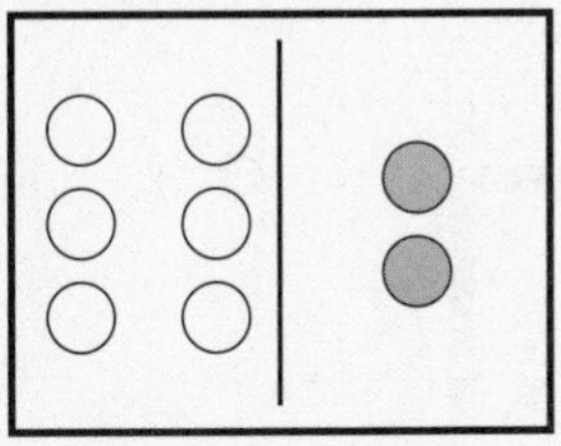

How many counters in all?

____ + ____ = ____

2.

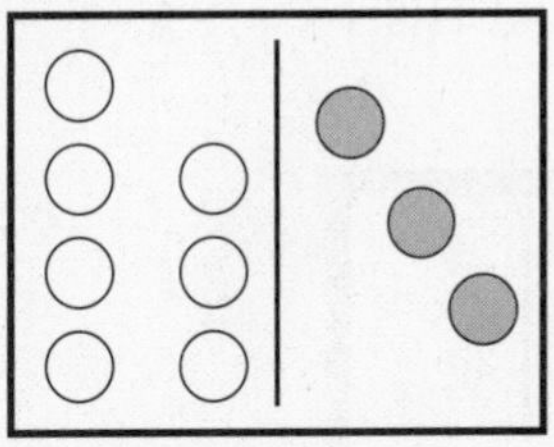

How many counters in all?

____ + ____ = ____

3.

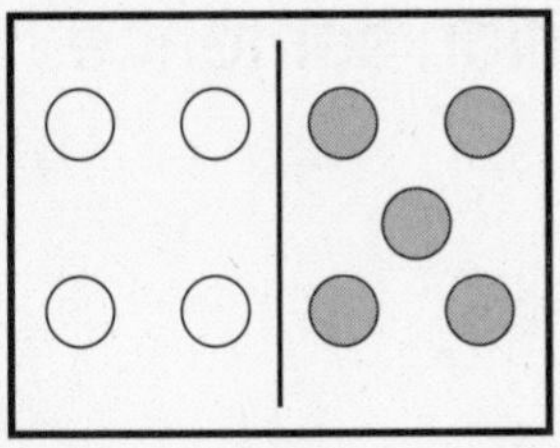

How many counters in all?

____ + ____ = ____

4.

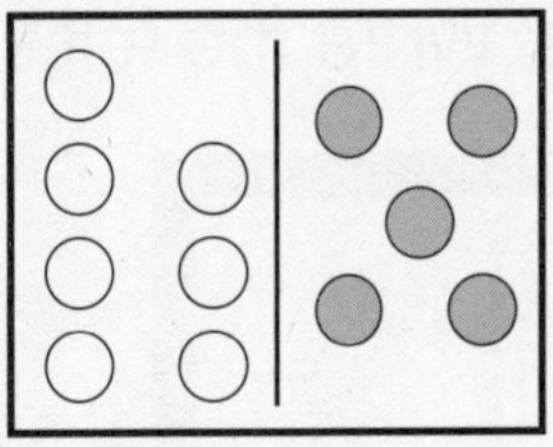

How many counters in all?

____ + ____ = ____

© Pearson Education, Inc. 2

Name ______________________

Practice
1-1

Writing Addition Number Sentences

Write an addition sentence for the picture.

1.

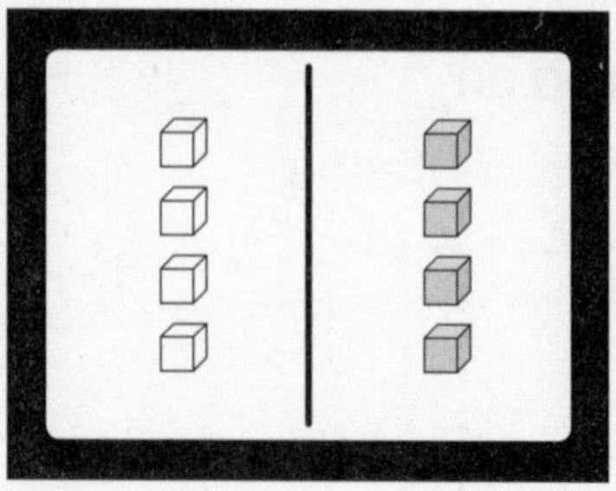

4 + 4 = 8

2.

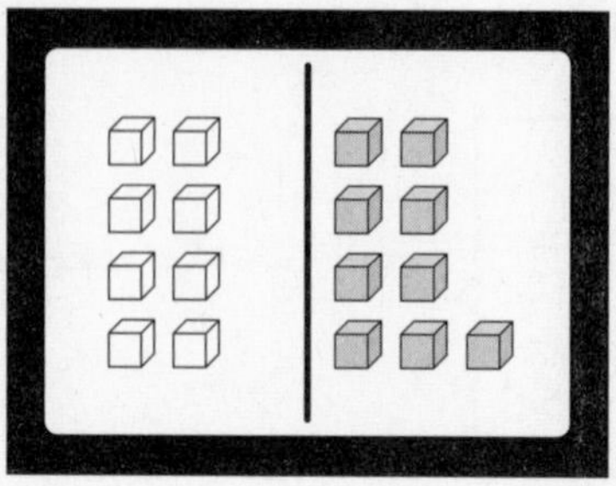

____ + ____ = ____

3. Ann has 5 white rocks. She also has 6 gray rocks. Which picture shows how many white and gray rocks Ann has?

○ 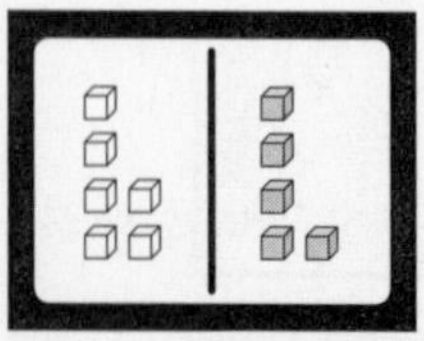

○ 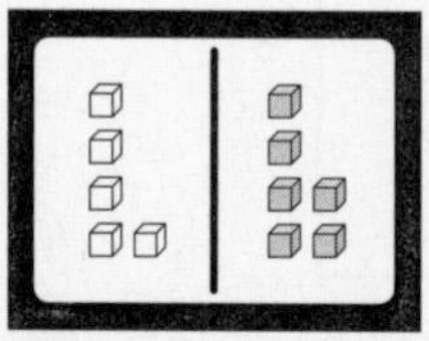

○ 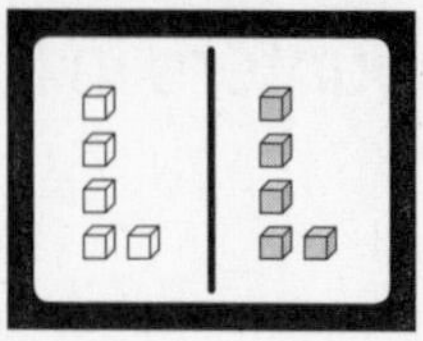

○ 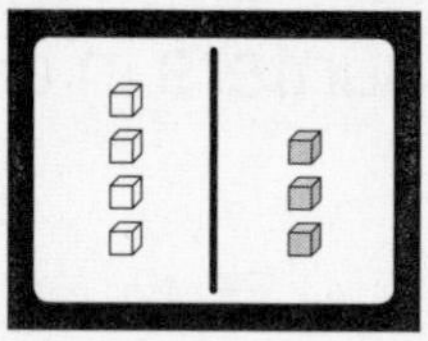

4. Algebra Write the missing number in the addition sentence.

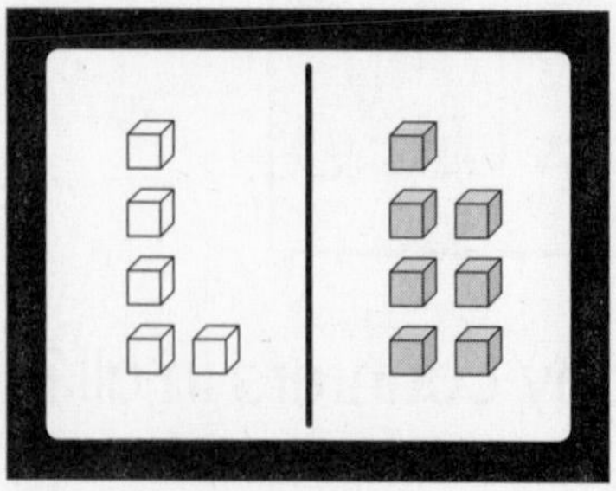

____ + 7 = 12

© Pearson Education, Inc. 2

Name ____________________

Stories About Joining

Follow the steps to solve this joining story.

You have 6 red crayons.
Your teacher gives you 3 blue crayons.
How many crayons do you have in all?

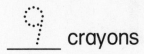

9 crayons

Write a number sentence for the story.

6 + 3 = 9

1. Draw 6 red crayons in the box.
2. Draw 3 blue crayons
3. Count the crayons.

Draw a picture to solve each story problem.
Write a number sentence to go with each story.

1. There are 7 black cats in the yard. 3 striped cats join them. How many cats are there in all?

____ + ____ = ____

2. You have 5 stickers. Your friend gives you 6 more stickers. How many stickers do you have in all?

____ + ____ = ____

© Pearson Education, Inc. 2

Name ________________________________

Practice
1-2

Stories About Joining

Draw a picture to find the sum.
Then write an addition sentence.

1. The monkey has 2 bananas.
He picks 9 more bananas.
How many bananas does
he have in all?

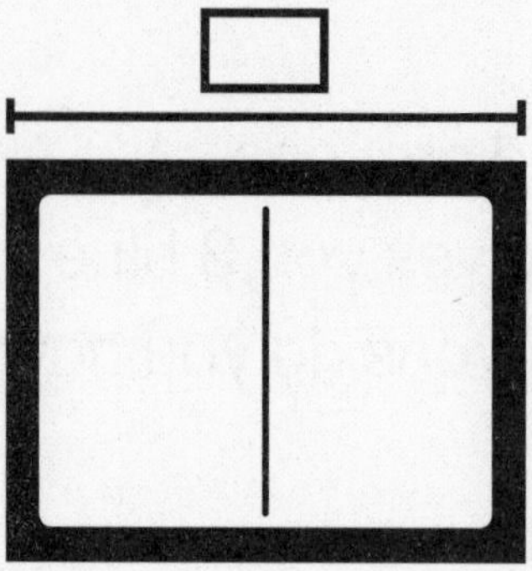

2 + 9 = 11   11 bananas

2. Morgan has 3 pennies.
She finds 8 more pennies.
How many pennies does
she have in all?

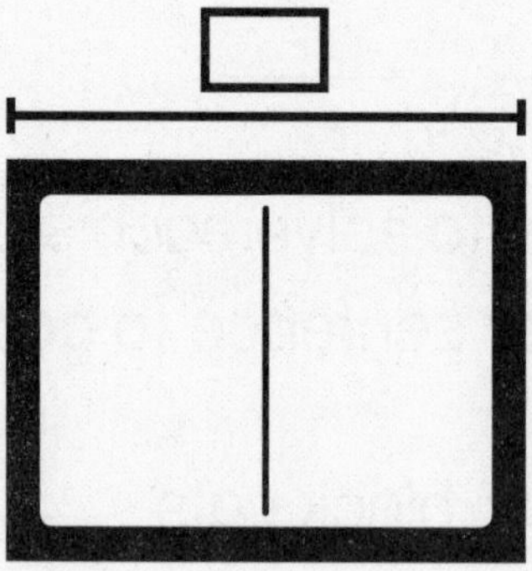

____ + ____ = ____   ____ pennies

3. Chad has 8 berries on his pancake. 7 more berries are in the bowl. How many berries are there in all?

○ 8 berries   ○ 15 berries

○ 10 berries   ○ 18 berries

4. Reasoning Write a joining story about the apples. Use pictures, numbers, or words.

© Pearson Education, Inc. 2

Name ______________________________

Writing Subtraction Number Sentences

Count all the cubes. How many?

6
____

Now count the cubes with Xs.
How many cubes have Xs?

2
____

How many cubes are left?

4
____

6 – 2 = 4

Count the cubes.
Write a subtraction sentence.

1. 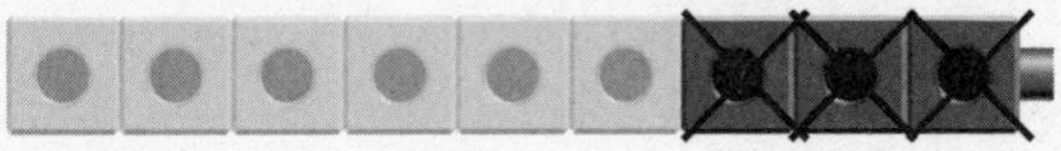

____ – ____ = ____

2. 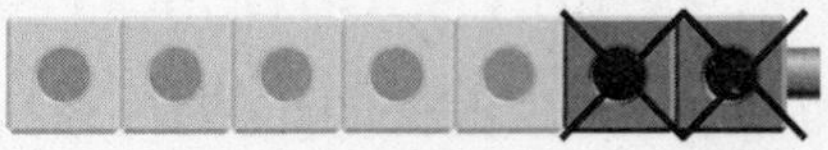

____ – ____ = ____

3. 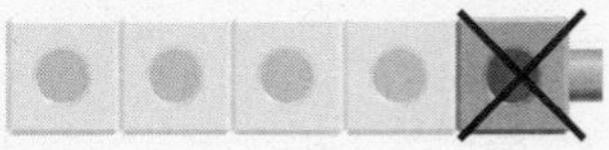

____ – ____ = ____

4. 

____ – ____ = ____

5. 

____ – ____ = ____

6. 

____ – ____ = ____

7. 

____ – ____ = ____

8. 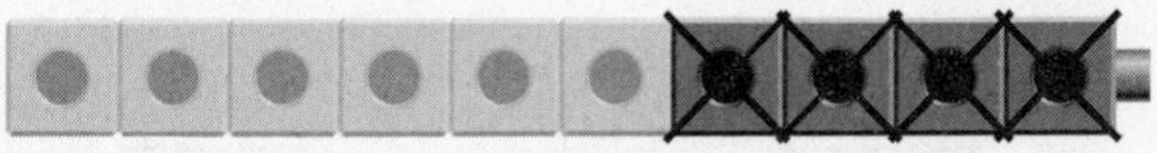

____ – ____ = ____

© Pearson Education, Inc. 2

Name ______________________________

Practice
1-3

Writing Subtraction Number Sentences

Draw the missing part. Write a subtraction sentence.

1.

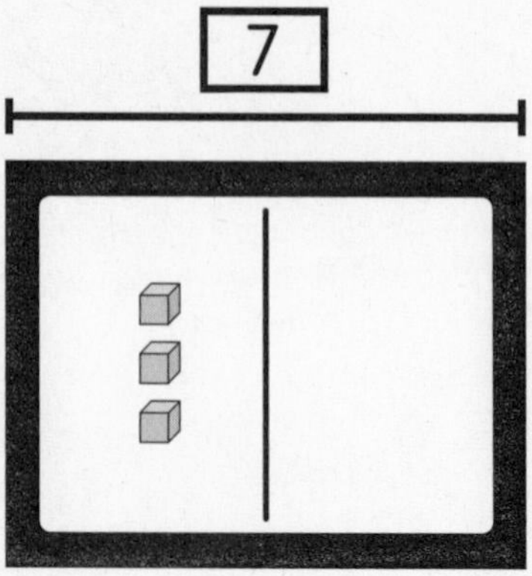

7 – 3 = ____

2.

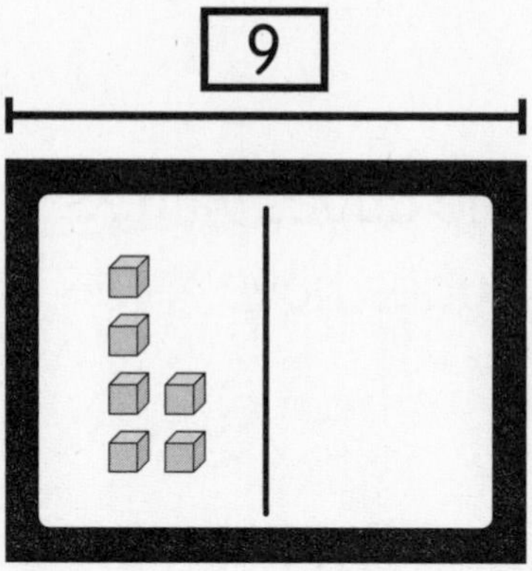

____ – ____ = ____

3. Kendra had 13 pencils. She took 4 pencils to school. Which subtraction sentence shows how many pencils Kendra left at home?

- ○ 17 – 4 = 13
- ○ 13 – 9 = 4
- ○ 13 – 4 = 9
- ○ 9 – 4 = 5

4. **Spatial Thinking** Draw a picture to show the story. Write a subtraction sentence.

14 mice are outside.
Then 7 mice go back in the den.
How many mice are still outside?

____ – ____ = ____

____ mice

© Pearson Education, Inc. 2

Name ______________________________

Stories About Separating

6 puppies are playing.
4 run away.
How many puppies are left?

6 – 4 = 2

Separate a group from the whole.
Then write a subtraction sentence.

1. There are 7 trucks in a lot.
5 trucks drive away.
How many trucks are left?

____ – ____ = ____

2. There are 8 apples.
You eat 3 apples.
How many apples are left?

____ – ____ = ____

3. **Journal** Write a separating story about cats.
Use pictures, numbers, or words. Show the answer.

____

____

____

© Pearson Education, Inc. 2

Name ____________________

Practice
1-4

Stories About Separating

Draw a picture to find the difference.
Write a subtraction sentence.

1. Pete has 16 stickers. He uses 9 of them. How many stickers does he have left?

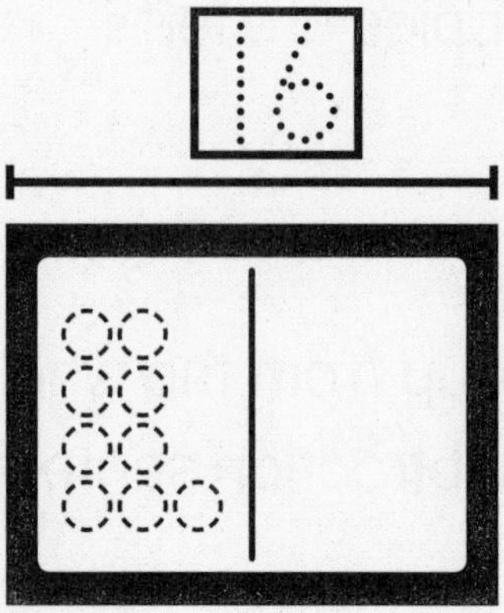

7 stickers

16 − 9 = ____

2. Hong has 10 stamps. She gives 6 stamps to Joe. How many stamps does she have left?

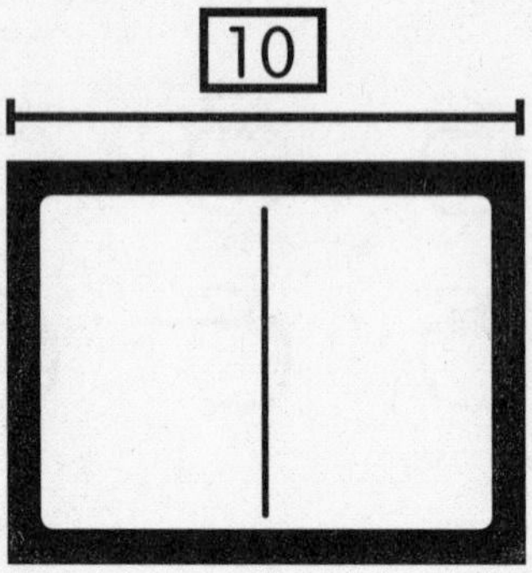

○ 4 stamps ○ 6 stamps

○ 5 stamps ○ 7 stamps

3. Reasonableness James has 12 rocks. He puts 7 rocks in Maria's garden. Which subtraction sentence tells how many rocks he has left?

○ 7 − 2 = 5 ○ 12 − 5 = 7

○ 7 − 4 = 3 ○ 12 − 7 = 5

© Pearson Education, Inc. 2

Name ______________________________

Reteaching
1-5

Stories About Comparing

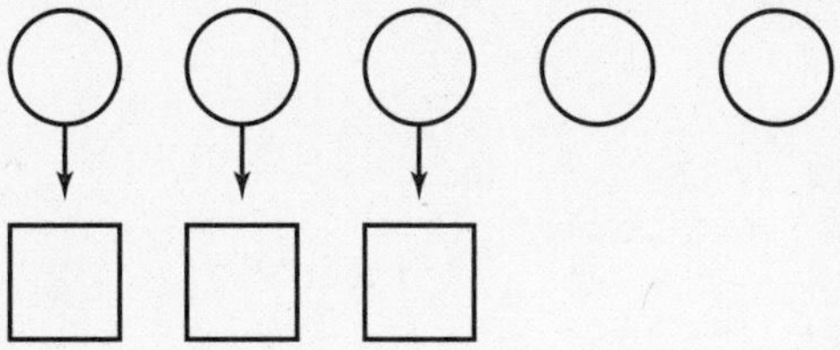

To compare the number of circles and squares, match each circle with a square. Are there more or fewer circles than squares?

There are 5 circles.

There are 3 squares.

How many *more* circles than squares? 2

5 − 3 = 2

Draw a picture for each story.
Compare the pictures.
Write a subtraction sentence.

1. There are 6 flowers.
There are 3 bees.
How many *more* flowers
than bees?

_____ more flowers _____ − _____ = _____

2. I have 7 juice boxes.
I have 5 straws.
How many *fewer* straws
than juice boxes?

_____ fewer straws _____ − _____ = _____

© Pearson Education, Inc. 2

Name ___________________________

Practice
1-5

Stories About Comparing

Draw a picture to find the difference.
Write a subtraction sentence.

1. A pond has 11 weeds and 7 lily pads. How many more weeds than lily pads does the pond have?

   4 more weeds   11 − 7 = 4

2. A vine has 8 red leaves and 5 brown leaves. How many fewer brown leaves does the vine have?

   _____ fewer brown leaves   _____ − _____ = _____

3. Mike plants 6 trees. Faye plants 4 trees. How many fewer trees does Faye plant than Mike?

   ○ 2 fewer trees   ○ 6 fewer trees
   ○ 4 fewer trees   ○ 10 fewer trees

4. **Journal** Write a math story about comparing to go with the picture.

____

____

© Pearson Education, Inc. 2

Name ____________________

Reteaching
1-6

Connecting Addition and Subtraction

1. Finish the model.
Draw 6 dots to make one part.
Draw 3 dots to make the other part.

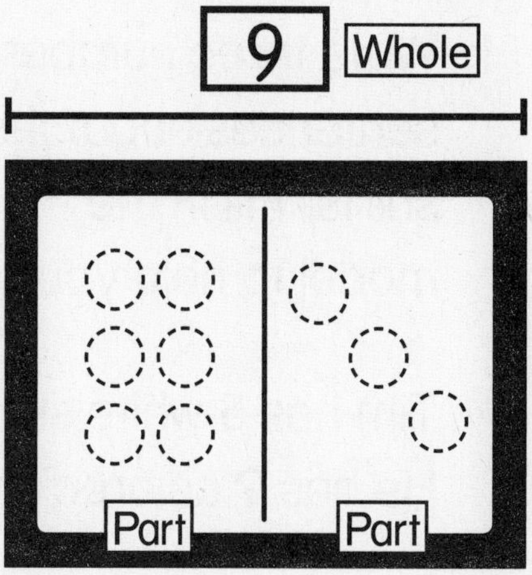

2. Show how the parts make the whole.
Write an addition sentence.

6 + 3 = 9
Part Part Whole

3. Write subtractions sentences.

9 − 3 = 6
Whole Part Part

9 − 6 = 3
Whole Part Part

Use the addition fact to help.
The addition sentence tells
the parts and the whole.

1. Add the parts to this model.
Draw 7 dots and 5 dots.

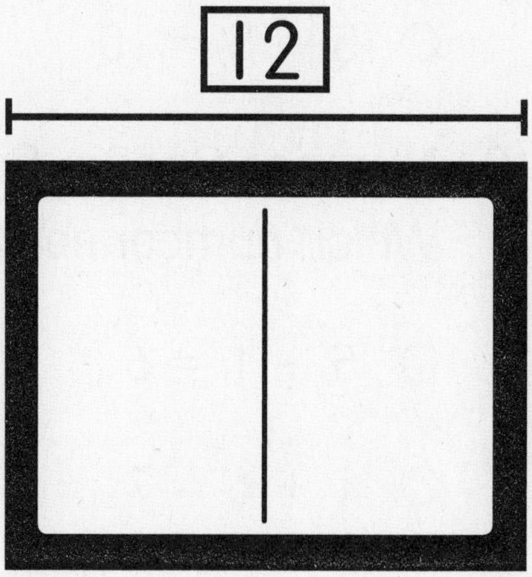

2. Write number sentences for the model.

____ + ____ = ____

____ − ____ = ____

____ − ____ = ____

© Pearson Education, Inc. 2

Name ______________________

Connecting Addition and Subtraction

1. Write three number sentences about the shirts. Fill in the model to help you.

Tim has 5 white shirts.
He has 9 colored shirts.

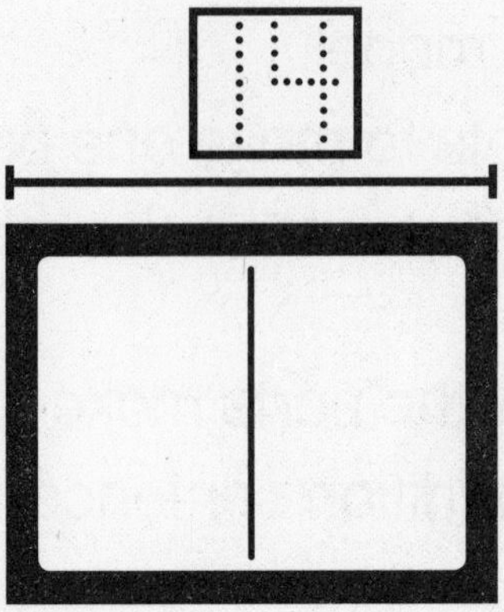

5 + 9 = 14

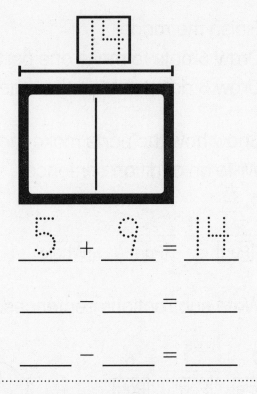

____ − ____ = ____

____ − ____ = ____

2. Connie has 2 pairs of jeans. She gets 3 more pairs of jeans. Which number sentence shows the story?

○ 2 + 3 = 5 ○ 3 − 2 = 1

○ 5 + 5 = 10 ○ 5 − 3 = 2

3. Number Sense Sarah had 5 caps. She lost 1 cap. Which number sentence shows the story?

○ 5 + 1 = 6 ○ 6 − 5 = 1

○ 1 + 6 = 7 ○ 5 − 1 = 4

© Pearson Education, Inc. 2

Name ______________________________

Problem Solving: Use Objects

You can use counters and your workmat to solve this story problem.

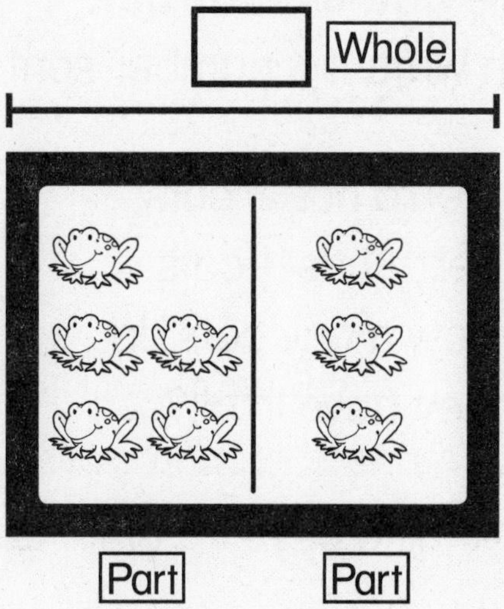

5 frogs are on a rock.
3 frogs join them.
How many frogs in all?

You need to find how many in all, or the whole.

Show 5 counters.
Show 3 more counters.
How many in all?

Do I need to add or subtract?
I will **add** because I need to find how many in all.

5 [+] 3 = 8
Part Part Whole

Use counters and your workmat to solve.
Circle add or subtract. Then write the number sentence.

1. 2 bugs are on a leaf.
4 bugs join them.
How many bugs in all?

add or subtract?

____ [ ] ____ = ____

2. 10 toads are in a pond.
5 toads jump out.
How many toads are left?

add or subtract?

____ [ ] ____ = ____

Name ______________________________

Practice
1-7

Problem Solving: Use Objects

Use counters and a workmat.
Circle **add** or **subtract**.
Then write the number sentence.

1. Sierra has 3 cats.
Perry has 4 cats.
How many cats do they have in all?

add   subtract

3 + 4 = 7 cats

2. Annika buys 10 gifts. Leroy buys 7 gifts.

Which number sentence shows how many more gifts Annika buys than Leroy?

○ $10 - 7 = 3$ ○ $7 + 3 = 10$

○ $10 - 3 = 7$ ○ $7 + 7 = 14$

3. 6 friends are playing a game.
Then 4 friends go home.

Which number sentence shows how many friends are playing now?

○ $6 + 4 = 10$ ○ $10 - 6 = 4$

○ $4 + 2 = 6$ ○ $6 - 4 = 2$

4. **Journal** Write a math story. Then write a number sentence to solve it.

____

____ ○ ____ ○ ____

Name ____________________

Adding 0, 1, 2

You can use a number line to add 0, 1, and 2.

Find 4 on the number line.
0 more than 4 is 4.

4 + 0 = 4

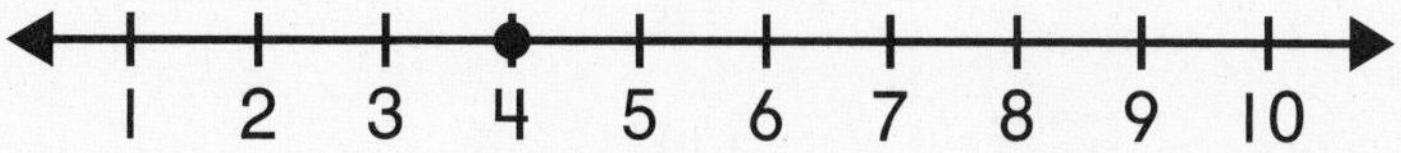

1 more than 4 is 5.

4 + 1 = 5

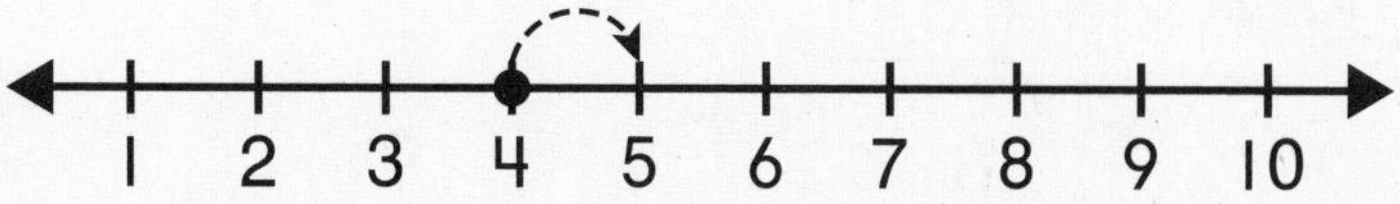

2 more than 4 is 6.

4 + 2 = 6

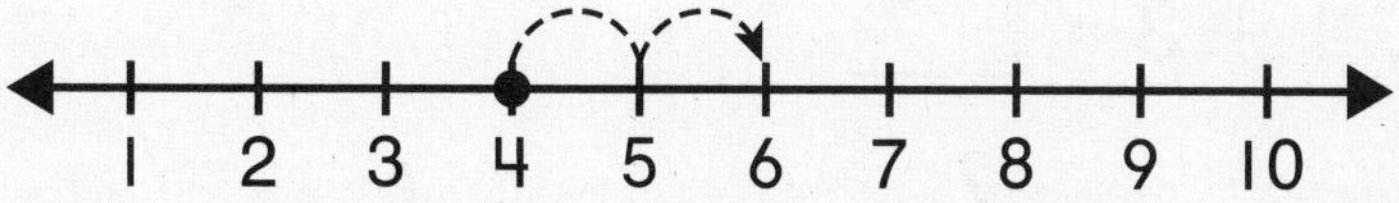

Add 0, 1, and 2.
Use the number line to help you.

1. 5 + 0 = ____

5 + 1 = ____

5 + 2 = ____

2. 7 + 0 = ____

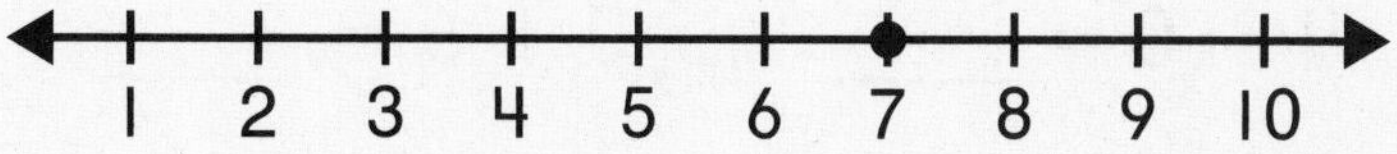

7 + 1 = ____

7 + 2 = ____

Name ____________________

Practice **2-1**

Adding 0, 1, 2

Circle the 0, 1, or 2. Then add.

1. $4 + 2 = 6$ (example: the 2 is circled)

2. $1 + 6 =$ ____

3. $7 + 2 =$ ____

4. $0 + 8 =$ ____

5. $1 + 8 =$ ____

6. $0 + 5 =$ ____

7. $2 + 8 =$ ____

8 ○   9 ○   10 ○   11 ○

8. $1 + 3 =$ ____

7 ○   6 ○   5 ○   4 ○

9. Solve. Write a number sentence.

Emily has 4 cats.
Troy does not have any cats.
How many cats do Emily and Troy have in all?

____ + ____ = ____

They have ____ cats in all.

Number Sense Add.

10. $4 + 0 =$ ____ $0 + 6 =$ ____ $5 + 0 =$ ____

11. What pattern do you notice in your answers?

____

12. Use your pattern to find these sums.

$17 + 0 =$ ____ $0 + 89 =$ ____ $253 + 0 =$ ____

Name ____________________

Doubles

Find 3 + 3.

Draw 3 more dots to show the double.
Then write the addition sentence.

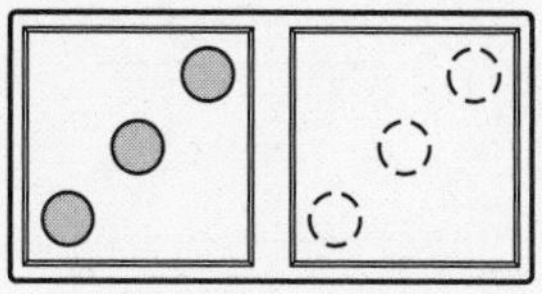

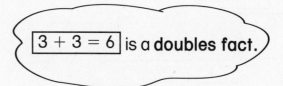

3 + 3 = 6 is a **doubles fact.**

3 + 3 = 6

Draw dots on the domino to show the double.
Then write the addition sentence.

1. 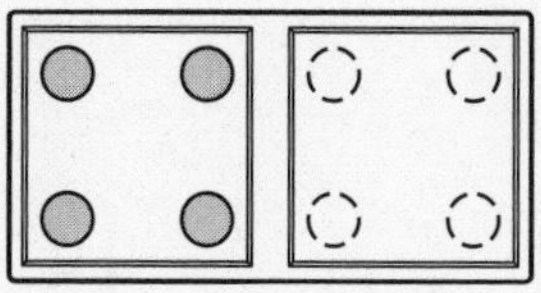

4 + 4 = 8

2. 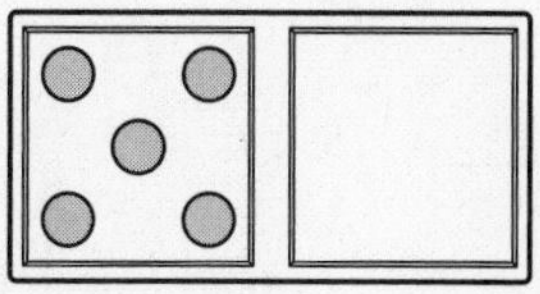

5 + ____ = ____

3. 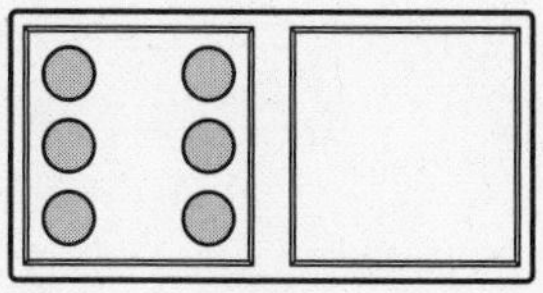

____ + ____ = ____

4. 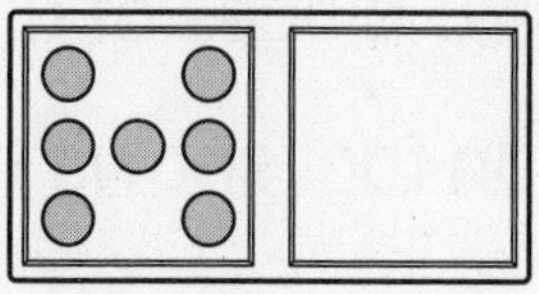

____ + ____ = ____

5. 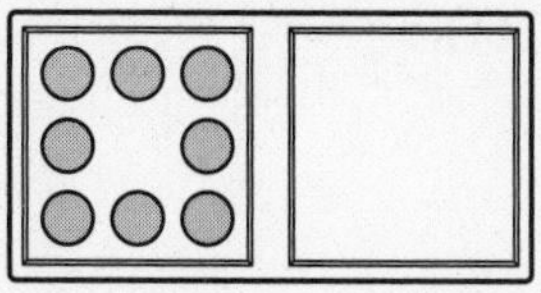

____ + ____ = ____

6. 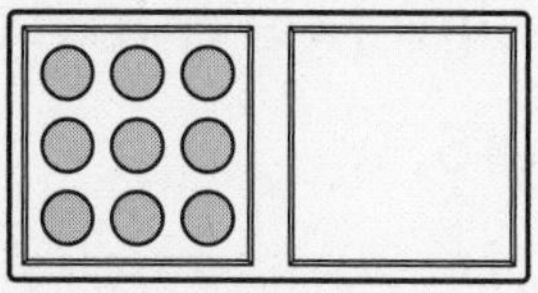

____ + ____ = ____

Name ____________________

Doubles

Complete the doubles.
Then solve.

1. $\begin{array}{r} 4 \\ + \boxed{4} \\ \hline 8 \end{array}$

2. $\begin{array}{r} \square \\ + 6 \\ \hline \end{array}$

3. $\begin{array}{r} 2 \\ + \square \\ \hline \end{array}$

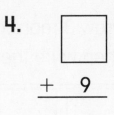

4. $\begin{array}{r} \square \\ + 9 \\ \hline \end{array}$

5. $8 + \square =$ ____

6. $\square + 5 =$ ____

7. $3 + 3 =$ ____

   ○ 8 ○ 7 ○ 6 ○ 5

8. $7 + 7 =$ ____

   ○ 10 ○ 11 ○ 12 ○ 14

9. Juana has two boxes of chalk.
   Each box has 8 pieces of chalk.

   Which addition fact shows the problem?

   ○ $4 + 4 = 8$ ○ $7 + 9 = 16$

   ○ $8 + 0 = 8$ ○ $8 + 8 = 16$

10. **Reasoning** Jim has 6 toy cars. Carl has the same number of cars.

    How many cars does Carl have?

    ○ 6 ○ 10 ○ 12 ○ 16

Name ______________________________

Adding in Any Order

You can add two numbers in any order.

The answer is the same.

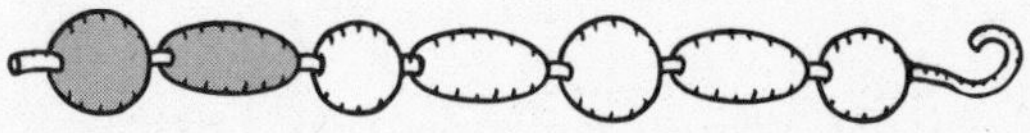

5 + 2 = 7

2 + 5 = 7

5 + 2 = 7 and 2 + 5 = 7 are turn around facts.

Write number sentences for each picture.

Solve the turn around facts.

1\.

____ + ____ = ____

____ + ____ = ____

2\.

____ + ____ = ____

____ + ____ = ____

3\.

□
\+ □
□

□
\+ □
□

Name ____________________

Practice **2-4**

Adding in Any Order

Write the sum. Then write the turn around fact.

1. 4 + 6 = 10

6 + 4 = 10

2. 5 + 3 = ____

____ + ____ = ____

3. 9 + 4 = ____

____ + ____ = ____

4. 2 + 5 = ____

____ + ____ = ____

5.

$\begin{array}{r} 3 \\ +\ 6 \\ \hline \end{array}$ $\begin{array}{r} \square \\ +\ \square \\ \hline \end{array}$

6.

$\begin{array}{r} 1 \\ +\ 9 \\ \hline \end{array}$ $\begin{array}{r} \square \\ +\ \square \\ \hline \end{array}$

Solve. Write two turn around facts.

7. A farm has 7 horses.
It gets 2 more horses.
How many horses does
the farm have now?

____ + ____ = ____

____ + ____ = ____

____ horses

8. **Geometry** Which shape belongs in the sentence?

Name ______________________________

Adding Three Numbers

There are different ways to add three numbers.

You can add any two numbers or try to make 10.
You can also look for doubles or near doubles.
Then add the third number.

Add any 2 numbers.	**Try to make 10.**	**Look for doubles.**
5 + 3 = [8]; 8 + [8] = [16]	4 + 6 = [10]; [10] + 3 = [13]	4 + 4 = [8]; 6 + [8] = [14]
5 3 + 8	4 3 + 6	4 6 + 4

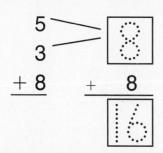

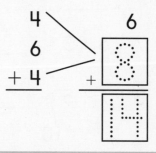

Find the sums.
Draw lines from the first two numbers you add.

1. 7, 4, + 3 → 4 + ☐ = ☐

2. 8, 2, + 5 → ☐ + 5 = ☐

3. 1, 6, + 9 → 6 + ☐ = ☐

4. 7, 7, + 5 → ☐ + 5 = ☐

5. 8, 4, + 8 → 4 + ☐ = ☐

6. 2, 6, + 7 → 2 + ☐ = ☐

7. Journal Use pictures, numbers, or words to show two different ways to add 2 + 4 + 6.

Name ______________________________

Practice
2-5

Adding Three Numbers

Write the sum.
Circle the numbers you added first.

1.	**2.**	**3.**	**4.**
4	6	2	7
3	0	9	4
+ 2	+ 5	+ 2	+ 1
9			

5. 7 + 6 + 3 = _____

6. 5 + 0 + 6 = _____

7. 3 + 7 + 5 = _____

○ 10 ○ 14 ○ 15 ○ 16

8. 3 + 8 + 2 = _____

○ 13 ○ 12 ○ 11 ○ 10

9. Lila cut out 3 rainbows. She cut out 4 moons. She cut out 7 stars. How many shapes did Lila cut out in all?

○ 7 ○ 10 ○ 11 ○ 14

10. Algebra Add across and down. Write the missing numbers.

9	3	2	14
	6		14
1		8	14
14	14	14	

Name ______________________________

Reteaching **2-6**

Making a 10 to Add 9

This shows 9 + 4.

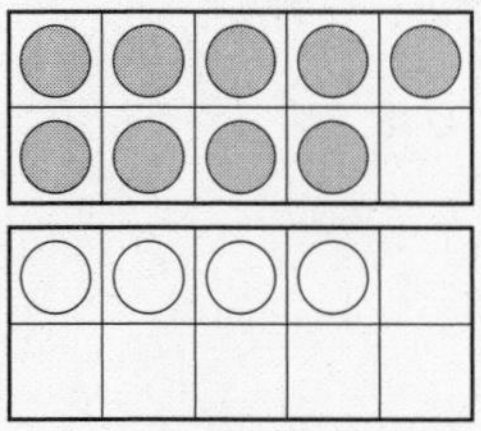

9 + 4 is the same as 10 + 3.

9 + 4 = 13

Show 10 + 3.
Move a counter to make 10.

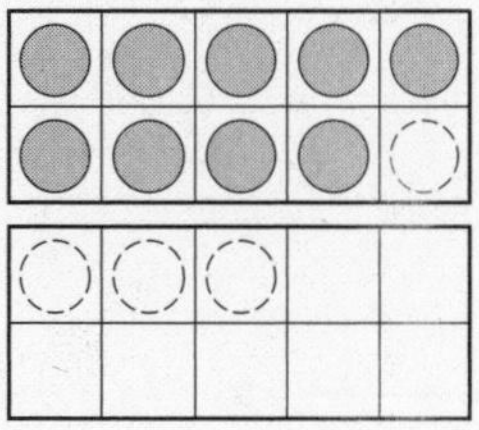

10 + 3 = 13

Make 10 to help you add.

1. Find 9 + 7.

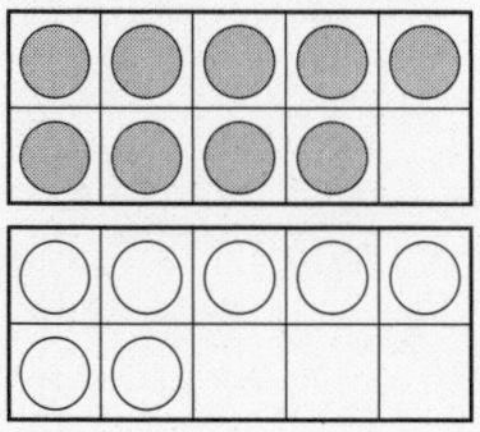

9 + 7 is the same as 10 + 6.

_____ + _____ = _____

Move a counter to make 10.

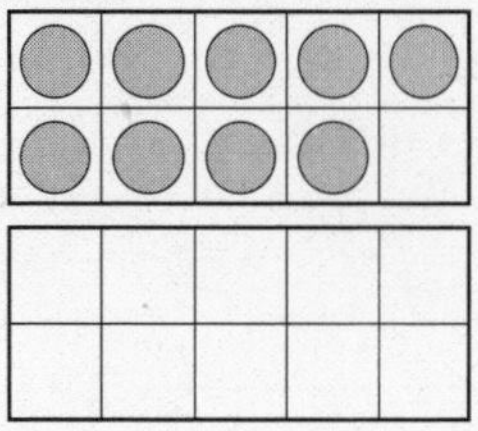

_____ + _____ = _____

2. Find 9 + 8.

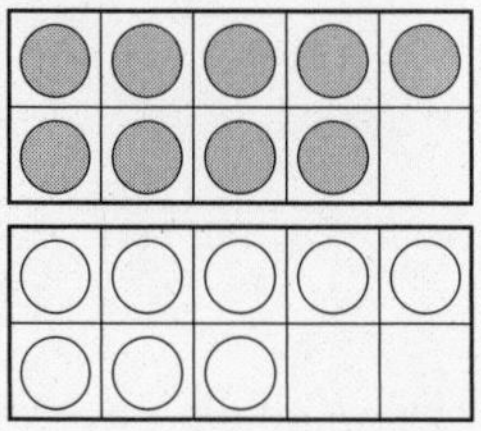

9 + 8 is the same as 10 + 7.

_____ + _____ = _____

Move a counter to make 10.

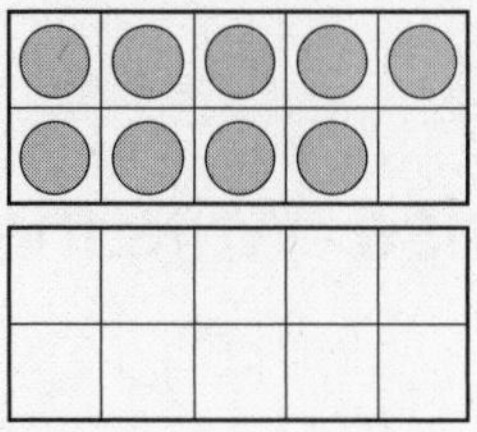

_____ + _____ = _____

Name ______________________

Practice
2-6

Making 10 to Add 9

Make 10 to add 9.
Use counters and your workmat.

1. $\begin{array}{r} 9 \\ +\ 1 \\ \hline 10 \end{array}$

2. $\begin{array}{r} 5 \\ +\ 9 \\ \hline \end{array}$

3. $\begin{array}{r} 2 \\ +\ 9 \\ \hline \end{array}$

4. $\begin{array}{r} 9 \\ +\ 7 \\ \hline \end{array}$

5. 9 + 4 = _____

6. 9 + 8 = _____

7. 3 + 9 = _____

○ 11 ○ 12 ○ 13 ○ 14

8. 6 + 9 = _____

○ 15 ○ 16 ○ 17 ○ 18

9. A mother robin pulls 9 worms from a garden.
A father robin pulls 6 worms from a garden.
How many worms do they have in all?

○ 18 worms ○ 15 worms

○ 17 worms ○ 14 worms

10. **Number Sense** Write the missing numbers.

7 + 9 = 10 + 6

9 + _____ = 10 + 3

_____ + 9 = 10 + 2

9 + 5 = 10 + _____

Name ________________________

Reteaching
2-7

Making 10 to Add 8

This shows 8 + 4.

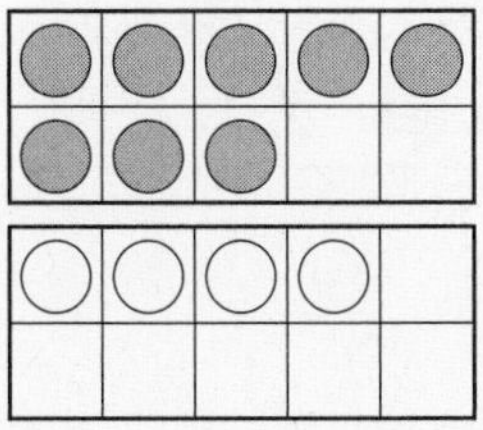

Show 10 + 2.
Move 2 counters to make 10.

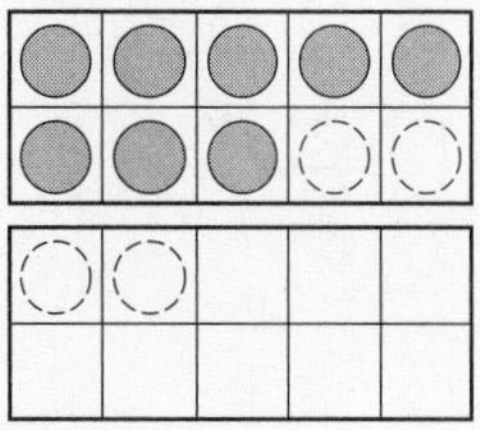

8 + 4 is the same as 10 + 2.

8 + 4 = 12

10 + 2 = 12

Make 10 to help you add.

1. Find 8 + 5.

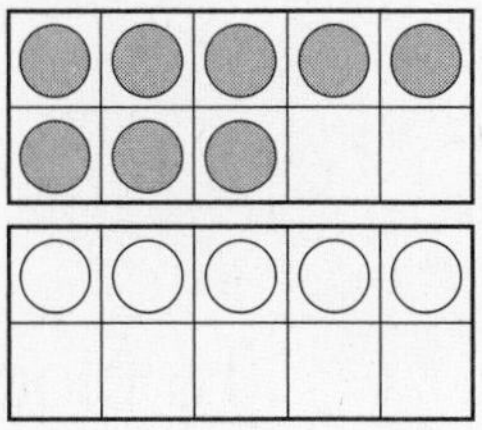

Move 2 counters to make 10.

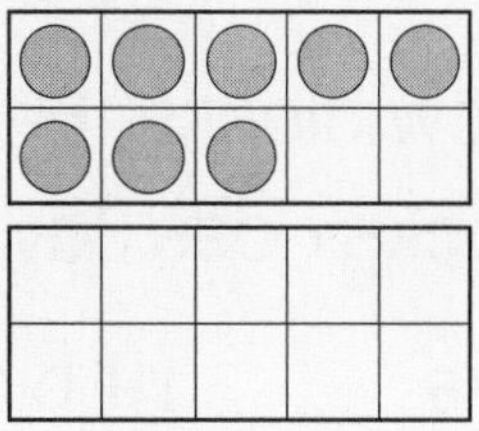

8 + 5 is the same as 10 + 3.

____ + ____ = ____ ____ + ____ = ____

2. Find 8 + 7.

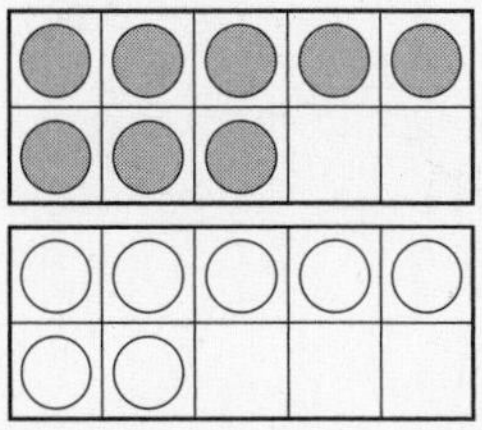

Move 2 counters to make 10.

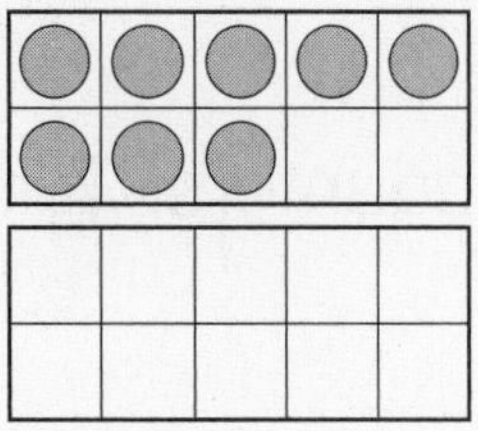

8 + 7 is the same as 10 + 5.

____ + ____ = ____ ____ + ____ = ____

Name ______________________

Practice
2-7

Making 10 to Add 8

Make 10 to add 8.
Use counters and your workmat.

1. $\begin{array}{r} 8 \\ +\ 3 \\ \hline \end{array}$

2. $\begin{array}{r} 5 \\ +\ 8 \\ \hline \end{array}$

3. $\begin{array}{r} 8 \\ +\ 9 \\ \hline \end{array}$

4. $\begin{array}{r} 8 \\ +\ 7 \\ \hline \end{array}$

5. $\begin{array}{r} 8 \\ +\ 1 \\ \hline \end{array}$

6. $\begin{array}{r} 4 \\ +\ 8 \\ \hline \end{array}$

7. $\begin{array}{r} 2 \\ +\ 8 \\ \hline \end{array}$

8. $\begin{array}{r} 0 \\ +\ 8 \\ \hline \end{array}$

9. 6 + 8 = ____

10. 8 + 8 = ____

11. Jay has 6 yellow blocks. He has 8 green blocks.
How many blocks does Jay have in all?

13 blocks ○ 14 blocks ○ 15 blocks ○ 16 blocks ○

12. Tia has 8 blue pens. She has 4 red pens.
How many pens does Tia have in all?

15 pens ○ 14 pens ○ 13 pens ○ 12 pens ○

13. **Journal** Use counters. Tell how to make 10 when adding 8 + 5.

____

____

Name ______________________________

Problem Solving: Draw a Picture and Write a Number Sentence

Tim and Rose played two games.
How many points in all did Tim and Rosa score in Game 1?

Players	Game 1	Game 2
Tim	////	//
Rosa	~~////~~	~~////~~ /

Use a part-part-whole mat to find out.

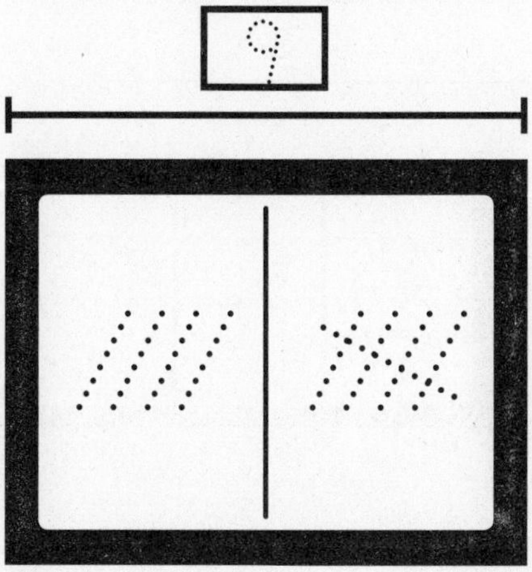

Write a number sentence.

4 + 5 = 9
Tim   Rosa   Points in all

In game 1, Tim and Rosa score 9 points in all.

Use a part-part-whole mat and write a number sentence to solve.

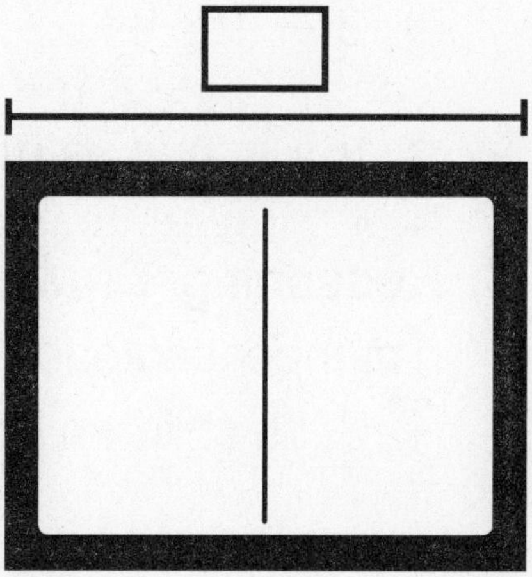

1. How many points in all did Tim and Rosa score in Game 2?

2. _____ + _____ = _____
Tim   Rosa   Points in all

3. In game 2, Tim and Rosa score _____ points in all.

Name ____________________

Practice
2-8

Problem Solving: Draw a Picture and Write a Number Sentence

Three children made a table to show how many stickers they have.

Stickers Collected			

Fernando	8	0	9
Kathleen	4	8	6
Mohammed	5	7	3

1. Draw counters and write a number sentence to solve. How many stickers does Fernando have?

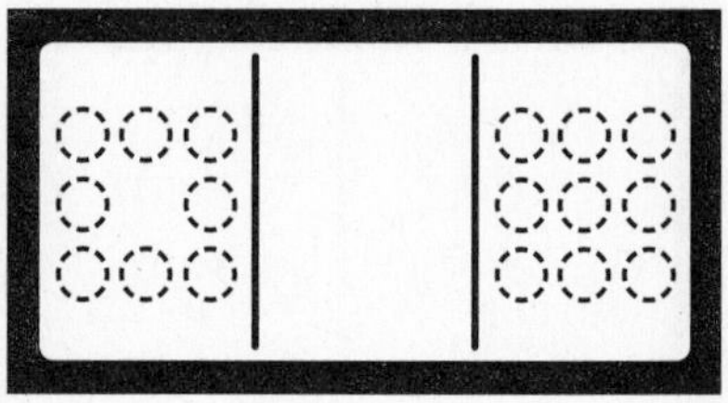

8 + 0 + 9 = 17 stickers

2. Which number sentence tells how many stickers Kathleen has?

○ 8 − 4 = 4 ○ 8 + 2 + 6 = 16

○ 4 + 8 + 2 = 14 ○ 4 + 8 + 6 = 18

3. Reasoning Draw counters and write a number sentence to show how many  the children have in all.

____ + ____ + ____ = ____

Name ______________________

Subtracting 0, 1, 2

You can use a number line to subtract 0, 1, and 2.

Find 6 on the number line.
0 less than 6 is 6.

6 − 0 = 6

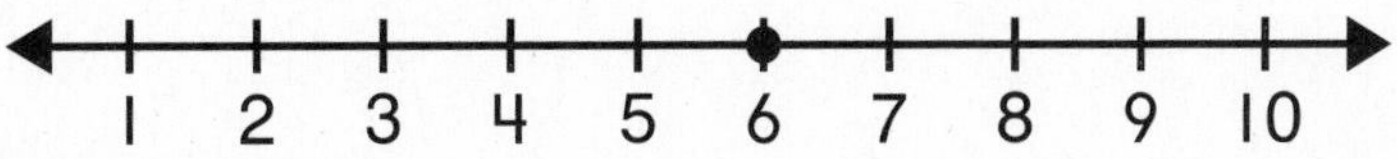

1 less than 6 is 5.

6 − 1 = 5

2 less than 6 is 4.

6 − 2 = 4

Subtract 0, 1, and 2.
Use the number line to help you.

1. 4 − 0 = _____

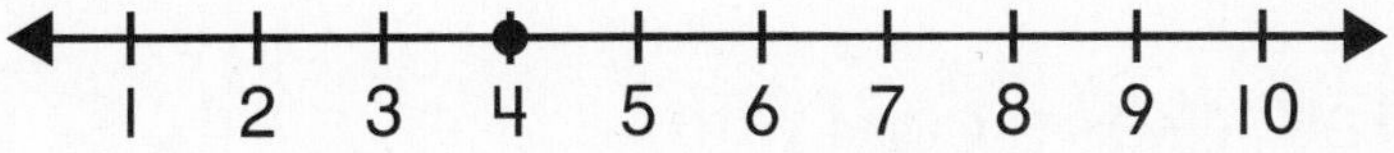

4 − 1 = _____

4 − 2 = _____

2. 7 − 0 = _____

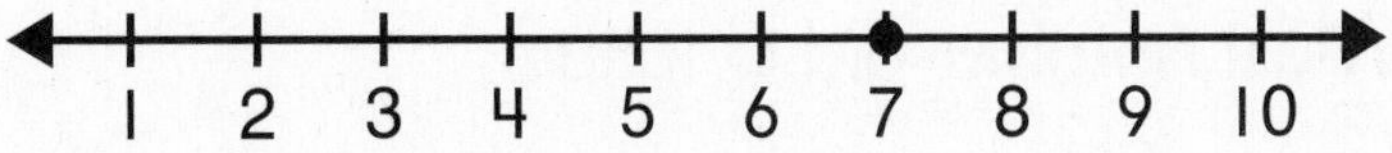

7 − 1 = _____

7 − 2 = _____

Name ______________________

Practice
3-1

Subtracting 0, 1, 2

Solve. Use cubes if needed.

1. $\begin{array}{r} 7 \\ -\ 2 \\ \hline 5 \end{array}$
2. $\begin{array}{r} 5 \\ -\ 1 \\ \hline \end{array}$
3. $\begin{array}{r} 2 \\ -\ 0 \\ \hline \end{array}$
4. $\begin{array}{r} 1 \\ -\ 1 \\ \hline \end{array}$

5. 4 − 0 = _____

6. 10 − 2 = _____

7. Kim has 5 teddy bears.
Jill has 1 less teddy bear than Kim.
How many teddy bears does Jill have?

○ 3 ○ 5

○ 4 ○ 6

8. **Spatial Thinking** Draw a picture to show the story.
Write a subtraction sentence.

Ted takes a card with
the number 10 on it.
Li takes a card that is
2 less than 10.

What number did Li take?

Li takes the number _____.   _____ − _____ = _____

Name ____________________

Reteaching **3-2**

Thinking Addition to Subtract Doubles

6 − 3 = ?

Think of a doubles fact.

3 + __3__ = 6

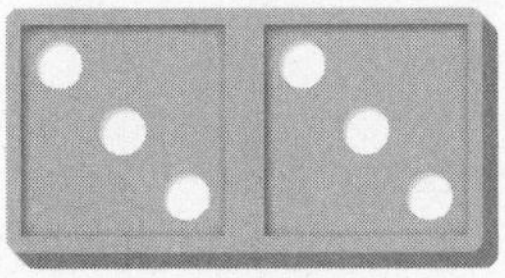

So, 6 − 3 = __3__.

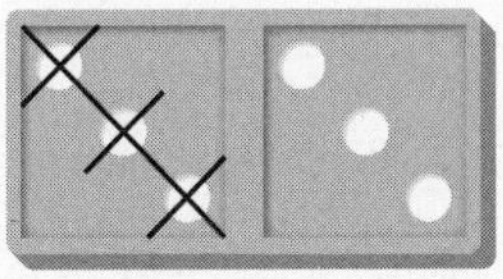

Use doubles facts to help you subtract.
Cross out the dots you take away.

1. 8 − 4 = ?

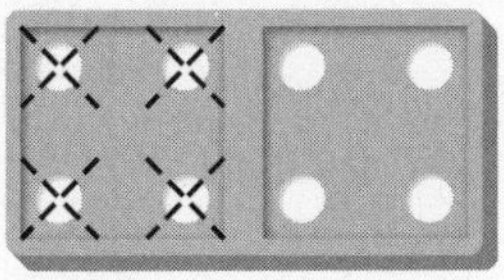

4 + __4__ = 8 8 − 4 = __4__

2. 10 − 5 = ?

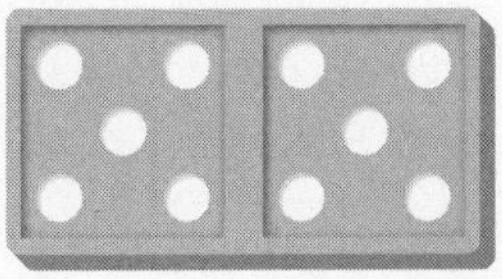

5 + ____ = 10 10 − 5 = ____

3. 12 − 6 = ?

6 + ____ = 12 12 − 6 = ____

4. 14 − 7 = ?

7 + ____ = 14 14 − 7 = ____

5. 16 − 8 = ?

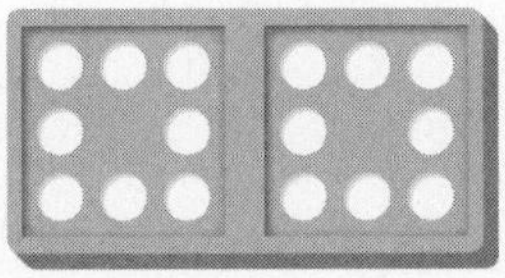

8 + ____ = 16 16 − 8 = ____

6. 18 − 9 = ?

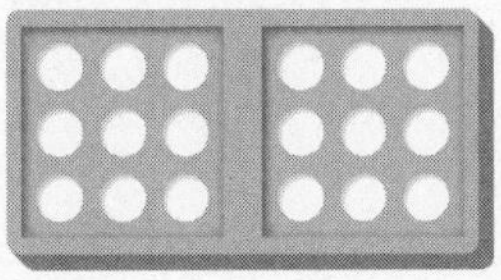

9 + ____ = 18 18 − 9 = ____

Name ____________________

Practice
3-2

Thinking Addition to Subtract Doubles

Subtract. Write the doubles fact that helped you.
Use cubes if you need to.

1.

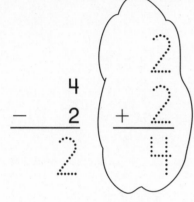

$$\begin{array}{r} 4 \\ -\ 2 \\ \hline 2 \end{array} \qquad \begin{array}{r} 2 \\ +\ 2 \\ \hline 4 \end{array}$$

2.

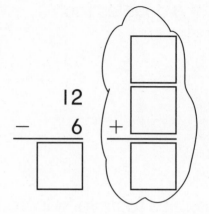

$$\begin{array}{r} 12 \\ -\ 6 \\ \hline \square \end{array} \qquad \begin{array}{r} \square \\ +\ \square \\ \hline \square \end{array}$$

3. 16 − 8 = ____

____ + ____ = ____

4. 18 − 9 = ____

____ + ____ = ____

5. David had 6 pizzas at his party.
His friends ate 3 pizzas.
Which doubles fact could you use
to find how many pizzas are left?

○ 3 + 3 = 6
○ 6 + 6 = 12
○ 6 − 6 = 0
○ 6 + 3 = 9

6. Reasoning Krista and Alan have 8 bookmarks.
How could they share the bookmarks so that they
each have the same number?

____

Name ______________________

Reteaching
3-3

Thinking Addition to 10 to Subtract

Addition facts can help you subtract.
Use the pictures to find the missing numbers.

Addition Fact

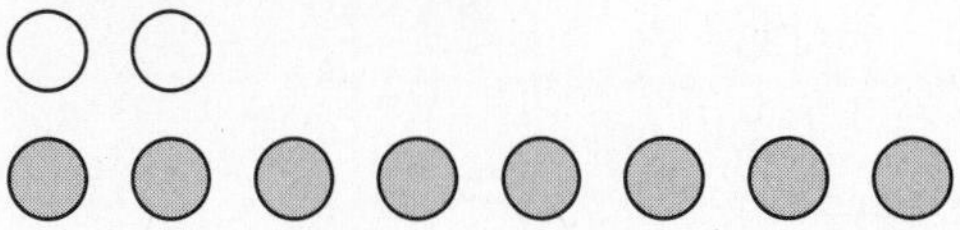

Think 2 + __8__ = 10.

Subtraction Fact

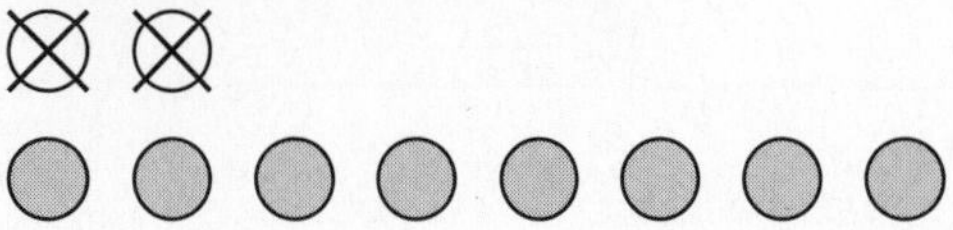

So, 10 − 2 = __8__

Use addition facts to help you subtract.

1. 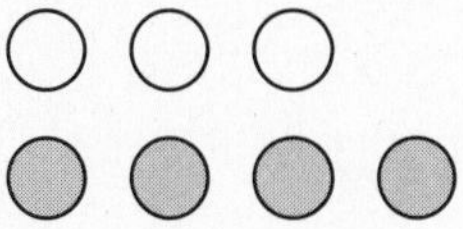

Think 3 + _____ = 7.

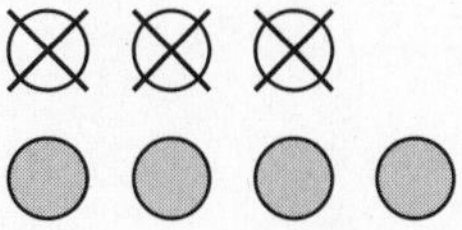

So, 7 − 3 = _____.

2. 

Think 7 + _____ = 8.

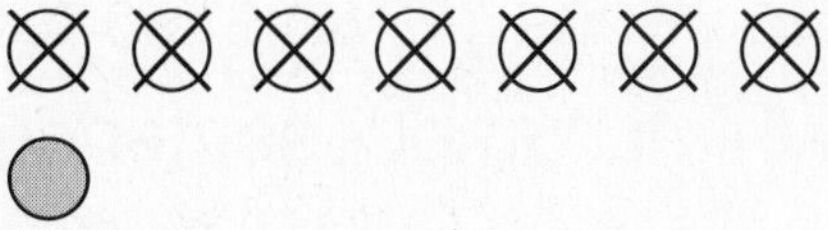

So, 8 − 7 = _____.

3. 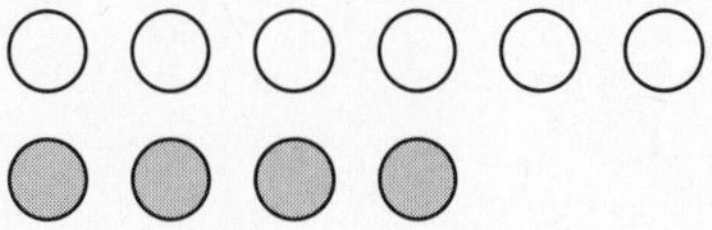

Think 6 + _____ = 10.

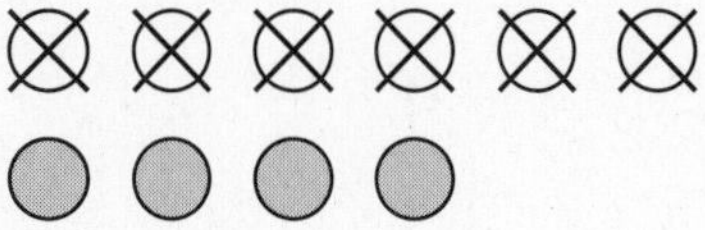

So, 10 − 6 = _____.

Name ____________________

Practice
3-3

Thinking Addition to 10 to Subtract

Use addition facts to help you subtract.
Use counters if you need to.

1.

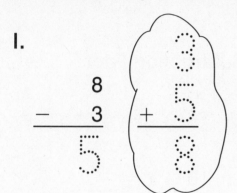

$$\begin{array}{r} 8 \\ -\ 3 \\ \hline 5 \end{array} \qquad \begin{array}{r} 3 \\ +\ 5 \\ \hline 8 \end{array}$$

2.

$$\begin{array}{r} 10 \\ -\ 6 \\ \hline \square \end{array} \qquad \begin{array}{r} 6 \\ +\ \square \\ \hline 10 \end{array}$$

3. 9 − 6 = ____

6 + ____ = 9

4. 6 − 2 = ____

2 + ____ = 6

5. Number Sense Chris has 7 whistles.
He needs 10 whistles for his party.
Which number sentence can help you find how many more whistles Chris needs?

○ 7 + 10 = 17

○ 7 + 3 = 10

○ 7 − 3 = 4

○ 4 + 3 = 7

Name ____________________

Thinking Addition to 18 to Subtract

Addition facts can help you subtract.
Use the pictures to find the missing numbers.

Addition Fact

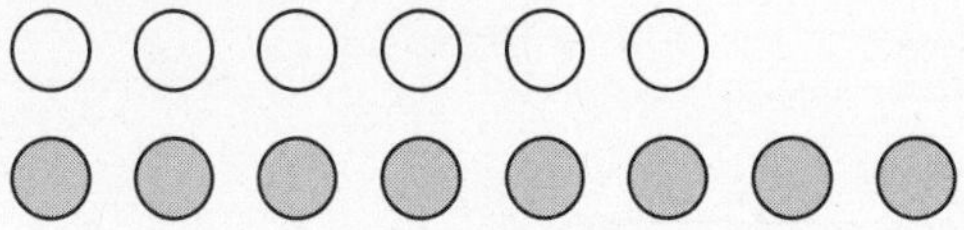

Think 6 + 8 = 14.

Subtraction Fact

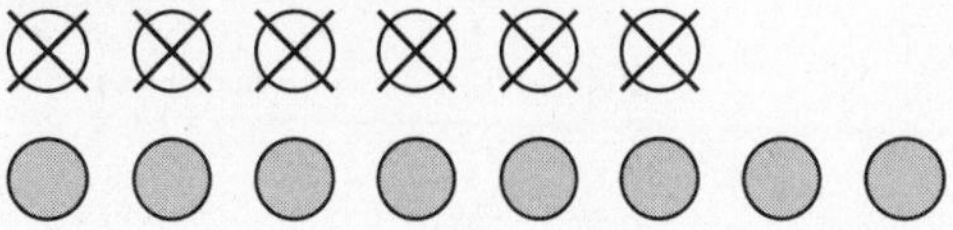

So, 14 − 6 = 8

Think addition to help you subtract.

1.

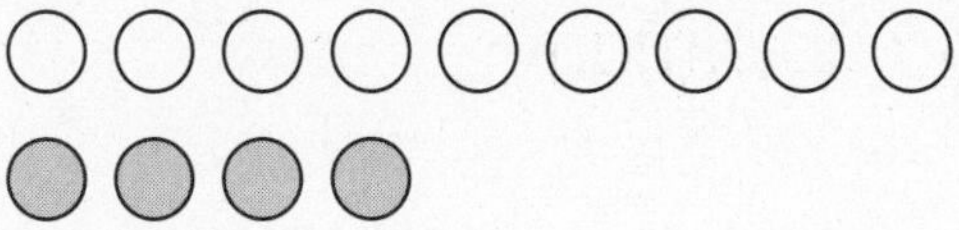

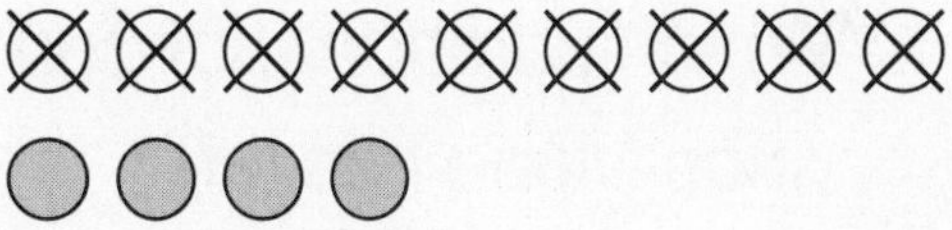

Think 9 + ____ = 13.

So, 13 − 9 = ____.

2.

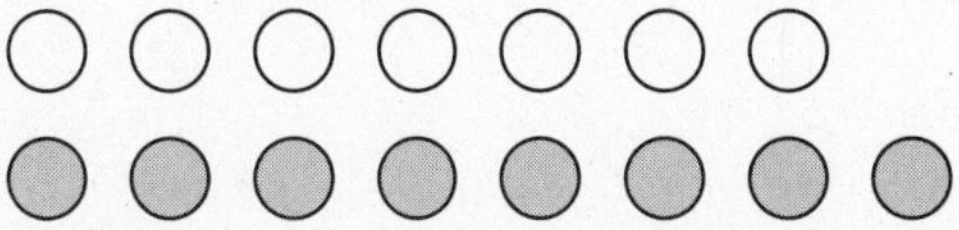

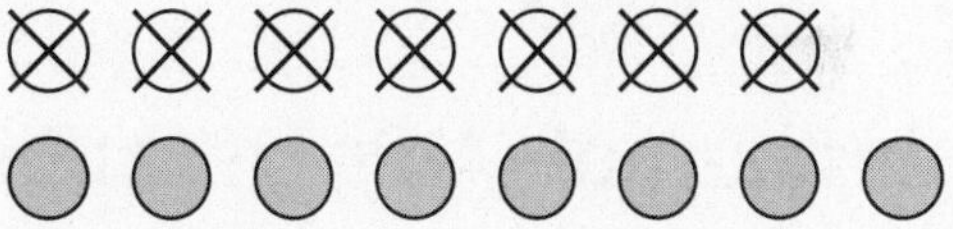

Think 7 + ____ = 15.

So, 15 − 7 = ____.

3.

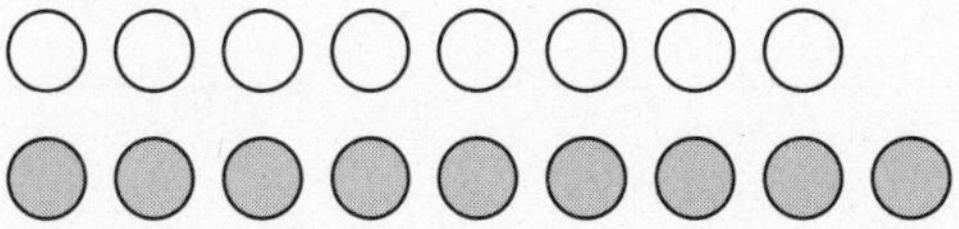

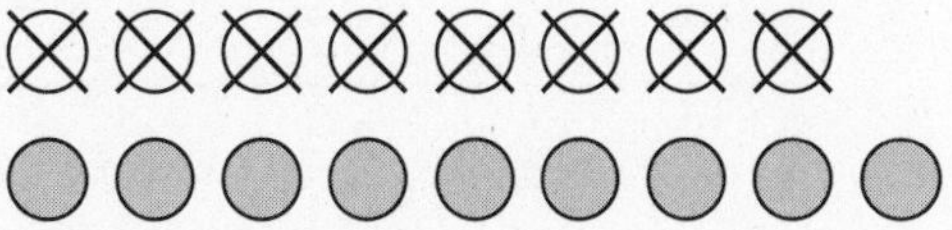

Think 8 + ____ = 17.

So, 17 − 8 = ____.

4. **Algebra** Use a related addition fact to complete the subtraction fact.

11 − 2 = ____

2+ ____ = 11

Name ____________________

Practice
3-4

Thinking Addition to 18 to Subtract

Use addition facts to help you subtract.
Use counters if you need to.

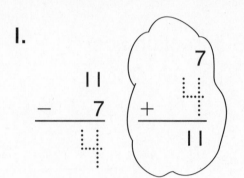

1.

$$\begin{array}{r} 11 \\ -\ 7 \\ \hline 4 \end{array} \qquad \begin{array}{r} 7 \\ +\ 4 \\ \hline 11 \end{array}$$

2. 15 − 6 = ____

6 + ____ = 15

---

3. Maria had 11 rings. She lost 3 rings.
Which addition fact can help you find how many rings Maria has left?

○ 3 + 1 = 4 ○ 3 + 8 = 11

○ 6 + 5 = 11 ○ 11 + 3 = 14

---

4. Journal Write a subtraction story for 12 − 9.
Then write the addition fact that can help you solve your story.

____

____

____

____ + ____ = ____ 12 − 9 = ____

Name ______________________

Finding the Missing Part

Miguel has 3 rocks. He needs 8 rocks.
How many more rocks does he need?

3 + ☐ = 8
Part Part Whole

This addition sentence shows what part is missing.

This is the related subtraction sentence.

8 − 3 = ☐
Whole Part Part

To find the answer, subtract a part from the whole. The whole is always the greater number.

Find the missing parts.

3 + 5 = 8
Part Part Whole

8 − 3 = 5
Whole Part Part

Find the missing parts.

1. 5 + 4 = 9
Part Part Whole

9 − 5 = 4
Whole Part Part

2. 7 + ☐ = 10

10 − 7 = ☐

3. 8 + ☐ = 15

15 − 8 = ☐

4. 2 + ☐ = 8

8 − 2 = ☐

5. **Journal** Write a story about missing parts.
Use 6 as the whole. Write an addition sentence and a subtraction sentence to go with your story.

Name ______________________________

Practice
3-5

Finding the Missing Part

Find and write the missing numbers.

1. 3 + ____ = 8

   8 − 3 = ____

2. 5 + ____ = 11

   11 − 5 = ____

3. 4 + ____ = 12

   12 − 4 = ____

4. 7 + ____ = 15

   15 − 7 = ____

5. Theo has 5 muffins.
   He needs 14 muffins to serve for breakfast.
   Which problem can help you find how many more muffins Theo needs?

   ○ 14 − 5 ○ 5 + 14

   ○ 14 + 5 ○ 5 − 14

6. **Algebra** Use the numbers on the cards. Write an addition sentence and a subtraction sentence.

   | 8 | 17 | 9 |

   ____ + ____ = ____ ____ − ____ = ____

Name ______________________________

Reteaching
3-6

Problem Solving: Two-Question Problems

Rachel and Ricky picked flowers.
Rachel picked 4 daisies.
How many daisies did Ricky pick?

Use a part-part-whole mat to find out.

Child	Daisy	Coneflower
Rachel		?
Ricky	?	
Total	6	8

Write a number sentence.

6 − 4 = 2

Ricky picked 2 daisies.

Use a part-part-whole mat and write a number sentence to solve.

1. Ricky picked 5 coneflowers. How many coneflowers did Rachel pick?

2. _____ − _____ = _____

3. Rachel picked _____ coneflowers.

Name ____________________

Practice **3-6**

Problem Solving: Two-Question Problems

Children made this chart to show what they ate at camp.

Lunches Sold			
	Saturday	Sunday	Total
	8	?	17
	?	7	16
	?	6	13

Draw a picture and write number sentences to solve.

1. How many hot dogs were sold on Sunday?

17 – 8 = 9 hot dogs

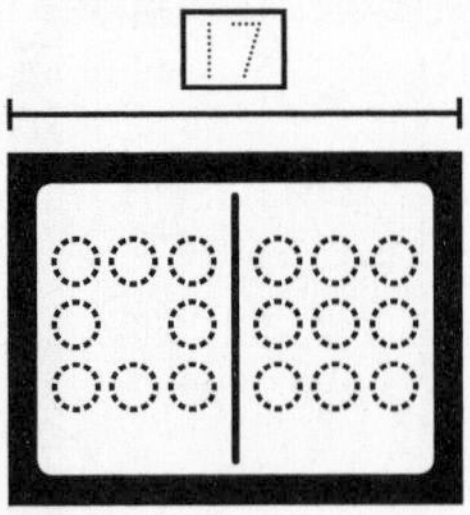

2. How many tacos were sold on Saturday?

_____ – _____ = _____ tacos

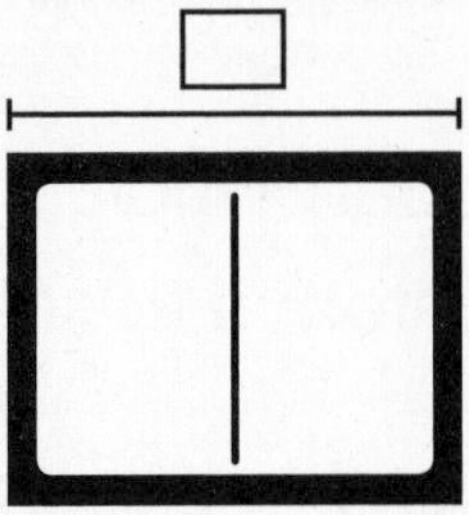

3. **Spatial Thinking** Draw a picture to solve. Which number sentence tells how many hamburgers were sold in all?

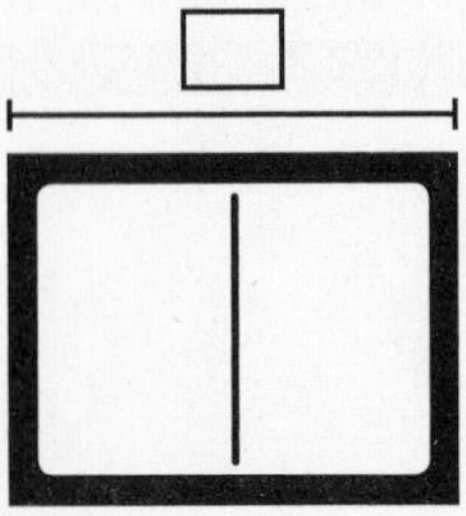

○ 7 – 6 = 1
○ 6 + 8 = 14
○ 6 + 7 = 13
○ 13 + 5 = 18

Name ______________________________

Models for Tens

Here are 20 ones.

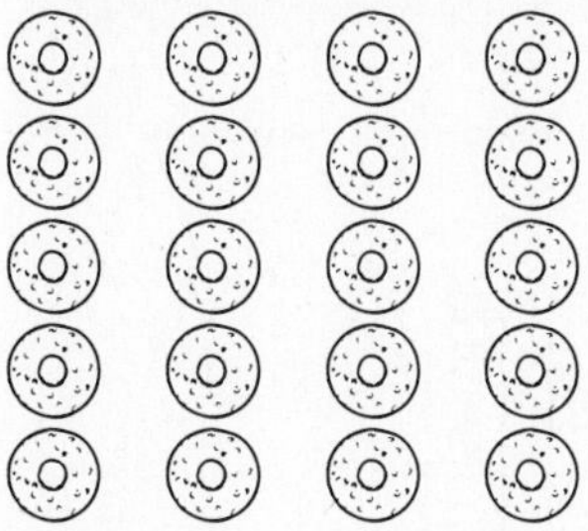

20 ones makes 2 tens.

Group the ones
to make 2 tens.

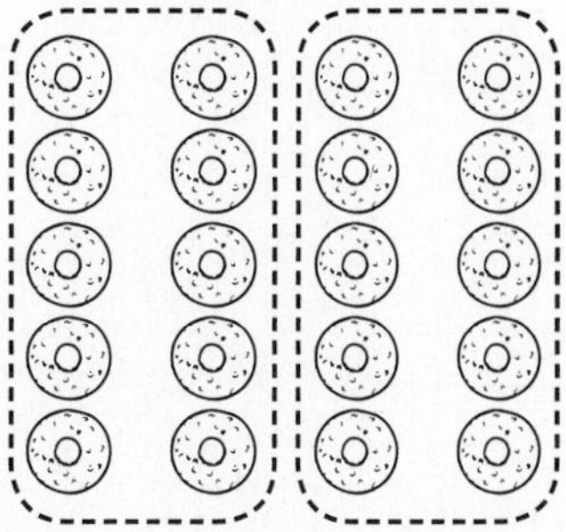

Count the ones. Group the ones to make tens.

1. There are _____ ones.

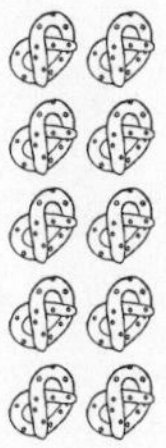

_____ ones makes _____ ten.

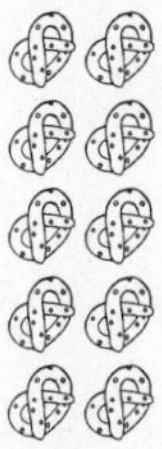

2. There are _____ ones.

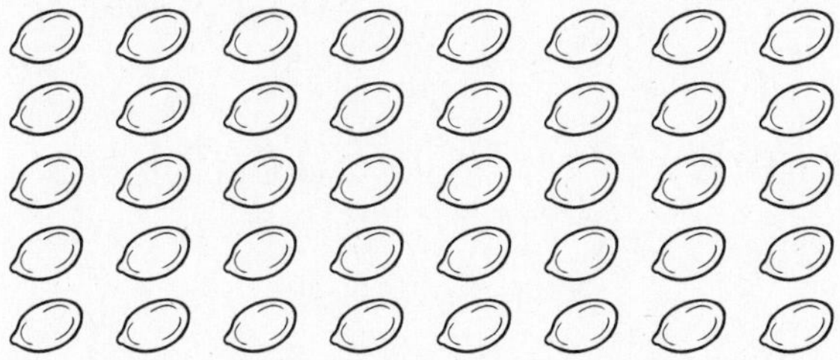

_____ ones makes _____ tens.

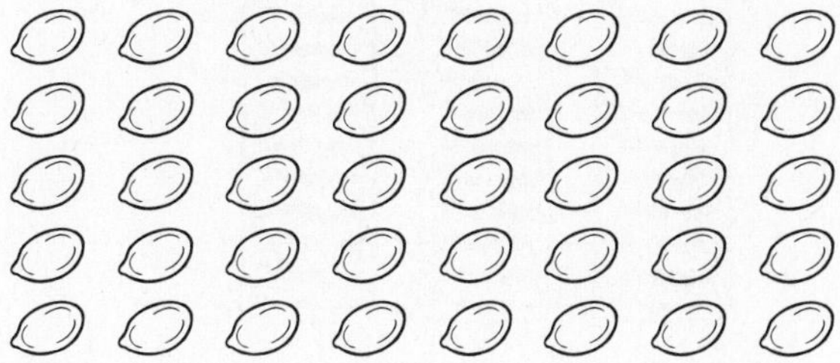

3. There are _____ ones.

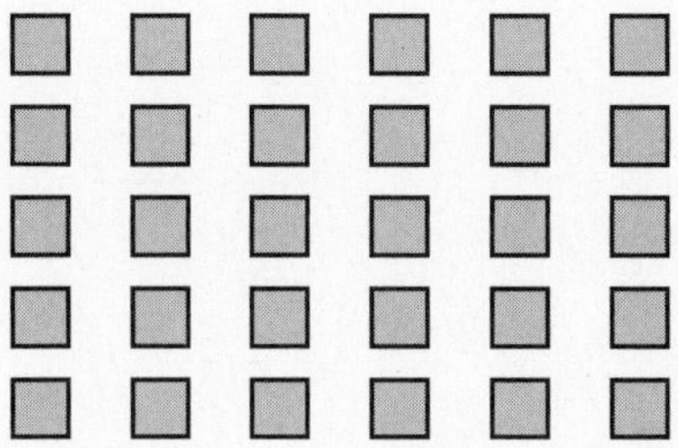

_____ ones makes _____ tens.

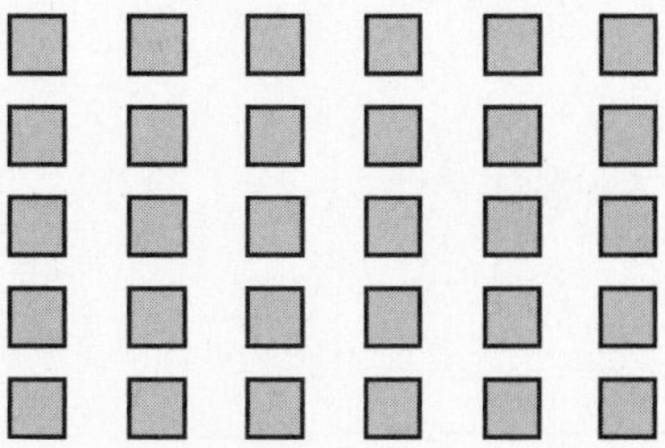

Name ____________________

Models for Tens

Write the number of ones.
Draw the tens that you can make.
Write the number of tens.

1.

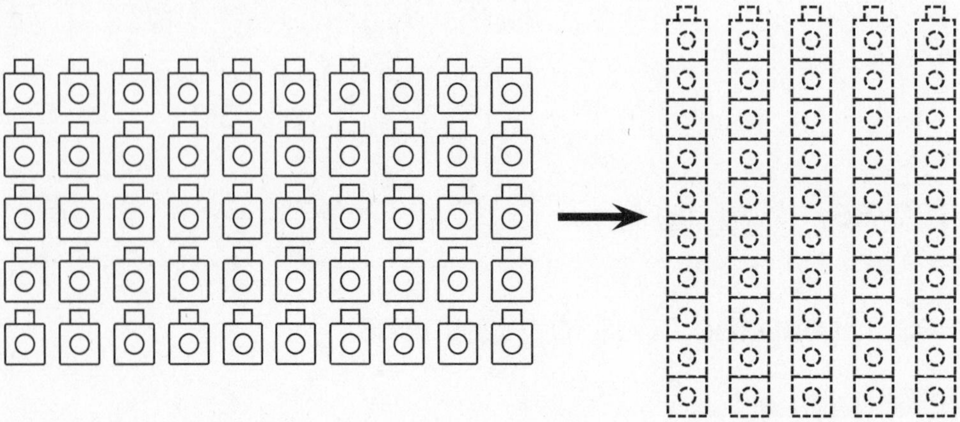

50 ones   5 tens

2. Serena has these packs of crackers. Each pack has 10 crackers. How many crackers does Serena have in all?

○ 20 crackers
○ 40 crackers
○ 30 crackers
○ 50 crackers

3. **Geometry** Which shape would you make if you pushed a cube into the sand?

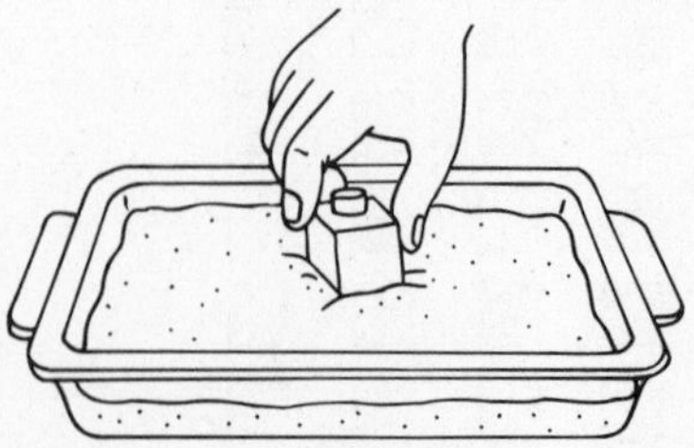

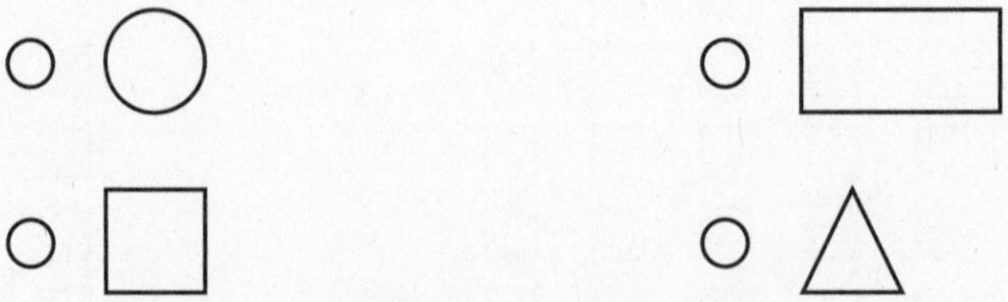

Name ____________________

Models for Tens and Ones

Ally had 35 raisins to make a snack.
She grouped the raisins into tens and ones.

The raisins on the celery show tens.

The leftover raisins show the ones.

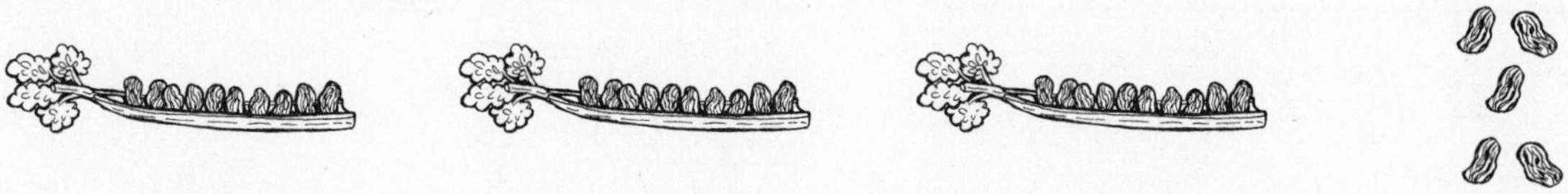

1 ten 1 ten 1 ten ones

3 tens and 5 ones is 35.

Count the tens and ones.
Write the numbers.

1. 

_____ ten and _____ ones is _____

2. 

_____ tens and _____ ones is _____

3. 

_____ tens and _____ ones is _____

Name ______________________________

Practice
4-2

Models for Tens and Ones

Circle groups of ten.
Tell how many tens and ones.
Write the number.

1. 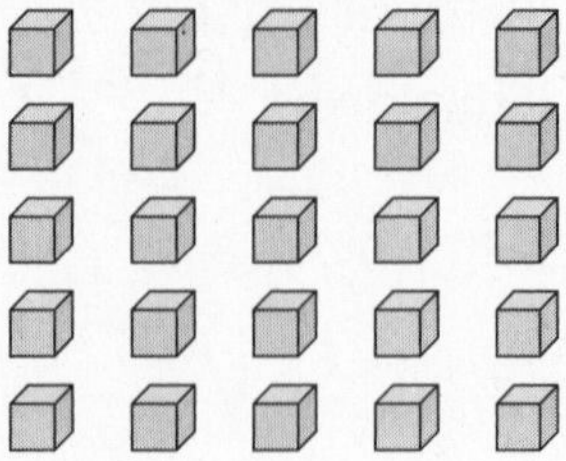

2 tens 5 ones

25

2. 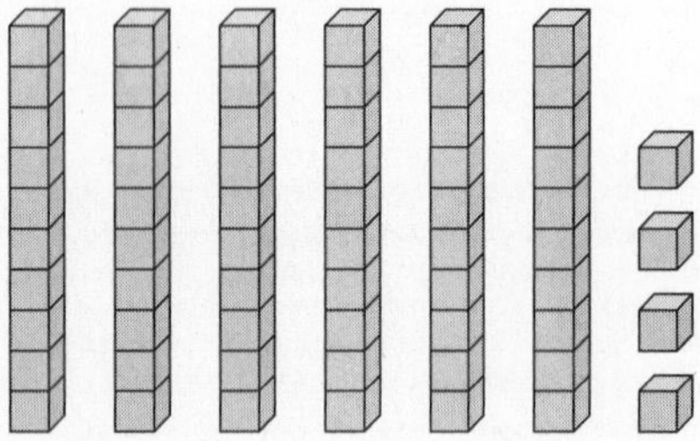

_____ tens _____ ones

_____

3. Sharon cut open this watermelon.
How many seeds can you see?

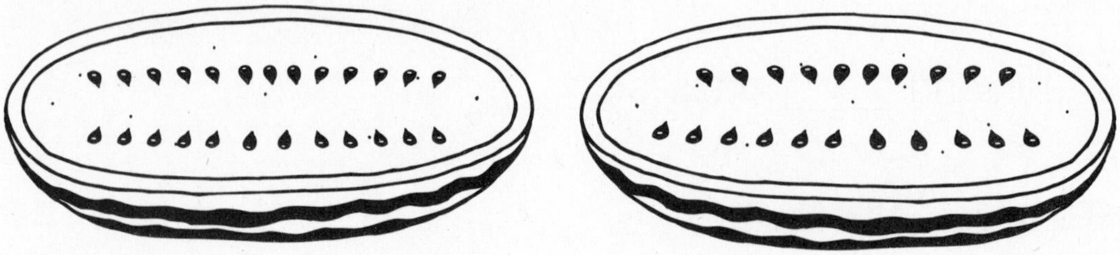

_____ tens _____ ones = _____ seeds

4. Estimation Terry has about 20 keys.

Which number could be the exact number of keys that Terry has?

9	21	35	42
○	○	○	○

Name ______________________

Reteaching
4-3

Reading and Writing Numbers

Ones	Teens	Tens
1 one	11 eleven	10 ten
2 two	12 twelve	20 twenty
3 three	13 thirteen	30 thirty
4 four	14 fourteen	40 forty
5 five	15 fifteen	50 fifty
6 six	16 sixteen	60 sixty
7 seven	17 seventeen	70 seventy
8 eight	18 eighteen	80 eighty
9 nine	19 nineteen	90 ninety

Write the number.

7 tens and 8 ones is 78.

78 has two **digits.**

Write the number word.

seventy and **eight** is

seventy-eight

Write the number and the number word.

1. 2 tens and 9 ones is _____. ______________________

2. 6 tens and 3 ones is _____. ______________________

3. 9 tens and 2 ones is _____. ______________________

4. 8 tens and 6 ones is _____. ______________________

Number Sense What is the number?

5. It is greater than 43 and less than 52. If you add the digits, the sum is 8. Write the number word.

____

6. It is less than 60 and greater than 55. If you add the digits, the sum is 13. Write the number.

_____

Name ______________________

Practice
4-3

Reading and Writing Numbers

Write the number.

1. forty-two 42

2. sixty-five _____

3. fifteen _____

4. fifty-one _____

Write the number word.

5. 33 thirty-three

6. 17 ______________________

7. 57 ______________________

8. 26 ______________________

9. 48 ______________________

10. 39 ______________________

11. What number do the cubes show?

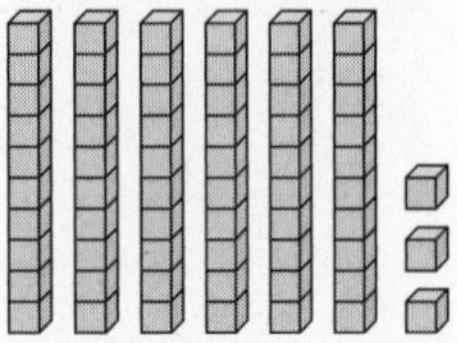

○ ten

○ sixty

○ thirty-six

○ sixty-three

12. Number Sense Write the number word to solve the riddle.

I am greater than 4 tens and less than 5 tens.
I have 9 ones. What number am I?

____

Name ___________________________

Reteaching
4-4

Using Models to Compare Numbers

Compare these numbers.
First compare the tens.

Tens	Ones
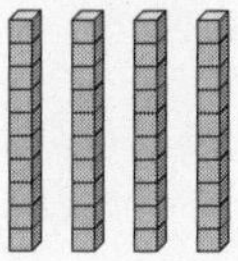	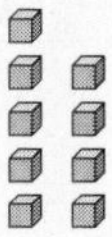

Tens	Ones
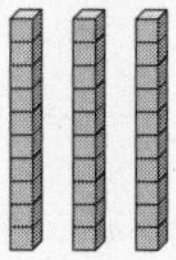	

49 is greater than 35

Compare these numbers.
If the tens are the same, compare the ones.

Tens	Ones
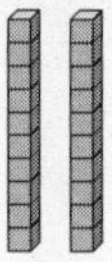	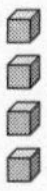

Tens	Ones
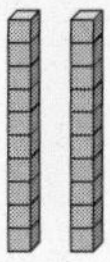	

24 is less than 25

Use cubes to show the numbers. Write **greater than** or **less than** to compare the numbers.

1. 40 is ______________ 50
2. 44 is ______________ 32
3. 37 is ______________ 34
4. 62 is ______________ 61

Name ____________________

Using Models to Compare Numbers

Write the numbers.

Circle **is greater than** or **is less than.**

1. 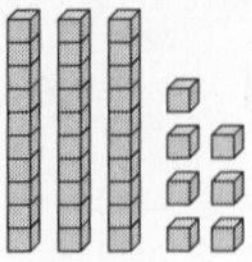 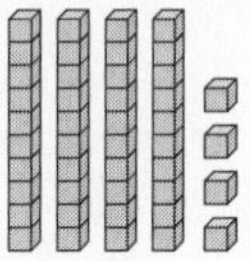

37 is greater than / (is less than) 44

2. 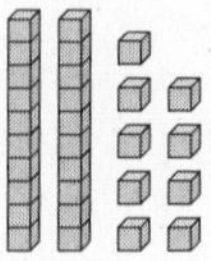 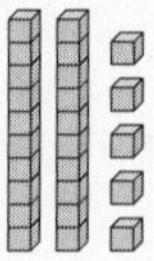

____ is greater than / is less than ____

3. Trevor saw 22 monkeys in a picture. He saw 29 birds in the same picture. Did Trevor see more birds or more monkeys?

more ________________

4. Kenya has 18 grapes. She has 21 berries. Does Kenya have more grapes or more berries?

more ________________

5. Laura counted 36 stars.
Andy counted more stars than Laura.
How many stars could Andy have counted?

○ 41 stars ○ 30 stars

○ 35 stars ○ 29 stars

6. **Reasoning** What number am I?

My tens digit is double my ones digit.
I am less than 70 and greater than 60.

____

Name ______________________________

Reteaching
4-5

Using Symbols to Compare Numbers

Compare numbers using >, <, and =.

> means "is greater than".
< means "is less than".
= means "equal to".

Tens	Ones
3	4

34 > 32
is more than

Tens	Ones
3	2

Tens	Ones
3	2

32 < 34
is less than

Tens	Ones
3	4

Tens	Ones
3	2

32 = 32
is equal to

Tens	Ones
3	2

Write less than, greater than, or equal to.
Circle >, <, or =.

1. 13 is ______________ 31.

13 > < = 31

2. 24 is ______________ 24.

24 > < = 24

3. 67 is ______________ 57.

67 > < = 57

4. 63 is ______________ 74.

63 > < = 74

Name ______________________________

Practice
4-5

Using Symbols to Compare Numbers

Write >, <, or = in the ◯.

1. 17 (<) 21

2. 59 ◯ 54

3. 29 ◯ 29

4. 12 ◯ 21

5. Solve. Write the numbers.
Write <, > or = in the ◯. A toy store has 38 red spiders. It has 43 black spiders. Does it have more red spiders or black spiders?

____ ◯ ____ more ________ spiders

6. A blue jar has 25 marbles. A red jar has 53 marbles. Which shows how to compare the number of marbles?

○ 25 = 53 ○ 53 < 25

○ 25 > 53 ○ 53 > 25

7. **Journal** One box holds 16 crayons. Another box holds 24 crayons. Write a sentence using words that compares the crayons in the two boxes.

____

____

Then write a number sentence that compares the two boxes. Use > or <.

____ ◯ ____

Name ______________________________

Before, After, Between

1	2	3	4	5	6	7	8	9	10
11	12	13	14	15	16	17	18	19	20
21	22	23	24	25	26	27	28	29	30
31	32	33	34	35	36	37	38	39	40
41	42	43	44	45	46	47	48	49	50
51	52	53	54	55	56	57	58	59	60
61	62	63	64	65	66	67	68	69	70
71	72	73	74	75	76	77	78	79	80
81	82	83	84	85	86	87	88	89	90
91	92	93	94	95	96	97	98	99	100

Use the words **before, after,** and **between** to help you find the numbers.

One **before** 66 is 65.

One **after** 66 is 67.

66 is between 65 and 67.

Write the numbers.

1. One before 12 is _____.

One after 12 is _____.

The number between

_____ and _____ is 12.

2. One before 70 is _____.

One after 70 is _____.

The number between

_____ and _____ is 70.

3. One before 45 is _____.

One after 45 is _____.

The number between

_____ and _____ is 45.

4. One before 91 is _____.

One after 91 is _____.

The number between

_____ and _____ is 91.

Name ______________________

Practice **4-6**

Before, After, and Between

Write the number that is 1 before, 1 after, or between.
You can use the hundred chart to help.

Before 1. 62, 63 2. _____, 51

After 3. 39, _____ 4. 98, _____

Between 5. 14, _____, 16 6. 71, _____, 73

7. The number on the white cap is 1 more than 52 and 1 less than 54. What number goes on the white cap?

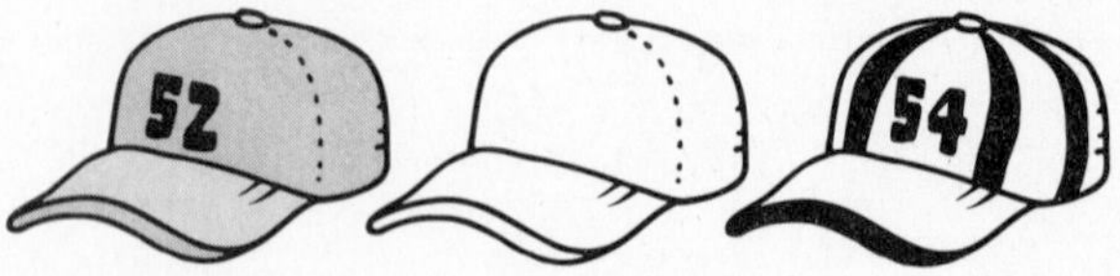

1	2	3	4	5	6	7	8	9	10
11	12	13	14	15	16	17	18	19	20
21	22	23	24	25	26	27	28	29	30
31	32	33	34	35	36	37	38	39	40
41	42	43	44	45	46	47	48	49	50
51	52	53	54	55	56	57	58	59	60
61	62	63	64	65	66	67	68	69	70
71	72	73	74	75	76	77	78	79	80
81	82	83	84	85	86	87	88	89	90
91	92	93	94	95	96	97	98	99	100

○ 25 ○ 53

○ 35 ○ 55

8. What number is it?

The number is **after** 45 and **before** 47.

74 ○ 48 ○ 46 ○ 44 ○

9. Spatial Thinking Which number comes **10 after** 76 on the hundred chart?

77 ○ 85 ○ 86 ○ 87 ○

Name ______________________________

Order Numbers

Order 54, 36, and 47 from least to greatest.

Look at the tens first.

54 **36** **47**

36, 47, 54

least greatest

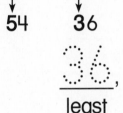

Compare two numbers at a time.

Now order 64, 52, and 63 from least to greatest.

If the tens are the same, look at the ones.

64 52 **63**

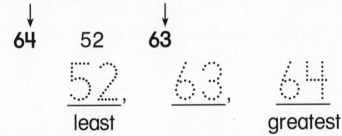

52, 63, 64

least greatest

Write the numbers in order from least to greatest.

1. 82, 46, 12

_____, _____, _____

least greatest

2. 32, 61, 22

_____, _____, _____

least greatest

3. 16, 24, 17

_____, _____, _____

least greatest

4. 89, 81, 85

_____, _____, _____

least greatest

5. Journal Draw three racecars with the numbers 25, 18, 77 in order from least to greatest.

Name ___________________________

Practice
4-7

Order Numbers

Write the numbers in order from least to greatest.

1. 80, 8, 51

8, 51, 80
least greatest

2. 24, 32, 16

____, ____, ____
least greatest

3. 96, 78, 87

____, ____, ____
least greatest

4. 44, 64, 62

____, ____, ____
least greatest

5. Reasonableness Which number is between 45 and 68?

○ 52 ○ 31

○ 69 ○ 43

45, ____, 68

6. The chart shows the points that three children earned. Which list shows their points in order from greatest to least?

Spelling Bee Points	
Tommy	21
Paige	34
Kris	17

○ 21, 34, 17 ○ 17, 34, 21

○ 17, 21, 34 ○ 34, 21, 17

Name ______________________________

Reteaching
4-8

Number Patterns on the Hundred Chart

1	2	3	4	5	6	7	8	9	10
11	12	13	14	15	16	17	18	19	20
21	22	23	24	25	26	27	28	29	30
31	32	33	34	35	36	37	38	39	40
41	42	43	44	45	46	47	48	49	50
51	52	53	54	55	56	57	58	59	60
61	62	63	64	65	66	67	68	69	70
71	72	73	74	75	76	77	78	79	80
81	82	83	84	85	86	87	88	89	90
91	92	93	94	95	96	97	98	99	100

Look for patterns on the hundred chart.

Start at 10.
Circle skip counts by 10s.

What is the ones digit in each number?

0
_____

1. Start at 5.
Shade skip counts by 5s with a yellow crayon.
What numbers do you find in the ones digit?

_____ _____

2. Start at 2.
Underline skip counts by 2s.
What numbers do you find in the ones digit?

_____ _____ _____ _____ _____

3. **Number Sense** Find the pattern.
Write the next three numbers.

20, 30, 40, _____, _____, _____

Name ______________________________

Number Patterns on the Hundred Chart

Finish skip counting.

1	2	3	4	5	6	7	8	9	10
11	12	13	14	15	16	17	18	19	20
21	22	23	24	25	26	27	28	29	30
31	32	33	34	35	36	37	38	39	40
41	42	43	44	45	46	47	48	49	50
51	52	53	54	55	56	57	58	59	60
61	62	63	64	65	66	67	68	69	70
71	72	73	74	75	76	77	78	79	80
81	82	83	84	85	86	87	88	89	90
91	92	93	94	95	96	97	98	99	100

1. Count by 2s.
   Circle each number.

2. Count by 3s.
   Put an X over each number.

3. Which numbers did you circle and put an X over?

____

____

Use the hundred chart. Find the pattern.

4. Which car comes next?

○ 

○ 

○ 

○ 

5. **Algebra** What is the next number in this pattern?
   16, 18, 20, _____

23	22	21	14
○	○	○	○

Name ____________________

Locating Numbers on the Number Line

Put 46, 41, and 49 in order.
Use a number line.

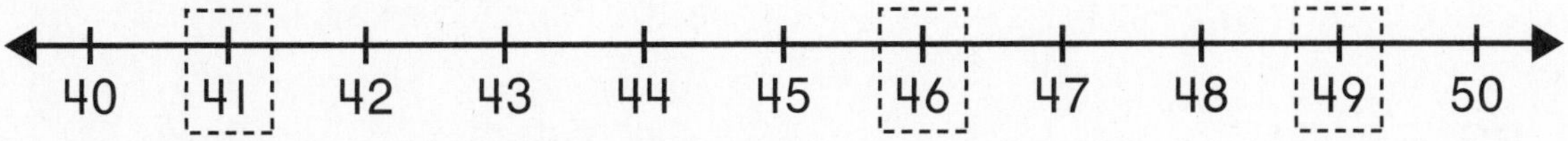

46 is **after** 41. It is **before** 49.
46 is **between** 41 and 49.

The numbers in order from least to greatest are:

41, 46, 49

Use the number line. Write the numbers in order from least to greatest.

1. 39, 22, 28

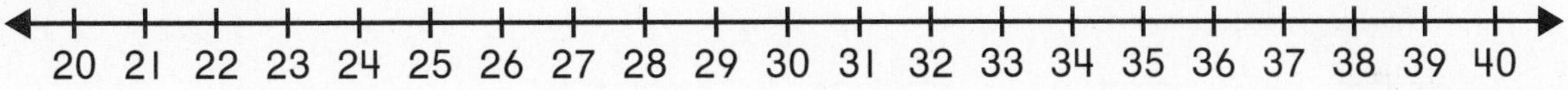

____, ____, ____

2. 67, 71, 77, 64

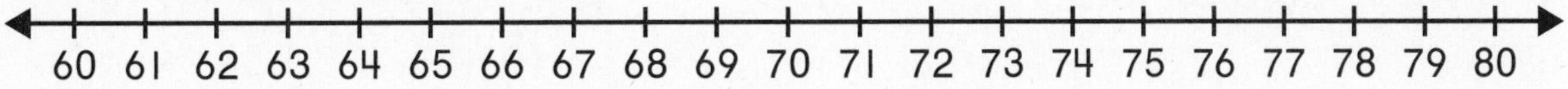

____, ____, ____, ____

3. 52, 48, 75, 69

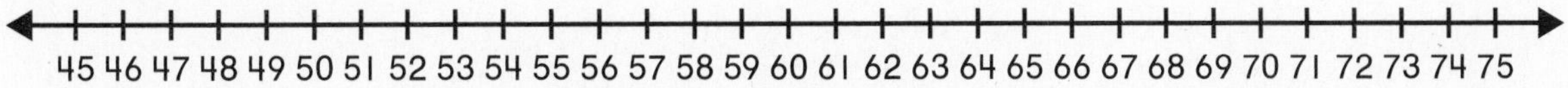

____, ____, ____, ____

Name ____________________

Locating Numbers on the Number Line

Use the number line below.
Write the numbers in order from least to greatest.

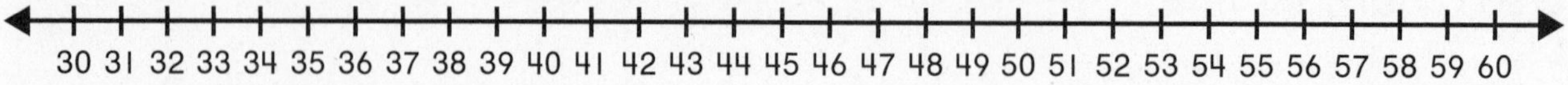

1. 45, 32, 59, 51

32 45 ____ ____
least greatest

2. 35, 45, 60, 30

____ ____ ____ ____
least greatest

3. 49, 37, 68, 55

____ ____ ____ ____
least greatest

4. What number am I? I am one number less than 30. My ones digit is a 9.

○ 39 ○ 31

○ 35 ○ 29

5. **Algebra** What is the missing number?

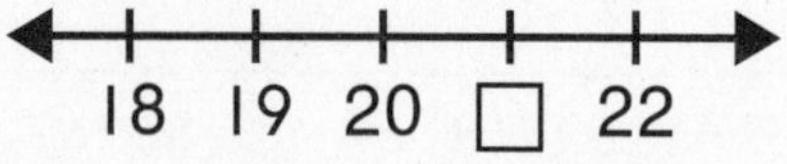

○ 15 ○ 21

○ 17 ○ 23

Name ______________________________

Reteaching
4-10

Problem Solving: Use Data From a Chart

Use clues to find the secret number on the chart.
Cross out numbers on the chart that do not fit each clue.

Clues:

It is greater than 25. → Cross out the numbers 25 and *less.*

It is less than 30. → Cross out the numbers 30 and *greater.*

It has a 7 in the ones place. → Cross out the numbers that don't have a 7 in the ones place. 26, 28, 29

11	12	13	14	15	16	17	18	19	20
21	22	23	24	25	26	27	28	29	30
31	32	33	34	35	36	37	38	39	40

The secret number is 27.

Use the clues to find the secret number.

31	32	33	34	35	36	37	38	39	40
41	42	43	44	45	46	47	48	49	50
51	52	53	54	55	56	57	58	59	60

It is greater than 40. → Cross out the numbers _____ and less.

It is less than 46. → Cross out the numbers _____ and greater.

It has a 5 in the ones place. → Cross out the numbers

______________________.

The secret number is _____.

Name ______________________________

Practice
4-10

Problem Solving: Use Data from a Chart

Use clues to find the secret number.
Cross out the numbers on the chart that do not fit the clues.

1. The secret number is an even number.
It is more than 50.
It has 4 ones.

31	32	33	34	35	36	37	38	39	40
41	42	43	44	45	46	47	48	49	50
51	52	53	54	55	56	57	58	59	60

The secret number is 54.

2. The secret number has a 7 in the ones place.
The tens number is an odd number.

61	62	63	64	65	66	67	68	69	70
71	72	73	74	75	76	77	78	79	80
81	82	83	84	85	86	87	88	89	90

The secret number is _____.

Use the clues and the chart to solve the problem.

3. Reasonableness The flag that Nico waves has an odd number in the ones place and an even number in the tens place.

Numbers on Racing Flags	
Red Flag	25
Blue Flag	14
Yellow Flag	32
Green Flag	6
Orange Flag	17

What flag does he wave?

○ Red ○ Blue ○ Yellow ○ Green

Name ____________________

Reteaching
5-1

Flat Surfaces, Vertices, and Edges

Some solid figures have **flat surfaces**. Some have **edges** and **vertices**.

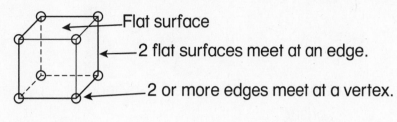

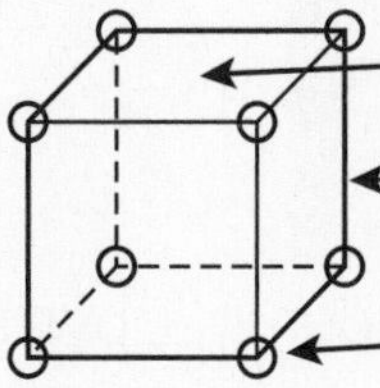

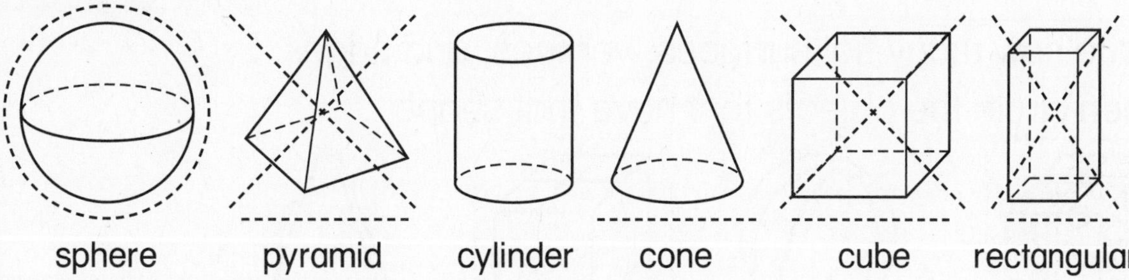

Put an X on the solid figures that have edges.
Underline the solid figures that have vertices.
Circle the solid figure that does not have a flat surface.

Write the number of flat surfaces or faces, edges, and vertices. Use solid figures to help you.

1.

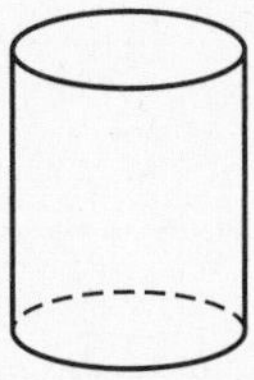

flat surfaces 2

edges ____

vertices ____

2.

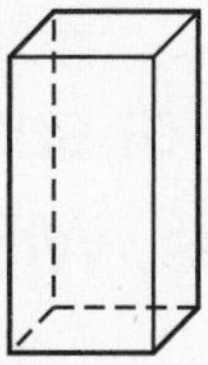

flat surfaces ____

edges ____

vertices ____

Name ______________________________

Practice
5-1

Flat Surfaces, Vertices, and Edges

rectangular prism | cube | cylinder | pyramid | sphere | cone

1. Write how many flat surfaces, vertices, and edges. Then circle the objects that have that shape.

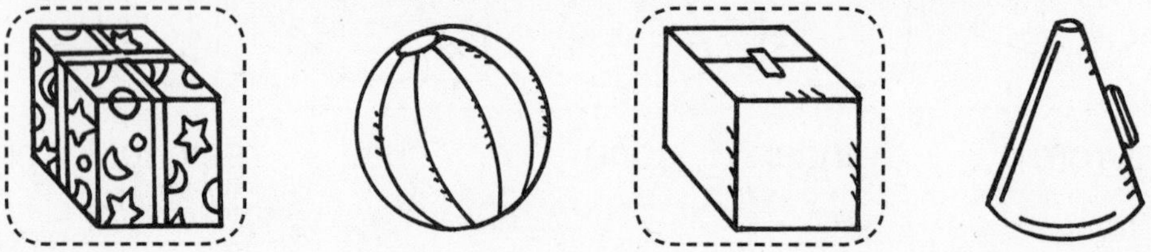

A cube has __6__ flat surfaces, _____ vertices, and _____ edges.

2. Ming's shape has 2 flat surfaces. It has no edges and no vertices. What shape is it?

○ ○ ○ ○

3. Kim's shape has no flat surfaces. It has no edges and no vertices. What shape is it?

○ ○ ○ ○

4. Algebra How many edges do these two shapes have in all? Write a number sentence.

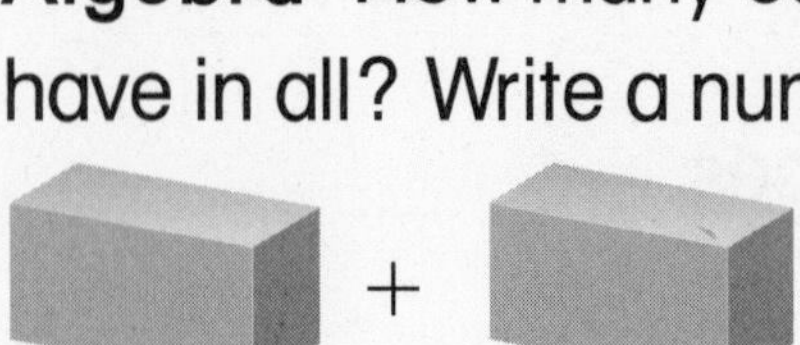

_____ + _____ = _____

The two shapes have _____ edges in all.

Name ______________________

Relating Plane Shapes to Solid Figures

If you trace the flat surfaces of solid figures, you will get these plane shapes.

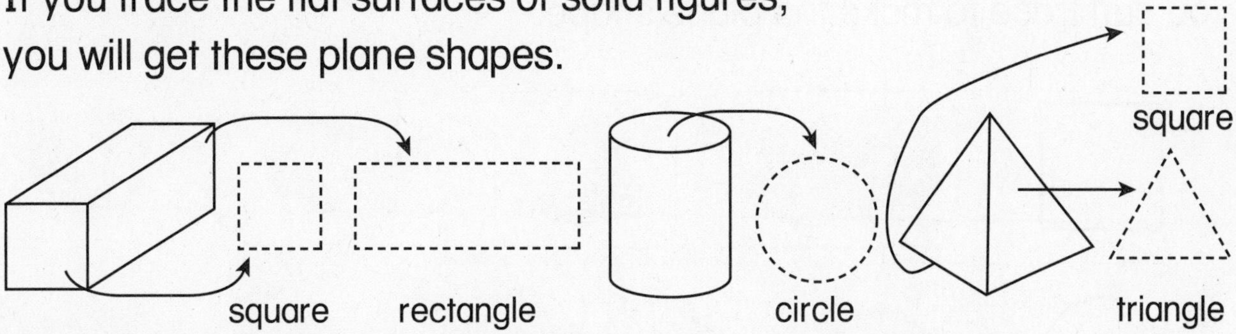

Use solid figures in your classroom.
Trace one flat surface.
Write the name of the shape you traced.

1. 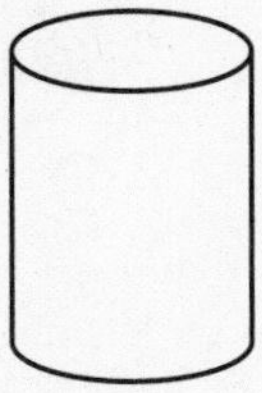 ______________________

2. 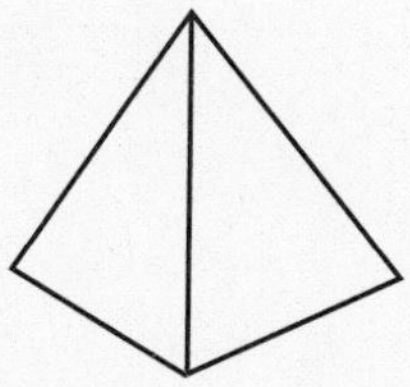 ______________________

3. 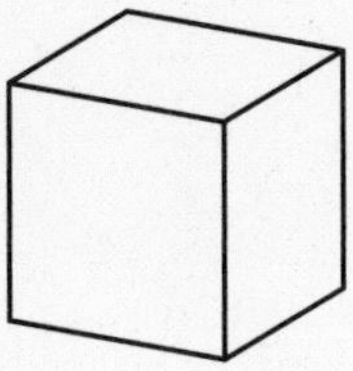 ______________________

4. 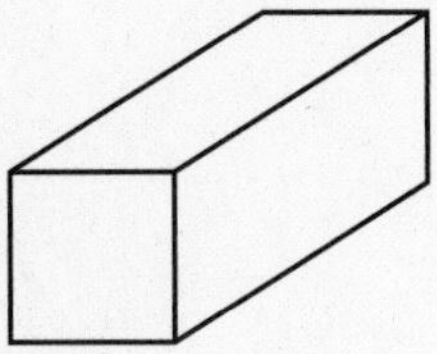 ______________________

Name ____________________

Practice
5-2

Relating Plane Shapes to Solid Figures

Circle the solid figure or figures that have flat surfaces you can trace to make the plane shape.

1. 

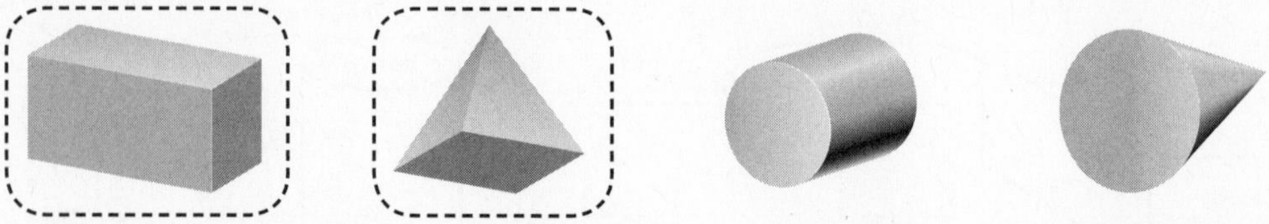

2. 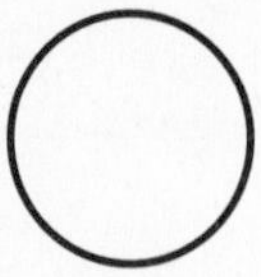

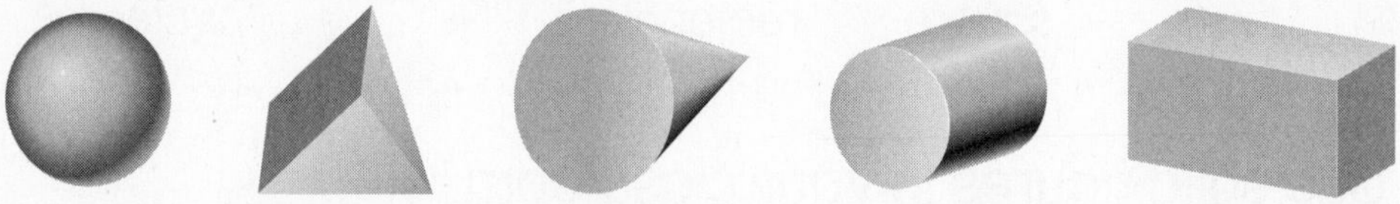

3. Dionne traces a square using a solid shape. Which solid shape does he have?

4. Which object did Maggie use to trace the rectangle?

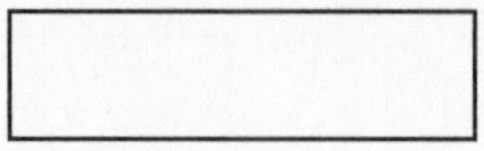

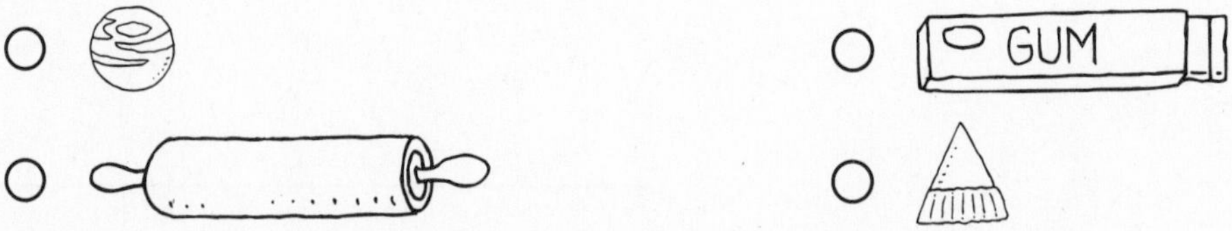

5. **Geometry** Circle the block or blocks Vincent can trace to draw the bug.

Name ______________________

Making New Shapes

You can make larger shapes from smaller shapes.

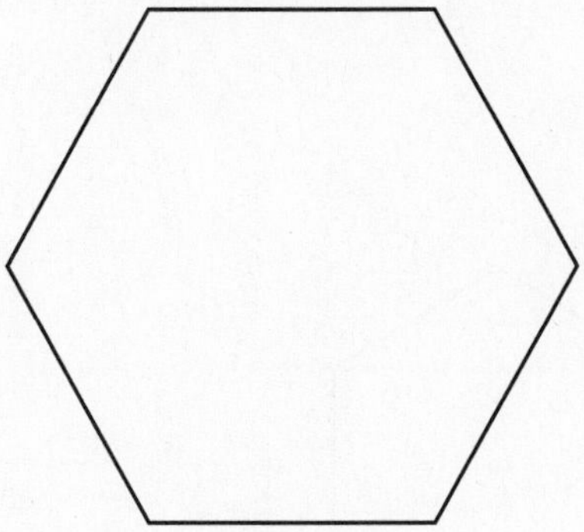

hexagon

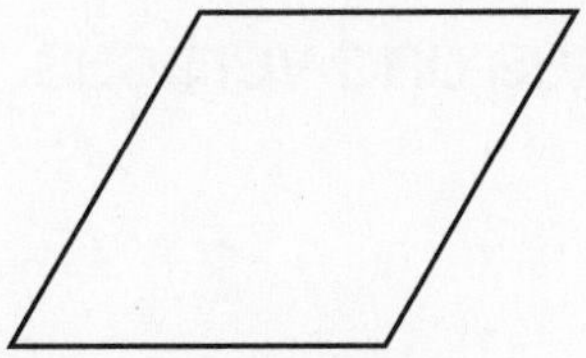

parallelogram

Use pattern blocks.

Put 2 parallelograms and a hexagon together to make this shape.

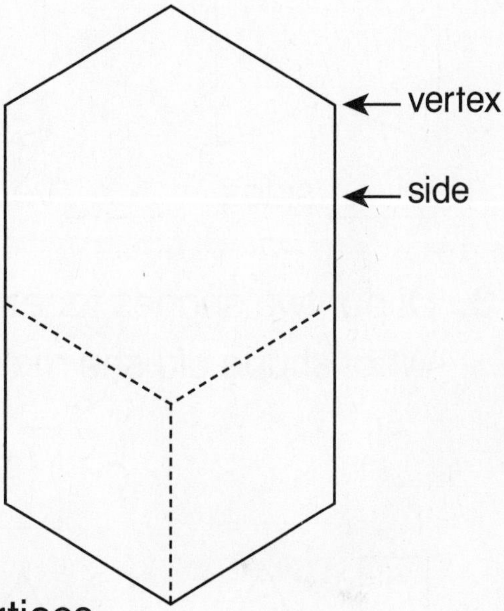

This shape has __6__ sides and __6__ vertices.

Spatial Thinking Use the pattern blocks shown to make a larger shape.
Trace the smaller shapes on the larger shape.
Write the number of sides and vertices.

I. 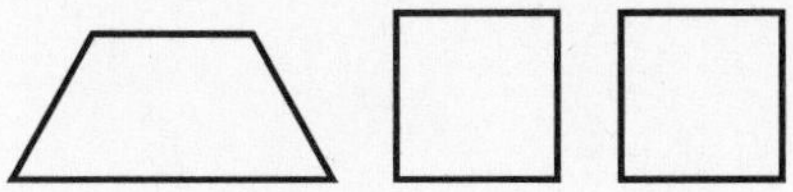

_____ sides

_____ vertices

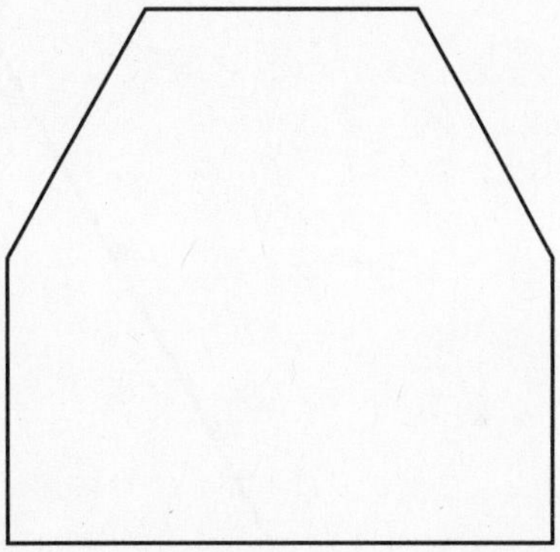

Name ____________________

Practice
5-3

Making New Shapes

Use pattern blocks to make the shape.
Trace and color to show one way to make it. Write the number of sides and vertices.

1.

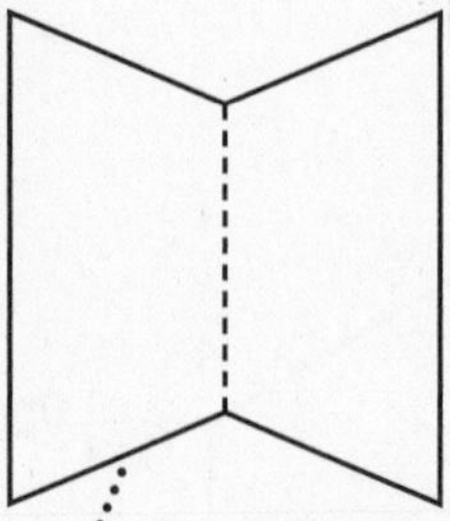

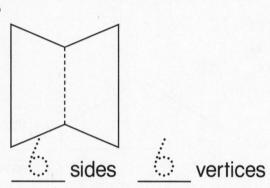

__6__ sides __6__ vertices

2.

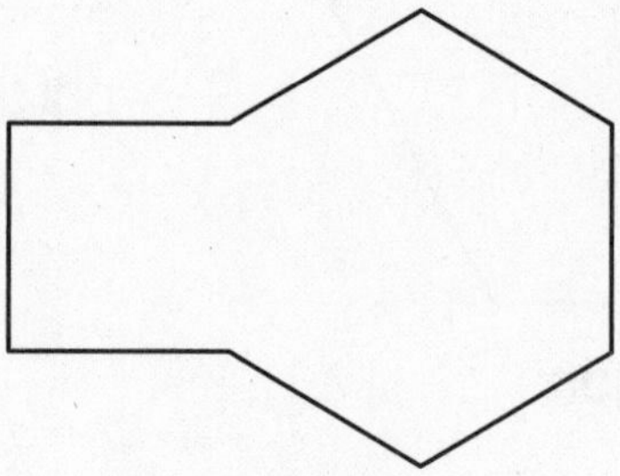

____ sides ____ vertices

3. Di put two shapes together.
What shape did she make?

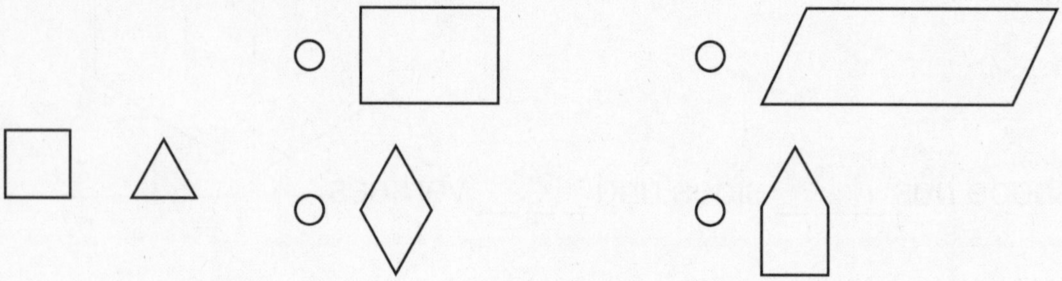

4. Spatial Thinking Make the triangle with 5 pattern blocks.

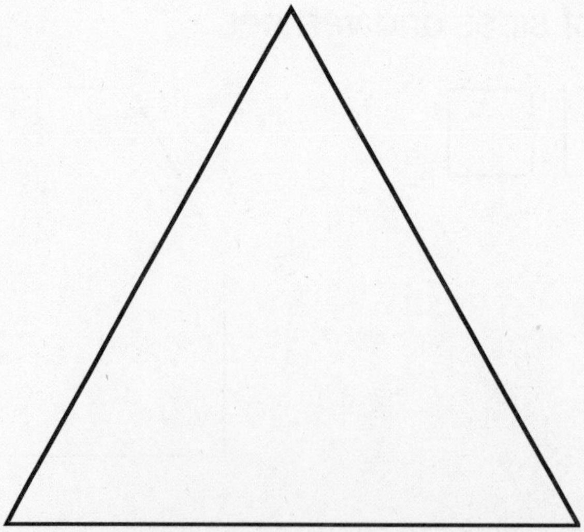

Name ________________________________

Cutting Shapes Apart

You can draw lines to cut a large shape into smaller shapes.

Draw 1 line to make

2 triangles.

Draw 2 lines to make

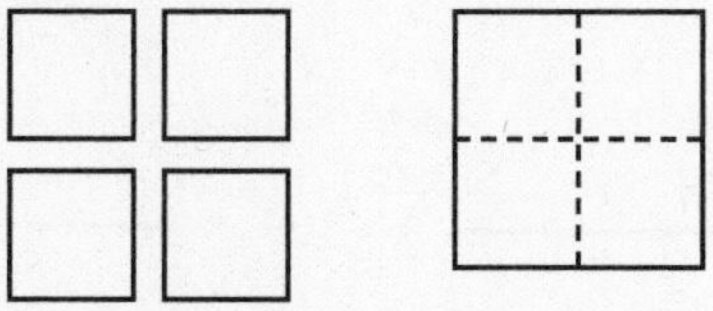

4 squares.

Draw lines to make the shapes shown.

1. Draw 2 lines to cut the square into

4 triangles.

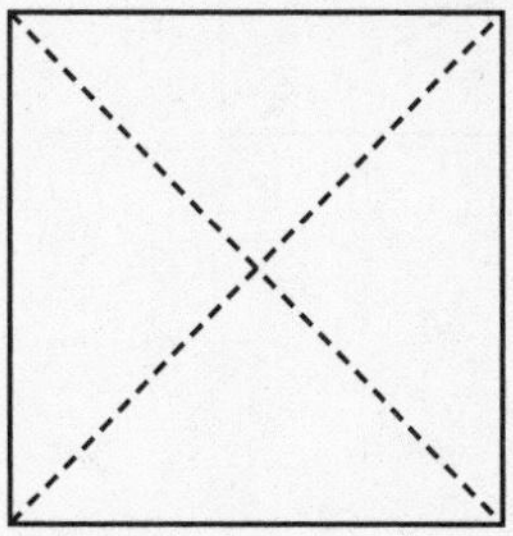

2. Draw 1 line to cut the hexagon into

2 trapezoids.

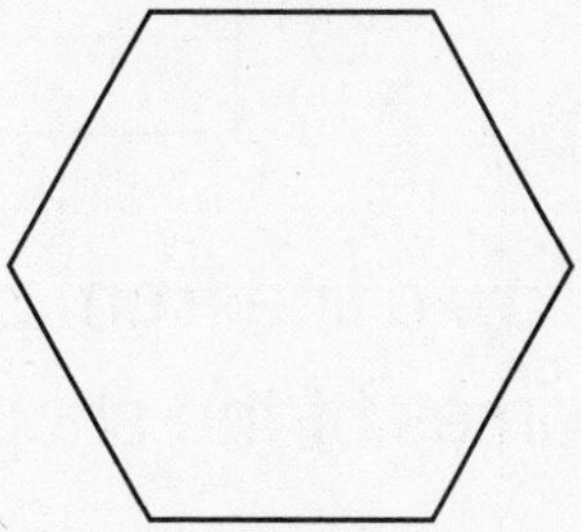

3. **Journal** Draw lines to cut the squares into rectangles.

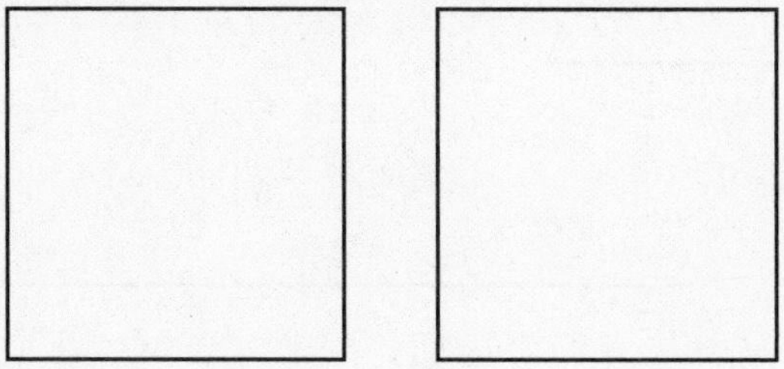

Name ______________________

Practice
5-4

Cutting Shapes Apart

Draw the number of lines shown to make new shapes.
Write the names of the shapes you made.

1. 2 lines

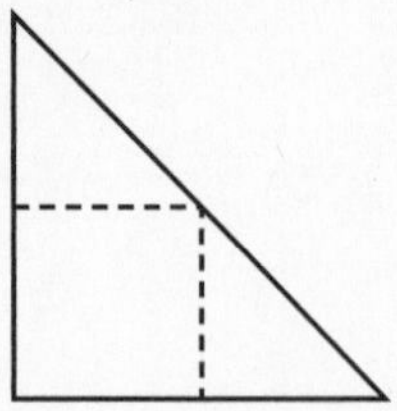

square

triangle

2. 1 line

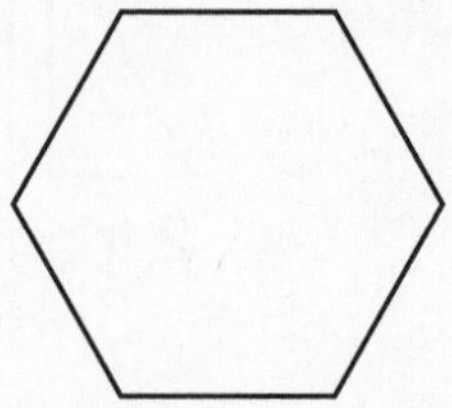

____

____

3. Dionne cut this shape into 2 triangles.
Which drawing shows how he cut it?

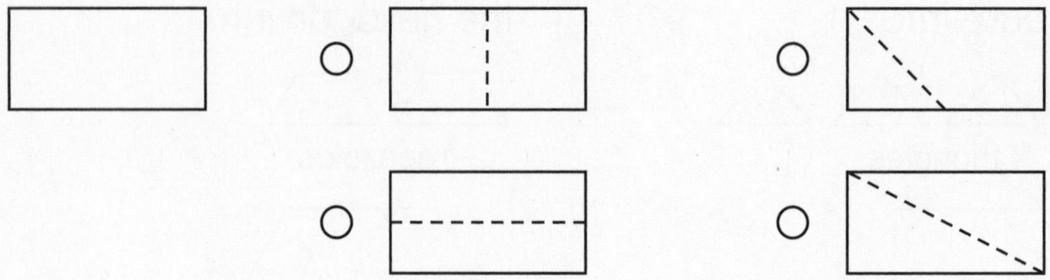

4. Journal Draw a line from point A to point B.
Write the names of the shapes you made.

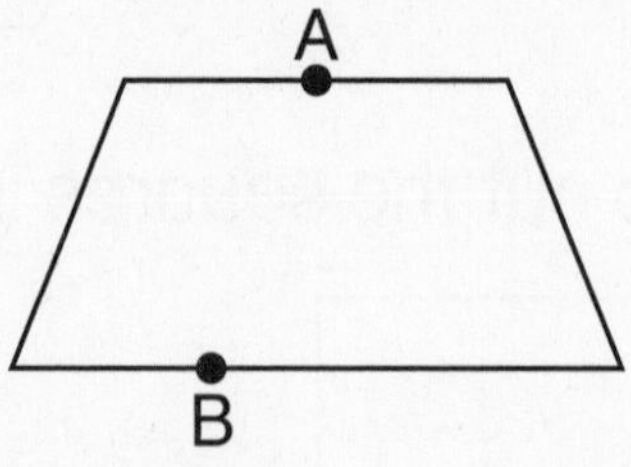

______________________ ______________________

Name ______________________________

Problem Solving: Use Reasoning

Read the clues.

I am not a square.
I do not have 4 sides.
Which shape am I?

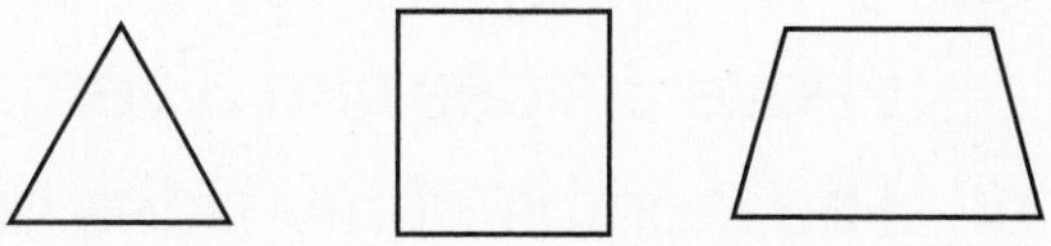

To find the shape, think:
It is not a square, so cross out the square.

It does not have 4 sides, so cross out the shape with 4 sides.

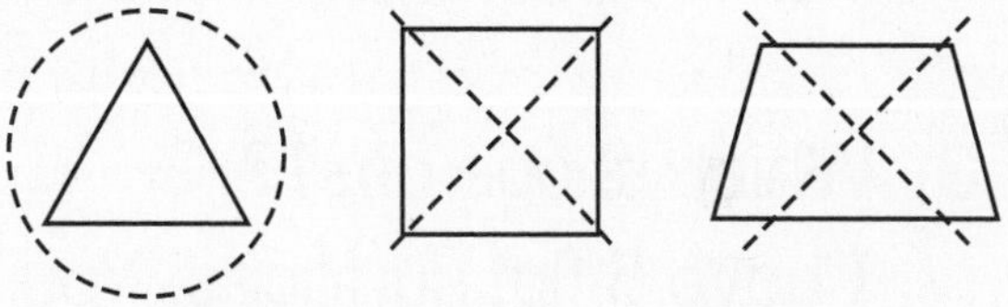

Circle the shape that fits the clues.

Cross out the solid figures or shapes that do not fit the clues. Circle the shape or solid figure that answers the question.

1. I do not have edges.
I am not a pyramid.
Which shape am I?

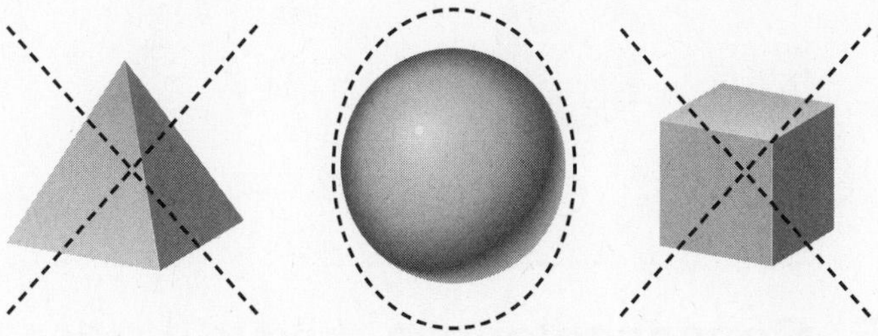

2. I do not have 6 sides.
I am not a circle.
Which shape am I?

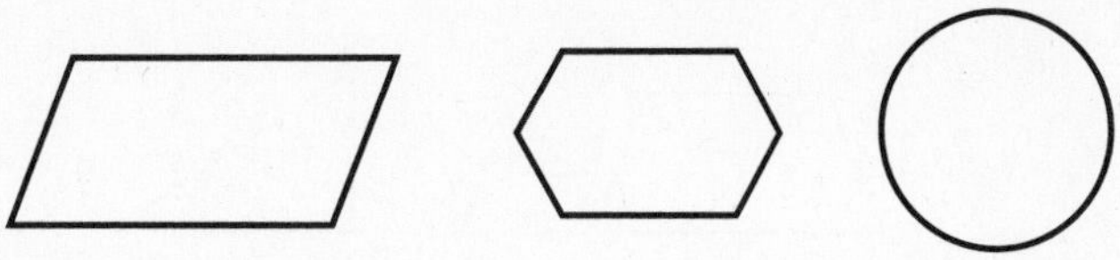

Name ______________________

Practice
5-5

Problem Solving: Use Reasoning

Cross out shapes that do not match the clues.
Circle the shape that answers the question.

1. Which shape am I?
I have 3 sides and 3 vertices.
The lengths of my sides are equal.

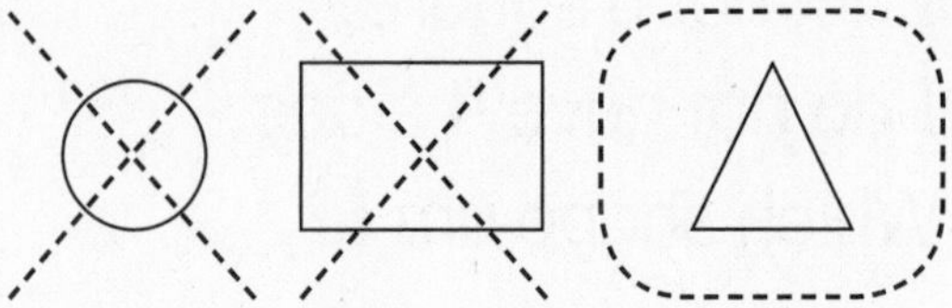

2. Which shape am I?
I have more than 5 sides.
The lengths of my sides are equal.

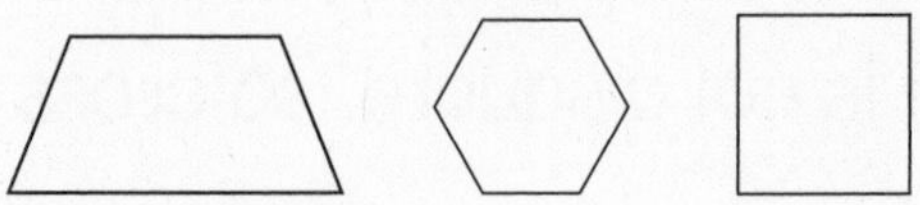

3. Which shape am I?
I have 5 flat surfaces. You can trace my flat surfaces to make a triangle and a rectangle.

4. I have no vertices or edges. I have 2 flat surfaces.
Which shows my shape?

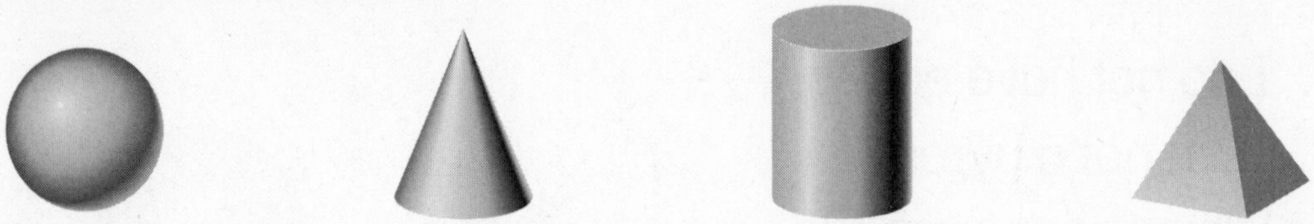

○ ○ ○ ○

5. **Reasonableness** I have 4 sides. The lengths of 2 of my sides are equal. Which shows my shape?

○ ○ ○ ○

Name ______________________

Reteaching
6-1

Adding Tens

To add tens, count on by tens.

When you add tens, only the digit in the tens place changes.

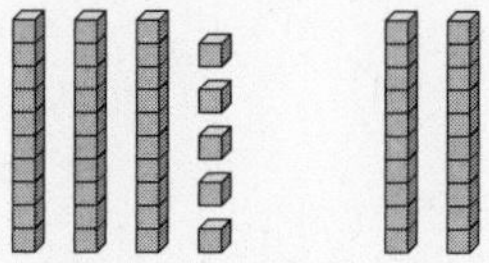

Think: Count on 2 tens.

Add: 35 and 20

35, 45, 55

So, 35 + 20 = 55.

Add tens. Use cubes or mental math.

1. 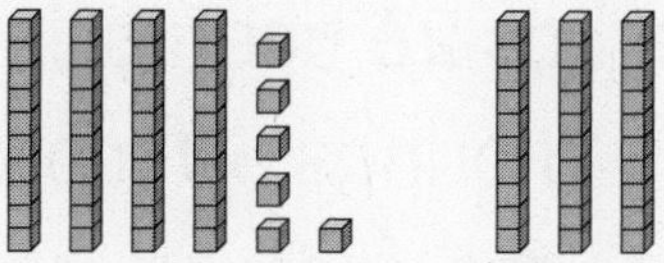

Count on 3 tens:

46, ___, ___, ___

46 and 30 = ___

46 + 30 = ___

2. 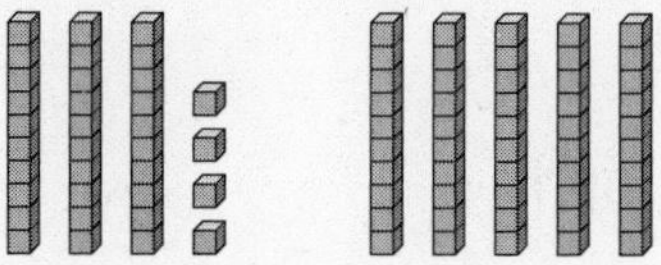

Count on 5 tens:

34, ___, ___, ___, ___, ___

34 and 50 = ___

34 + 50 = ___

3. 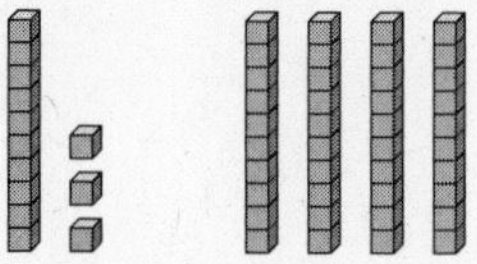

Count on 4 tens:

13, ___, ___, ___, ___

13 and 40 = ___

13 + 40 = ___

Name ______________________

Practice
6-1

Adding Tens

Add using mental math.

1. 20 + 42 = 62

2. 53 + 30 = _____

3. 50 + 19 = _____

4. 35 + 40 = _____

5. 36 + 10 = _____

47	46	40	37
○	○	○	○

6. 21 + 40 = _____

29	41	60	61
○	○	○	○

7. Nellie had 14 rubber bands. Then she bought a pack of 30 rubber bands.

How many rubber bands does Nellie have now?

_____ rubber bands

8. A squirrel has 26 acorns in its nest. It brings 50 more acorns into the nest.

How many acorns does the squirrel have in all?

_____ acorns

9. Spatial Thinking Draw tens and ones to solve.

69 + 20 = _____

Name ______________________

Adding Ones

36 + 7 = ____

Circle the ones to make the next ten.

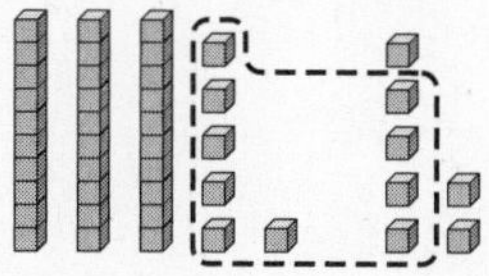

Think: 6 and 4 more make 10.
40 and 3 more make 43.

So, 36 + 7 = 43

Circle the ones to make the next ten.
Add the ones to the tens.

1. 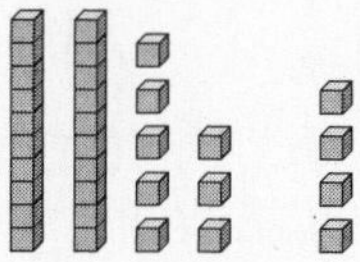

28 + 4 = ____

2. 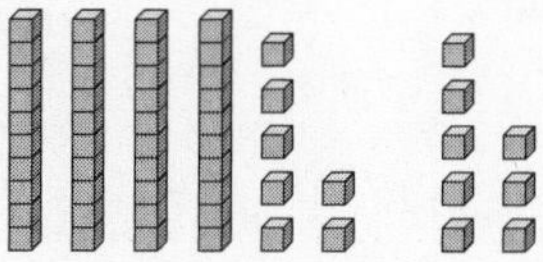

47 + 8 = ____

3. 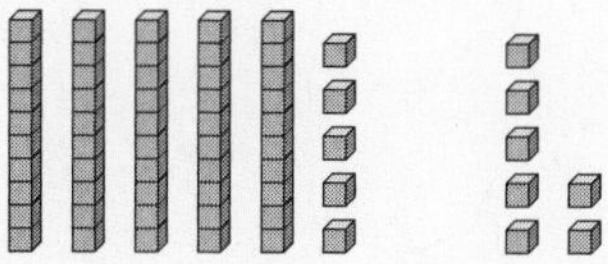

55 + 7 = ____

4. 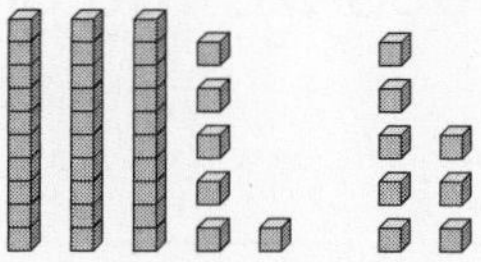

36 + 8 = ____

5. 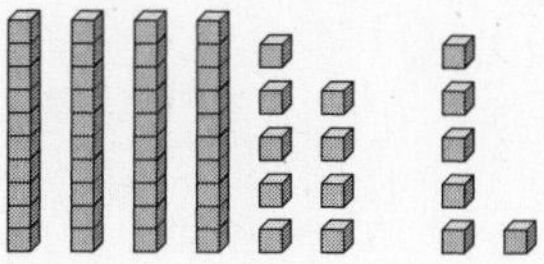

49 + 6 = ____

6. 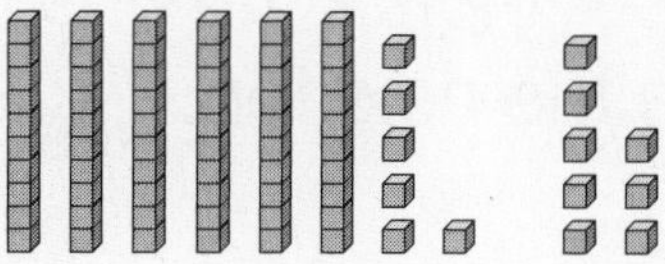

66 + 8 = ____

Name ______________________

Practice **6-2**

Adding Ones

Add the ones. Use mental math.

1. 17 + 4 = 21

2. 38 + 5 = ____

3. 49 + 3 = ____

4. 23 + 2 = ____

5. 65 + 7 = ____

6. 52 + 8 = ____

7. 38 + 9 = ____

47	41	31	17
○	○	○	○

8. 65 + 6 = ____

11	59	61	71
○	○	○	○

9. Janna made a necklace using 18 beads.

   Leah made a necklace using only 9 beads.

   How many beads did the girls use in all?

   ____ + ____ = ____

   ____ beads

10. **Algebra** Find the missing number that will make the next ten.

    53 + ____ = 60

6	7	8	9
○	○	○	○

Name ______________________________

Reteaching
6-3

Adding Tens and Ones

Find 25 + 34.

25 and 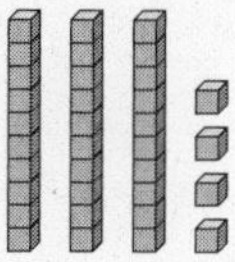

First, count on by tens to add the tens:

Think: 25 and 3 tens

25, 35, 45, 55

Then add the ones.

55 and 4 ones is 59.

So, 25 + 34 = 59.

Add. Use mental math or cubes.

1. 34 + 23

34 and 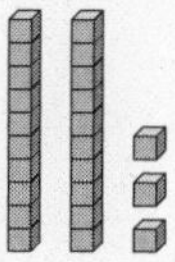

34, _____, _____

54 and _____ ones is _____.

So, 34 + 23 = _____.

2. 52 + 33

52 and 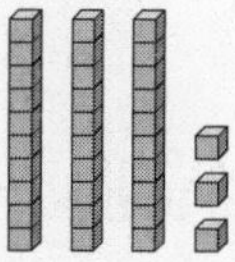

52, _____, _____, _____

_____ and _____ ones is _____.

So, 52 + 33 = _____.

3. 42 + 12 = _____

4. 25 + 21 = _____

Name ______________________

Practice
6-3

Adding Tens and Ones

Add using mental math.

1. 41 + 24 = 65

2. 53 + 15 = _____

3. 56 + 33 = _____

4. 62 + 25 = _____

5. 43 + 36 = _____

6. 50 + 25 = _____

7. 37 + 21 = _____

8. 17 + 52 = _____

9. 46 + 32 = _____

○ 68 ○ 70 ○ 74 ○ 78

10. 61 + 13 = _____

○ 78 ○ 74 ○ 70 ○ 63

11. Tad has 72 seashells. He finds 15 more shells.

How many seashells does Tad have in all?

○ 82 ○ 83 ○ 87 ○ 92

12. **Estimation** One bunch has 31 grapes.
Another bunch has 28 grapes.
About how many grapes are there in all?

○ about 30 grapes

○ about 60 grapes

○ about 50 grapes

○ about 70 grapes

Name ____________________

Reteaching
6-4

Adding on a Hundred Chart

Find 16 + 23.

1. Start on square 16.
2. Move down 2 rows to show the tens in 23.
3. Move 3 squares to the right to show the ones in 23.
4. Where did you stop? 39

So, 16 + 23 = 39

1	2	3	4	5	6	7	8	9	10
11	12	13	14	15	16	17	18	19	20
21	22	23	24	25	26	27	28	29	30
31	32	33	34	35	36	37	38	39	40
41	42	43	44	45	46	47	48	49	50
51	52	53	54	55	56	57	58	59	60
61	62	63	64	65	66	67	68	69	70
71	72	73	74	75	76	77	78	79	80
81	82	83	84	85	86	87	88	89	90
91	92	93	94	95	96	97	98	99	100

Add using the hundred chart.

1. 12 + 11 = _____
2. 31 + 45 = _____
3. 81 + 14 = _____
4. 48 + 51 = _____
5. 24 + 23 = _____
6. 33 + 56 = _____
7. 52 + 15 = _____
8. 15 + 14 = _____
9. **Number Sense** Write the number of tens in each number.

67 _____ tens   85 _____ tens   94 _____ tens

Name ____________________

Practice
6-4

Adding on a Hundred Chart

Add using the hundred chart.

1	2	3	4	5	6	7	8	9	10
11	12	13	14	15	16	17	18	19	20
21	22	23	24	25	26	27	28	29	30
31	32	33	34	35	36	37	38	39	40
41	42	43	44	45	46	47	48	49	50
51	52	53	54	55	56	57	58	59	60
61	62	63	64	65	66	67	68	69	70
71	72	73	74	75	76	77	78	79	80
81	82	83	84	85	86	87	88	89	90
91	92	93	94	95	96	97	98	99	100

1. 47 + 31 = 78

2. 18 + 25 = _____

3. 28 + 43 = _____

4. 37 + 56 = _____

5. 35 + 28 = _____

○ 65 ○ 63 ○ 62 ○ 60

6. 64 + 26 = _____

○ 80 ○ 82 ○ 90 ○ 92

7. Geometry Choose the shapes that answer the question.

What weights can you put on the scale to make it balance?

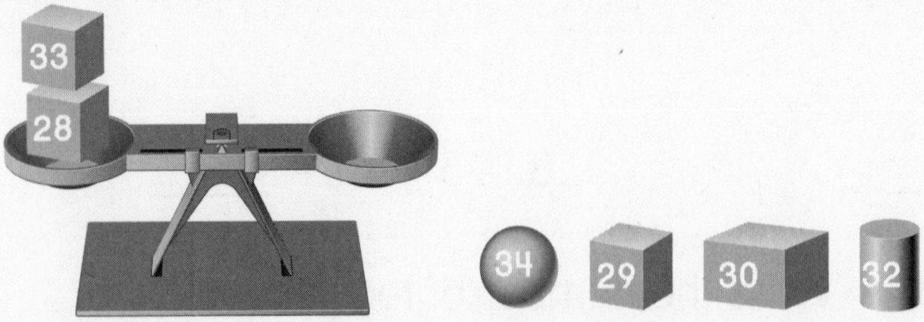

○ cube and cylinder

○ pyramid and cube

○ sphere and cube

○ rectangular prism and pyramid

Name ______________________________

Problem Solving: Look for a Pattern

Look for a pattern in these rows of buttons.
Draw buttons to finish the pattern.

2

4

6

8

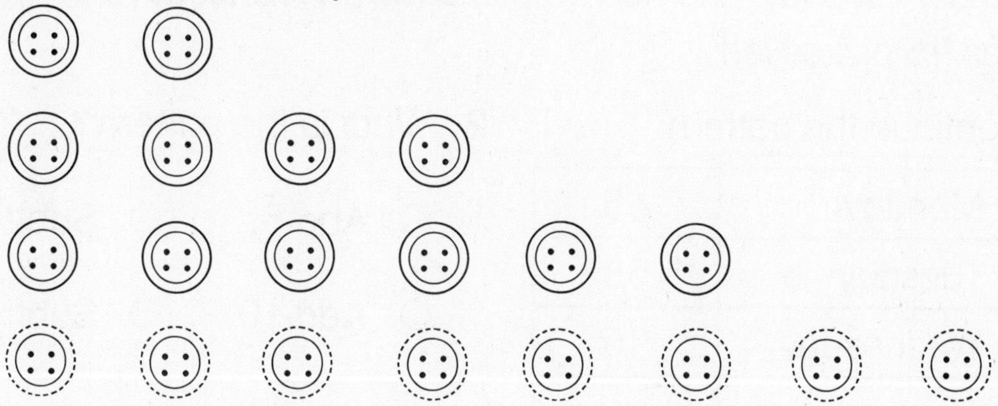

The pattern is to add 2 buttons each time.

Look for a pattern. Solve.

1. Emma is collecting cans for a recycling project. The chart shows how many cans she plans to collect each week.
What is the pattern?

Week 1	10 cans
Week 2	20 cans
Week 3	30 cans
Week 4	? cans
Week 5	? cans

_____ more cans each week

2. What is Emma's goal for week 4 and week 5?

Week 4: _____ Week 5: _____

3. **Journal** Create a pattern problem for a friend to solve. Draw a picture or write a story problem.

Name ____________________

Problem Solving: Look for a Pattern

Finish the pattern. Solve.
On Monday, a cook has 65 pizzas. Each day she cooks 10 pizzas. Tuesday, she has 55 pizzas left. Wednesday, she has 45 pizzas left.

1. Continue the pattern.

Monday	65
Tuesday	55
Wednesday	45
Thursday	35
Friday	25

2. What is the pattern?

○ Add 5. ○ Subtract 5.

○ Add 10. ○ Subtract 10.

In Week 1, Cleo picked 2 tomatoes. In Week 2, she picked 7 tomatoes. In Week 3, she picked 12 tomatoes.

3. Continue the pattern.

Week 1	2
Week 2	7
Week 3	12
Week 4	
Week 5	

4. What is the pattern?

○ Add 5. ○ Subtract 5.

○ Add 7. ○ Subtract 7.

5. Journal Patty made 4 headbands last week. She made 8 this week. Next week, she will make 12. What is the pattern? How many headbands will Patty make the following week?

____________________ _____ headbands

Name ______________________

Subtracting Tens

Here are two ways you can find 57 − 30.

When you subtract tens, only the tens digit changes.

1. Count back 3 tens, or 30.

57, 47, 37, 27

2. Use cubes to subtract the tens.

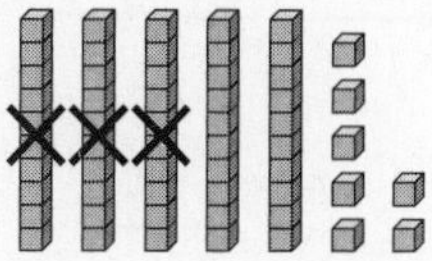

50 − 30 = 20

Then subtract the ones.

7 − 0 = 7

So, 57 − 30 = 27.

Count back to subtract tens. Use cubes if needed.

1. 64 − 30 =

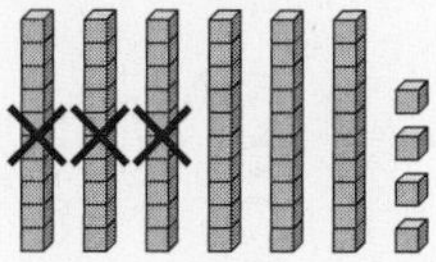

64, _____, _____, _____

64 − 30 = _____

2. 62 − 40 = _____

3. 76 − 20 = _____

4. 84 − 50 = _____

5. 95 − 70 = _____

Name ______________________

Subtracting Tens

Subtract. Use mental math.

1. 76 − 40 = 36

2. 98 − 50 = ____

3. 94 − 60 = ____

4. 33 − 20 = ____

5. 65 − 10 = ____

6. 52 − 30 = ____

7. 47 − 30 = ____

37	30	20	17
○	○	○	○

8. 61 − 40 = ____

20	21	30	41
○	○	○	○

9. Use mental math to solve.

A box holds 48 crackers. Austin ate 10 of them.

How many crackers are left in the box?

18	28	38	58
○	○	○	○

10. **Number Sense** Allie had 36¢. On Thursday she spent 10¢, and on Friday she spent 10¢ more.

How much money does she have now?

46¢	36¢	26¢	16¢
○	○	○	○

Name ______________________________

Reteaching
7-2

Finding Parts of 100

Find parts for 100.
Draw more tens to make 100.

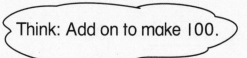

Think: Add on to make 100.

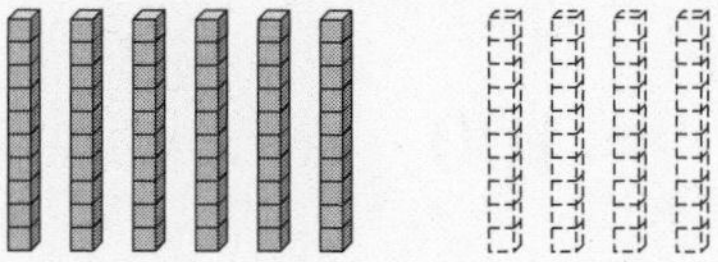

60 and __40__ is 100.

60 + __40__ = 100

Now draw tens and ones to make 100.

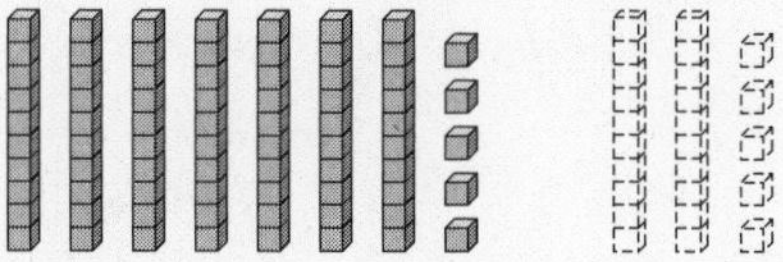

75 and __25__ is 100.

75 + __25__ = 100

Draw tens to find the other part of 100.

1. 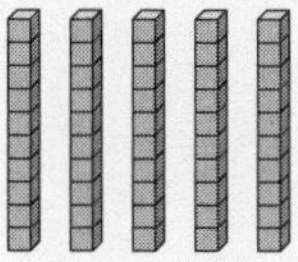

50 and _____ is 100.

50 + _____ = 100

Draw tens and ones to make 100. Add on.

2. 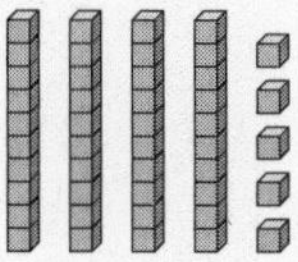

45 and _____ is 100.

45 + _____ = 100

Name ______________________

Practice
7-2

Finding Parts of 100

Add on to find the other part of 100.

1. 54 + __46__ = 100
2. 29 + ____ = 100
3. 43 + ____ = 100
4. 72 + ____ = 100
5. 89 + ____ = 100
6. 18 + ____ = 100
7. 37 + ____ = 100
8. 61 + ____ = 100
9. 65 + ____ = 100
10. 46 + ____ = 100

Solve.

11. Latisha had a box of 100 birthday cards. So far, she has sent out 47 cards.

    How many cards are left in the box?

    ○ 51 cards
    ○ 53 cards
    ○ 52 cards
    ○ 54 cards

12. **Reasonableness** Do not add or subtract. Read each answer. Choose the reasonable answer.

    A store had 100 class rings. They sold 37 rings. How many are left?

    ○ 63 rings
    ○ 35 rings
    ○ 50 rings
    ○ 10 rings

Name ______________________

Reteaching
7-3

Subtracting on a Hundred Chart

A hundred chart can help you subtract.

1	2	3	4	5	6	7	8	9	10
11	12	13	14	15	16	17	18	19	20
21	22	23	24	25	26	27	28	29	30
31	32	33	34	35	36	37	38	39	40
41	42	43	44	45	46	47	48	49	50
51	52	53	54	55	56	57	58	59	60
61	62	63	64	65	66	67	68	69	70
71	72	73	74	75	76	77	78	79	80
81	82	83	84	85	86	87	88	89	90
91	92	93	94	95	96	97	98	99	100

Find 36 − 24.

1. Start at 24.
2. Move down to 34.
   This is the row that 36 is in.
   One row down makes __10__.
3. Move right from 34 to 36 to count __2__ ones.
4. Count the tens down and ones across.
   __10__ + __2__ = __12__, so 36 − 24 = 12.

Subtract using the hundred chart.

1. 87 − 72 = ____
2. 79 − 48 = ____
3. 65 − 41 = ____
4. 99 − 52 = ____
5. 35 − 13 = ____
6. 84 − 33 = ____

Name ______________________

Practice
7-3

Subtracting on a Hundred Chart

Subtract using the hundred chart.

1. 47 − 31 = 16

2. 78 − 25 = _____

3. 99 − 43 = _____

4. 37 − 16 = _____

5. 55 − 23 = _____

6. 64 − 26 = _____

1	2	3	4	5	6	7	8	9	10
11	12	13	14	15	16	17	18	19	20
21	22	23	24	25	26	27	28	29	30
31	32	33	34	35	36	37	38	39	40
41	42	43	44	45	46	47	48	49	50
51	52	53	54	55	56	57	58	59	60
61	62	63	64	65	66	67	68	69	70
71	72	73	74	75	76	77	78	79	80
81	82	83	84	85	86	87	88	89	90
91	92	93	94	95	96	97	98	99	100

7. A pan holds 36 biscuits. Kiana put 12 biscuits on the pan.

How many more biscuits will fit on the pan?

- ○ 24 biscuits
- ○ 22 biscuits
- ○ 23 biscuits
- ○ 21 biscuits

8. A garden has room for 22 flowers.
Dan needs to plant 11 more flowers.

How many flowers did Dan already plant?

- ○ 10 flowers
- ○ 12 flowers
- ○ 11 flowers
- ○ 13 flowers

9. Journal Explain how to use a hundred chart to subtract.

____

____

Name ____________________

Adding On to Subtract

If you have 57 and take away 32, how many are left?

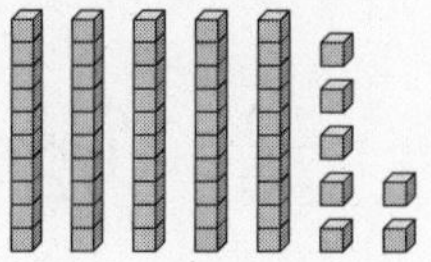

Find 57 − 32.

First, count back by tens to subtract 3 tens.

57, 47, 37, 27

Then, count back to subtract 2 ones.

27, 26, 25

So, 57 − 32 = 25

Here is another way to subtract.

First, add 8 cubes to make the next ten, 40.

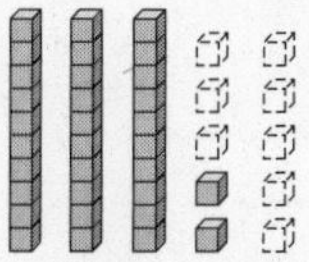

Then, count up from 40 to 57.

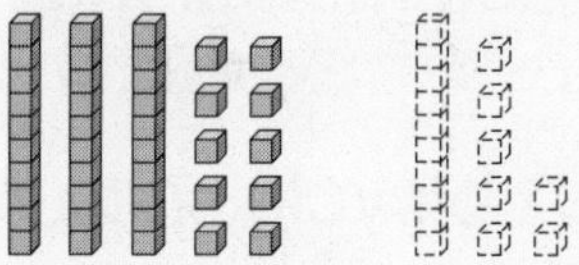

Add. 8 + 17 = 25

So, 57 − 32 = 25

Count back and add on to find the difference.

1. 23 − 11 = ____

11 + ____ = 23

2. 68 − 34 = ____

34 + ____ = 68

3. Journal Write an addition sentence to go with this subtraction sentence.

48 − 23 = 25

Name ______________________________

Practice
7-4

Adding On to Subtract

Subtract and add on to find the difference.

1. 76 − 42 = 34

42 + 34 = 76

2. 62 − 41 = ____

41 + ____ = 62

3. 58 − 33 = ____

33 + ____ = 58

4. 45 − 22 = ____

22 + ____ = 45

5. 37 − 15 = ____

15 + ____ = 37

6. 26 − 12 = ____

12 + ____ = 26

7. Use mental math to solve.

A bicycle shop had 38 bicycles.
It sold 24 bikes the first week of June.

How many bicycles are left?

○ 4 bicycles

○ 24 bicycles

○ 14 bicycles

○ 28 bicycles

8. Reasoning Use the numbers on the cards to write 2 two-digit numbers that make a difference of 25.

1 3 5 6

☐ ☐
− ☐ ☐
2 5

Name ________________________________

Reteaching
7-5

Problem Solving: Missing or Extra Information

Solve.

Sometimes you do not have enough information to solve a problem. Sometimes you have too much information and you do not need it to solve a problem.

There are 4 children on a bowling team.
Mike bowls a score of 55.
Sherry bowls a score of 30.
How much higher is Mike's score?

1. What do you need to find out?

The difference between Mike's and Sherry's score.

2. What information do you need to solve the problem?

Mike's score and Sherry's score:

55 – 30 = 25

3. What information is extra?

There are 4 children on the team.

Cross out the extra information.
Solve the problem if you have the information you need.

1. There are 39 adults at the bowling alley.
   There are 9 children at the bowling alley.
   ~~Mark bowls a score of 82.~~

   How many more adults than children are there?

   Solve if you can: _____ – _____ = _____

Name ______________________________

Practice
7-5

Problem Solving: Missing or Extra Information

Circle **Extra Information** or **Missing Information.**
Then write a number sentence if the problem can be solved.

1. Julia painted 12 pictures and made 3 clay baskets at school. Julia took 5 pictures home. How many pictures are left at school?

   Extra Information

   Missing Information

   12 − 5 = 7 pictures

2. Nico cut out 15 red circles and 10 yellow circles. Then he gave away some red circles. How many red circles does Nico have left?

   Extra Information

   Missing Information

   _____ − _____ = _____ red circles

Spatial Thinking Draw a picture to solve each problem. Then choose the correct answer.

3. A bush had 18 berries. A raccoon ate 9 of the berries. Then the raccoon ate 6 fish. How many berries are left?

   ○ 11 berries ○ 9 berries

   ○ 10 berries ○ 8 berries

4. A bowl holds 16 oranges and 4 apples. Children eat 9 oranges. How many oranges are left in the bowl?

   ○ 7 oranges ○ 9 oranges

   ○ 8 oranges ○ 10 oranges

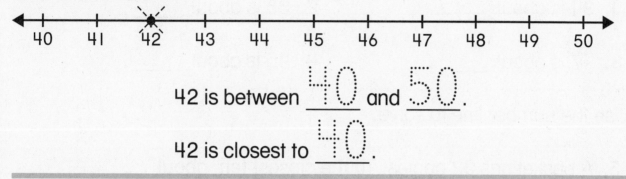

Finding the Closest Ten

Are there **about** 40 or 50 pumpkins?

Use tens to tell **about** how many.

Find the closest ten.

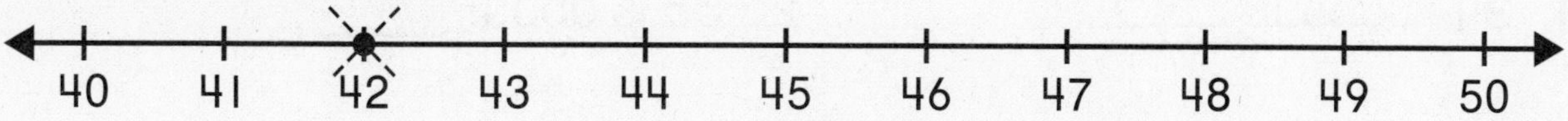

42 is between 40 and 50.

42 is closest to 40.

Find the number on the basket on the number line.

Mark it with an X. Write the closest ten.

1. 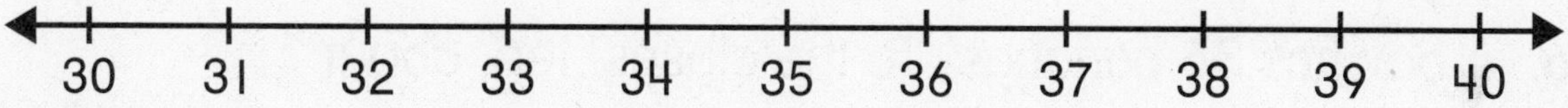

38 is between _____ and _____.

38 is closest to _____.

2. 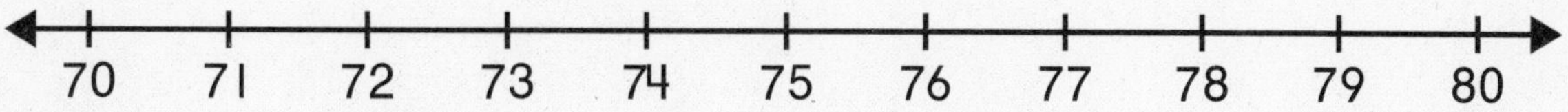

74 is between _____ and _____.

74 is closest to _____.

Name ________________________________

Practice
8-1

Finding the Closest Ten

Find the number on the number line.
Write the closest ten.

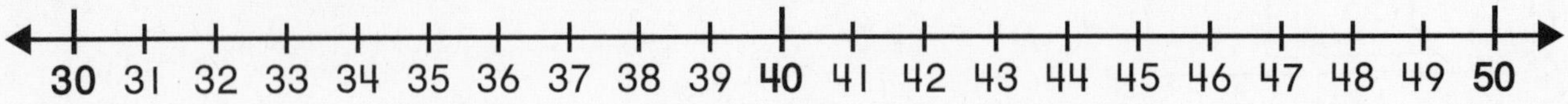

1. 34 is about 30.

2. 35 is about _____.

3. 47 is about _____.

4. 45 is about _____.

Use the number line to solve.

5. A basket has 32 apples. To the closest ten, about how many apples are in the basket?

   ○ 20 ○ 30 ○ 40 ○ 50

6. A box has 36 bananas. To the closest ten, about how many bananas are in the box?

   ○ 50 ○ 40 ○ 30 ○ 20

7. **Journal** Explain how to find the closest ten for a number using a number line.

____

____

____

Name ______________________________

Estimating Sums

Use mental math to **estimate.**

and

Think: Add the tens first.

20¢ and 10¢ is __30__¢.

Think: Add the ones next.

__2__¢ and __6__¢ is __8__¢ more.

You have 40¢.

Do you have enough money?

(yes) no

Estimate. Circle **yes** or **no** to answer the question.

1.

and

_____¢ and _____¢ is _____¢.

_____¢ and _____¢ is _____¢ more.

You have 50¢.

Do you have enough money?

yes no

2.

and

_____¢ and _____¢ is _____¢.

_____¢ and _____¢ is _____¢ more.

You have 60¢.

Do you have enough money?

yes no

Name ____________________

Estimating Sums

Estimate. Circle **yes** or **no** to answer the question.

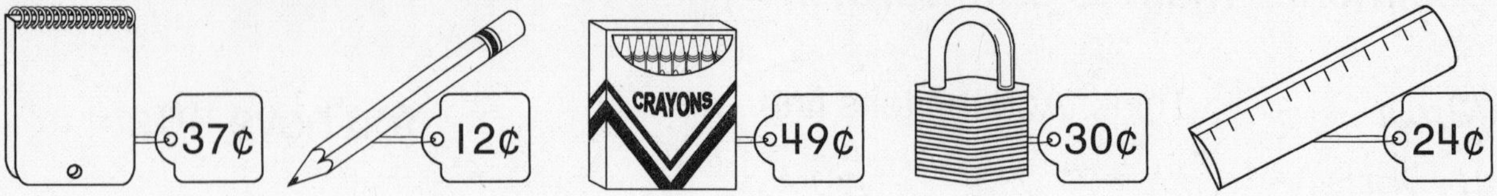

1. Can you buy  and  with 50¢? | yes (circled) | no

2. Can you buy 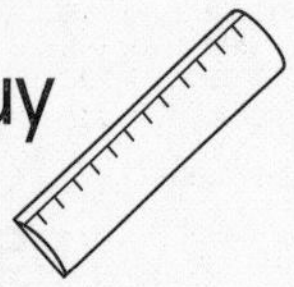 and  with 70¢? | yes | no

3. Can you buy 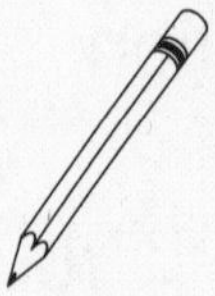 and  with 50¢? | yes | no

4. Can you buy  and  with 80¢? | yes | no

5. Reanna wants to buy the ruler and the lock.
How much money does she need?

- ○ 30¢
- ○ 50¢
- ○ 40¢
- ○ 60¢

6. **Reasoning** Sam has 45¢. He has exactly enough money to buy the lock for 30¢ and an apple. How much does the apple cost?

10¢	15¢	20¢	25¢
○	○	○	○

Name ____________________

Estimating Differences

Estimate to solve.

Subtract the tens first.

You have 46¢.
You buy:

$40¢ -$ 20¢ is 20¢

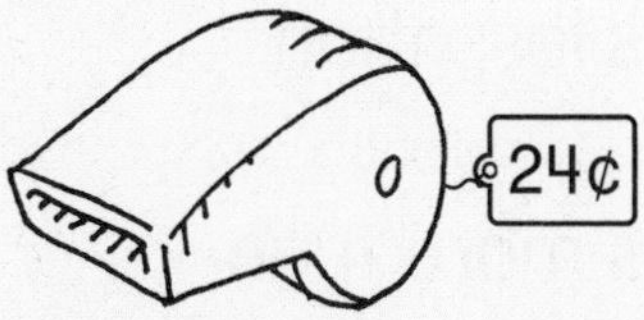

Think about the ones.

Will you have more or less than 20¢ left?

46¢ − 24¢ is (more) / less than 20¢.

Estimate to solve.
Circle **more** or **less** to complete each sentence.

1. You have 68¢.
You buy:

Subtract the tens first.

60¢ − _____¢ is _____¢

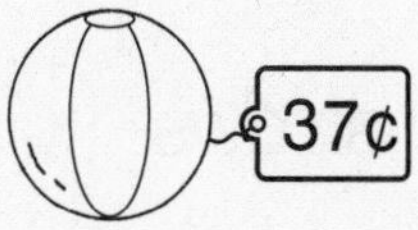

Think about the ones.

Will you have more or less than 30¢ left?

68¢ − 37¢ is more / less than 30¢.

2. You have 70¢.
You buy:

Subtract the tens first.

70¢ − _____¢ is _____¢

Think about the ones.

Will you have more or less than 30¢ left?

70¢ − 42¢ is more / less than 30¢.

Name ______________________________

Practice
8-3

Estimating Differences

Estimate. Circle **is more than** or **is less than** to complete each sentence.

1. 71 − 33 is more than / is less than 40.

2. 70 − 42 is more than / is less than 30.

3. 56 − 24 is more than / is less than 30.

4. 85 − 17 is more than / is less than 70.

5. 64 − 23 is more than / is less than 40.

6. 48 − 26 is more than / is less than 20.

7. A stand had 93 straws. It sold 45 cans of juice. Each can had one straw. How many straws were left?

- ○ less than 20 straws
- ○ less than 40 straws
- ○ less than 30 straws
- ○ less than 50 straws

8. Estimate There were 40 people at the movie. 18 people left. About how many people are still at the movie?

- ○ about 10 people
- ○ about 30 people
- ○ about 20 people
- ○ about 40 people

Name ______________________________

Reteaching
8-4

Problem Solving: Use Reasoning

Pat has 42 stamps.
He gets 20 more stamps.
Does Pat have more than or fewer than 60 stamps?

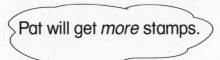

Pat will get *more* stamps.

To find out, do you need to add or subtract? add
Then estimate.

Add the tens:

4 tens and 2 tens = 6 tens = 60

There are ones to add so you know the answer will be greater than 60.

Circle the answer.

1. Eric has 67 pennies.
He gives 30 away.
Does Eric have more than or fewer than 40 pennies?

The answer is __________.

greater than 40

less than 40

2. Mary has 35 stickers.
She buys 17 more.
Does Mary have more than or fewer than 50 stickers?

The answer is __________.

greater than 50

less than 50

Name ___________________________________

Practice
8-4

Problem Solving: Use Reasoning

Use reasoning and estimation to solve.

1. 72 people are at the fair.
45 of them are on the rides.
Are there more or fewer than 30 people who are not on rides?

72 – 45   is greater than / (is less than)   30.

The number of people who are not on the rides   is greater than / is less than   30.

2. 29 people ride on the Ferris wheel.
38 more people join them.
Are there more or fewer than 50 people on the Ferris wheel?

__________   is greater than / is less than   60.

The number of people who are riding the Ferris wheel   is greater than / is less than   60.

3. Sid sells 48 tickets. Lynn sells 29 tickets. Which is the best way to estimate how many tickets they sold altogether?

○ 48 + 29   ○ 48 + 19

○ 29 – 48   ○ 48 – 29

4. Estimation Stella sells 28 hot dogs. Brent sells 35 hot dogs. Together, did they sell more or fewer than 60 hot dogs?

They sold __________ than 60 hot dogs.

Name ______________________________

Reteaching
9-1

Regrouping 10 Ones for 1 Ten

Find the sum.

24 + 8 = ____

Regroup 10 ones as 1 ten.

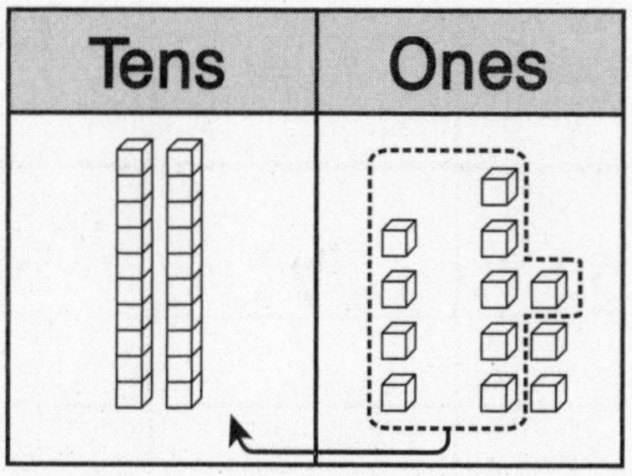

There are 3 tens and 2 ones

24 + 8 = 32

Regroup 10 ones as 1 ten.
Add. Count the tens and the ones.

1.

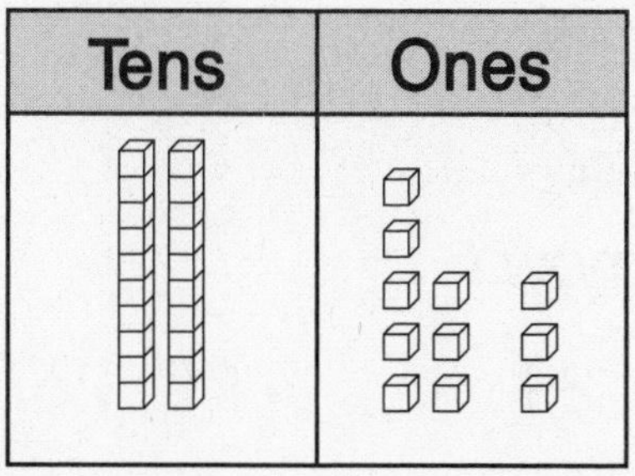

28 + 3 = ____

2.

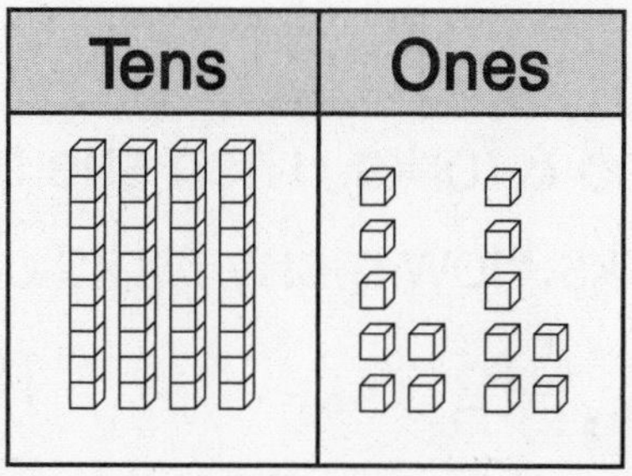

47 + 7 = ____

3.

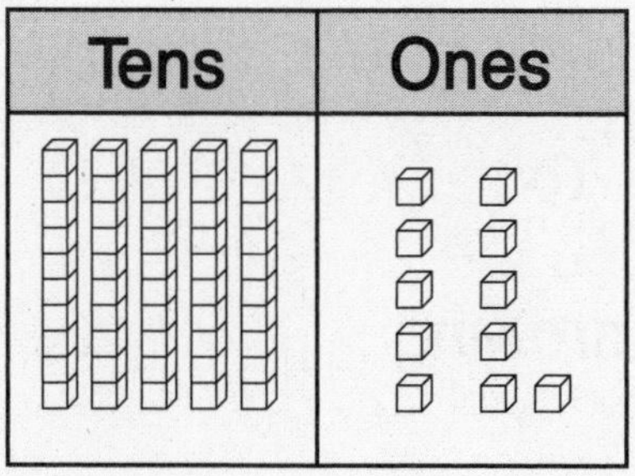

55 + 6 = ____

4.

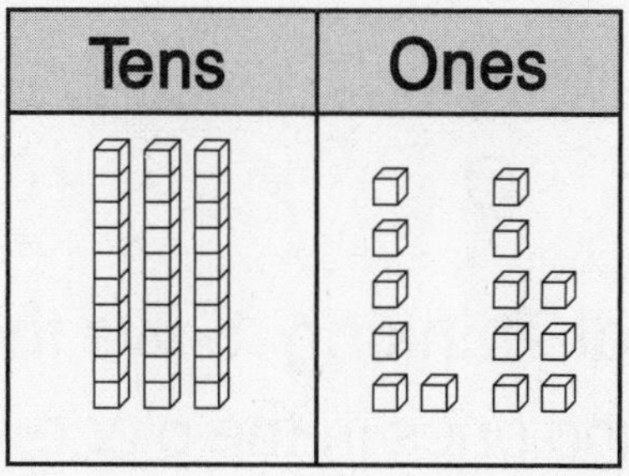

36 + 8 = ____

Name ______________________

Regrouping 10 Ones for 1 Ten

Use cubes and a workmat.
Add. Regroup if you need to.

Show.	Add.	Do you need to regroup?		Show.
1. 24	7	(Yes)	No	24 + 7 = 31
2. 56	9	Yes	No	56 + 9 = ____
3. 92	6	Yes	No	92 + 6 = ____

4. Pat had 6 forks. Then she bought a pack of 18 forks. How many forks does she have now?

12	14	24	26
○	○	○	○

5. Theo counted 69 red plates. Then he counted 8 blue plates. How many plates did he count in all?

79	77	71	61
○	○	○	○

6. **Spatial Thinking** Solve the problem by drawing tens and ones in the place-value chart.

48 + 5 = ____

Tens	Ones

Name ______________________

Models to Add Two- and One-Digit Numbers

Add 35 + 7.

Step 1:
How many ones?

5 + 7 = 12

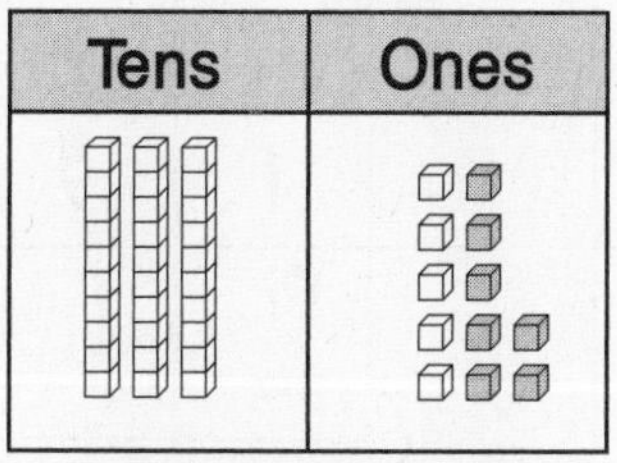

	Tens	Ones
	☐	
	3	5
+		7
		2

Step 2:
Regroup 12 as 1 ten and 2 ones.
Write 2 ones.

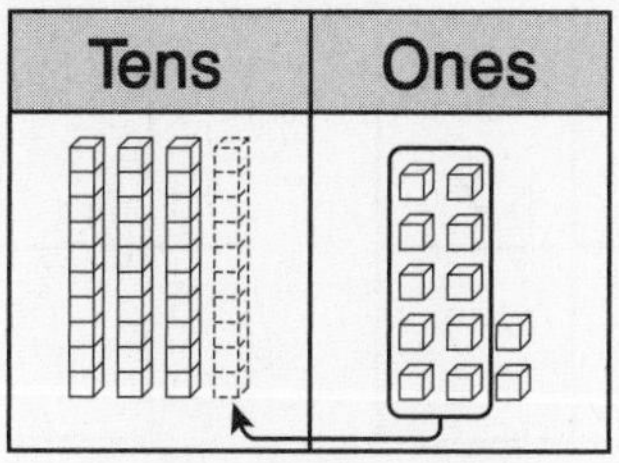

	Tens	Ones
	1	
	3	5
+		7
		2

Step 3:
How many tens?

3 + 1 = 4 tens

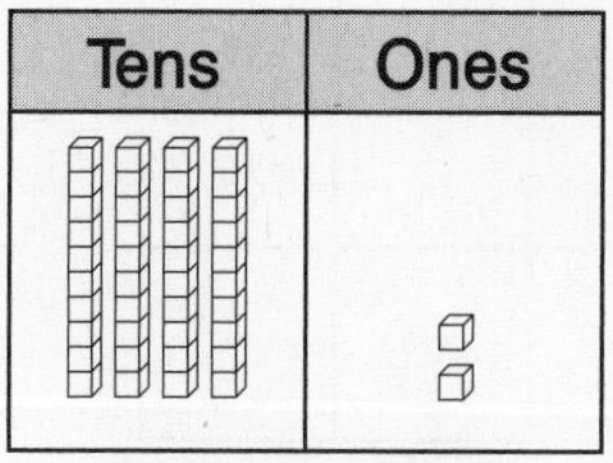

	Tens	Ones
	1	
	3	5
+		7
	4	2

So, 35 + 7 = 42.

Use connecting cubes and the workmat. Add.
Did you need to regroup? Circle **yes** or **no.**

	Tens	Ones
	☐	
	4	6
+		9

Yes No

	Tens	Ones
	☐	
	5	2
+		7

Yes No

	Tens	Ones
	☐	
	3	8
+		5

Yes No

	Tens	Ones
	☐	
	6	7
+		3

Yes No

Name ______________________________

Practice **9-2**

Models to Add Two- and One-Digit Numbers

Use connecting cubes and a workmat. Add.
Do you need to regroup? Circle **Yes** or **No**.

1.

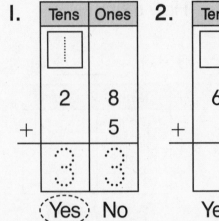

	Tens	Ones
	1	
	2	8
+		5
	3	3

Yes No

2.

	Tens	Ones
	☐	
	6	4
+		9

Yes No

3.

	Tens	Ones
	☐	
	5	2
+		5

Yes No

4.

	Tens	Ones
	☐	
		7
+	1	9

Yes No

5. A crow ate 22 kernels of corn. Then it ate 4 more kernels. How many kernels did it eat in all?

○ 18 kernels
○ 24 kernels
○ 20 kernels
○ 26 kernels

6. Algebra Write the missing numbers in the boxes.

	☐	
	4	9
+		☐
	5	2

Name ______________________

Adding Two- and One-Digit Numbers

Remember the steps for adding.

Step 1: Add the ones.

Step 2: Regroup if there are more than 10 ones.

Step 3: Add the tens.

	Tens	Ones
	1	
	3	7
+		6
	4	3

37 + 6 = ?

There are more than 10 ones.

Regroup 13 as 1 ten and 3 ones. Add the tens.

Use paper and pencil to add.

1. Do you need to regroup?

Yes No

	Tens	Ones
	☐	
	2	8
+		4

2. Do you need to regroup?

Yes No

	Tens	Ones
	☐	
	3	6
+		9

3. Do you need to regroup?

Yes No

	Tens	Ones
	☐	
	3	4
+		5

4. Do you need to regroup?

Yes No

	Tens	Ones
	☐	
	4	6
+		4

Name ______________________

Practice
9-3

Adding Two- and One-Digit Numbers

Add. Regroup if you need to.

1.

	Tens	Ones
	1	
	7	6
+		7
	8	3

2.

	Tens	Ones
	6	4
+		3

3.

	Tens	Ones
	8	3
+		6

4.

	Tens	Ones
	3	7
+		9

5.

	Tens	Ones
	7	5
+		7

6.

	Tens	Ones
	5	0
+		8

7.

	Tens	Ones
	7	6
+		4

8.

	Tens	Ones
	8	3
+		5

9. Bessie has 25 flowers. Then she picks 9 more flowers. How many flowers does Bessie have in all?

33	34	35	36
○	○	○	○

10. Journal Tell how you know when to regroup.

____

____

Name ____________________

Models to Add Two-Digit Numbers

Add 46 + 18.

Step 1:
How many ones?

6 + 8 = 14

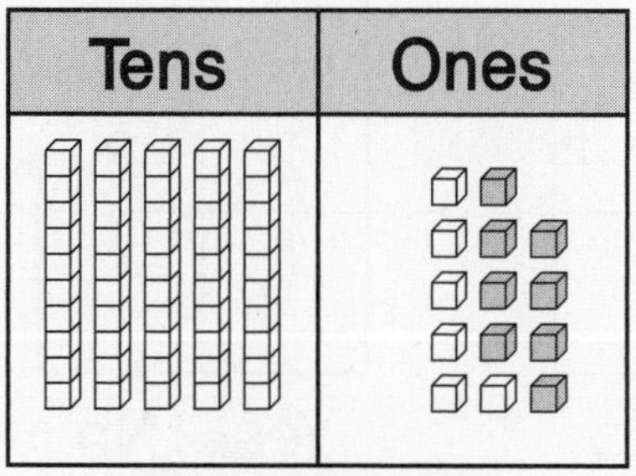

	Tens	Ones
	☐	
	4	6
+	1	8
		4

Step 2:
Do I need to regroup?

(yes) no

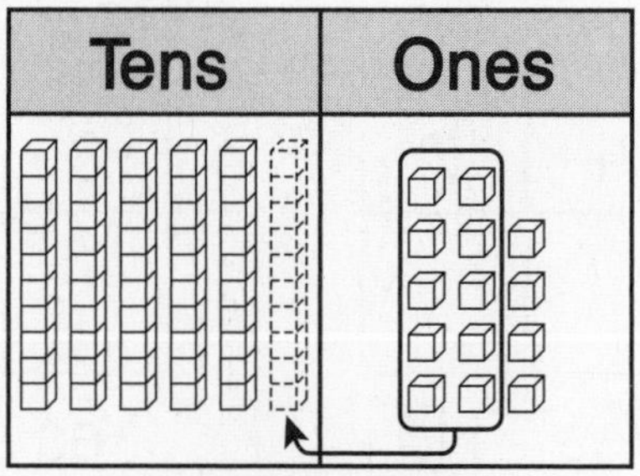

	Tens	Ones
	1	
	4	6
+	1	8
		4

Step 3:
How many tens?

5 + 1 = 6 tens

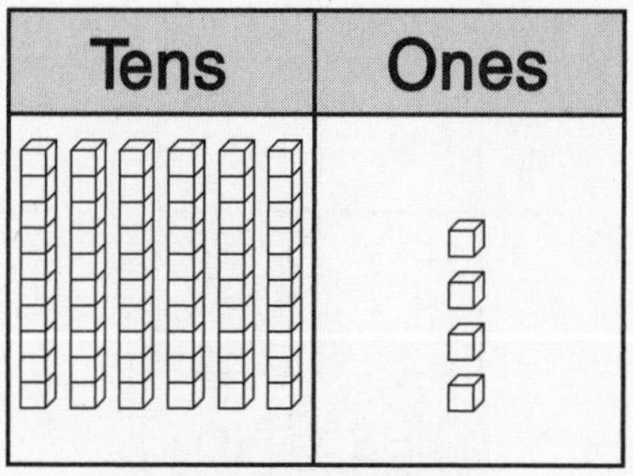

	Tens	Ones
	1	
	4	6
+	1	8
	6	4

So, 46 + 18 = 64.

Follow the steps. Use connecting cubes and the workmat. Add.

	Tens	Ones
	☐	
	2	4
+	2	9

	Tens	Ones
	☐	
	5	2
+	1	7

	Tens	Ones
	☐	
	3	8
+	4	5

	Tens	Ones
	☐	
	1	7
+	6	3

Name ___________________________

Models to Add Two-Digit Numbers

Use connecting cubes and the workmat. Add.
Do you need to regroup? Circle **Yes** or **No**.

1.

	Tens	Ones
	1	
	3	3
+	4	9
	8	2

(Yes) No

2.

	Tens	Ones
	5	1
+	4	7

Yes No

3.

	Tens	Ones
	2	3
+	3	7

Yes No

4.

	Tens	Ones
	4	4
+	2	8

Yes No

5. Lia counts 38 red paper cups and 25 blue paper cups. How many paper cups did she count in all?

○ 13 ○ 53

○ 43 ○ 63

	Tens	Ones
+		

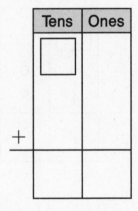

6. Reasonableness Use the clues to solve the riddle.
I am between 24 and 34.
You say my name when you count by twos from zero.
You say my name when you count by fives from zero.
What number am I?

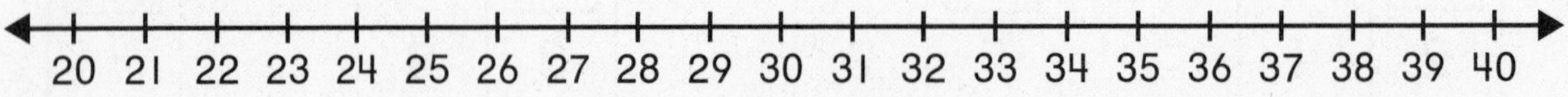

I am the number _____.

Name ______________________________

Reteaching
9-5

Adding Two-Digit Numbers

Remember the steps for adding:

Step 1: Add the ones.

Step 2: Regroup if you need to.

Step 3: Add the tens.

34 + 27 = ?
Regroup 11 ones as 1 ten and 1 one.

	Tens	Ones
	[1]	
	3	4
+	2	7
	6	1

12 + 36 = ?
You do not need to regroup 8 ones.

	Tens	Ones
	[ ]	[ ]
	1	2
+	3	6
	4	8

Write the addition problem. Find the sum.

1. 15 + 26

	Tens	Ones
	[ ]	
	1	5
+	2	6

32 + 24

	Tens	Ones
	[ ]	
	3	2
+	2	

28 + 15

	Tens	Ones
	[ ]	
	2	8
+		

49 + 13

	Tens	Ones
	[ ]	
+		

2. **Algebra** Begin with 39. Find the number that gives you a sum of 56. Use connecting cubes to help.

The number is _____.

	Tens	Ones
	[ ]	
	3	9
+		
	5	6

Name ____________________

Practice
9-5

Adding Two-Digit Numbers

Write the addition problem. Find the sum.

1. 26 + 52

	Tens	Ones
	☐	
	2	6
+	5	2
	7	8

2. 31 + 19

	Tens	Ones
	☐	
+		

3. 47 + 28

	Tens	Ones
	☐	
+		

4. 56 + 34

	Tens	Ones
	☐	
+		

5. 63 + 26

	Tens	Ones
	☐	
+		

6. 75 + 13

	Tens	Ones
	☐	
+		

7. 68 + 29

	Tens	Ones
	☐	
+		

8. 54 + 37

	Tens	Ones
	☐	
+		

9. Paul has a stack of 43 pennies and a stack of 36 pennies. How many pennies does he have altogether?

○ 47 pennies
○ 79 pennies
○ 66 pennies
○ 89 pennies

10. Estimate One jar has 38 buttons. Another jar has 43 buttons. About how many buttons are in both jars?

○ about 80 buttons
○ about 60 buttons
○ about 70 buttons
○ about 50 buttons

Name ______________________________

Reteaching
9-6

Problem Solving: Draw a Picture and Write a Number Sentence

Look for clue words to help you solve a story problem.

Tina has 23 counters.
She gets 27 more counters.
How many counters does Tina have in all?

"How many in all" tells you to add.

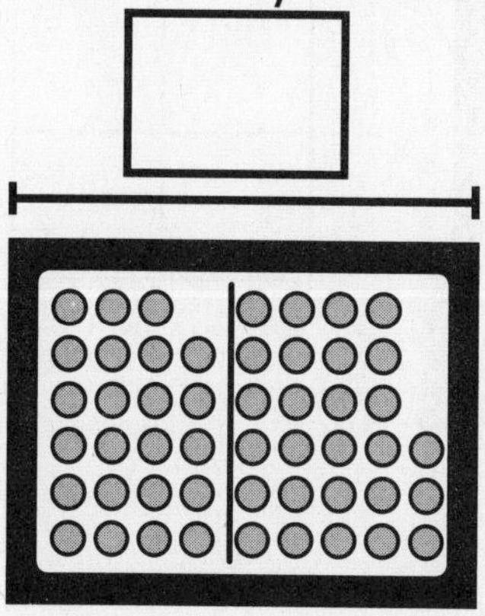

23 + 27 = 50

	Tens	Ones
	1	
	2	3
+	2	7
	5	0

Draw pictures to solve the problem.
Then write a number sentence.

1. Raul has 15 counters.
   He gets 19 more counters.
   How many does he have in all?

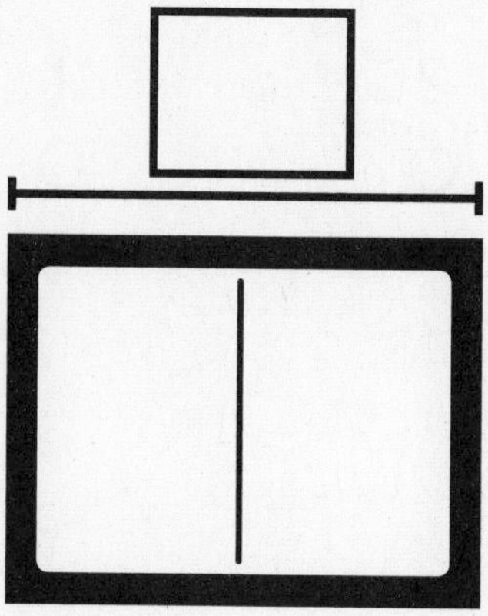

____ + ____ = ____

	Tens	Ones
+		

Name ____________________

Problem Solving: Draw a Picture and Write a Number Sentence

Write a number sentence to solve the problem.
Use the part-part-whole mat if needed.

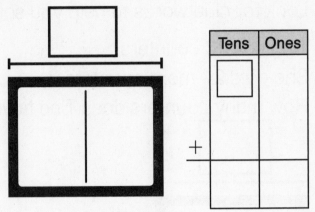

1. Jordan had 19¢. Then he found 17¢ more. How much money does he have now?

19 + 17 = ____ ¢

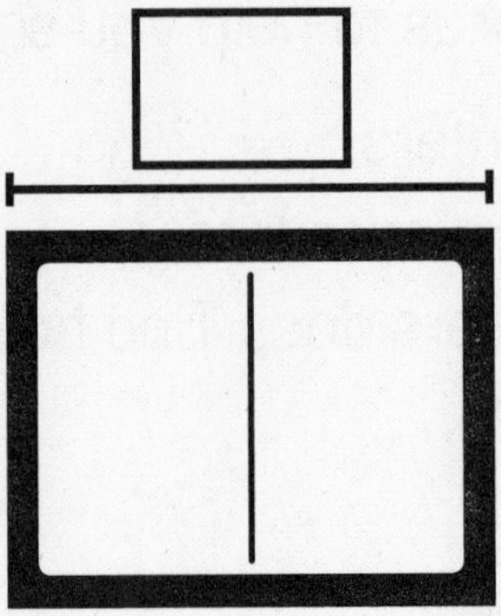

	Tens	Ones
	☐	
+		

2. Curt made paper cranes. He made 45 blue cranes. He made 17 green cranes.

Which number sentence shows how many paper cranes he made in all?

○ 45 − 17 = 28 ○ 45 + 17 = 62

○ 17 + 17 = 34 ○ 45 + 45 = 90

3. Algebra Which number is missing?

	Tens	Ones
	1	☐
	2	8
+	1	4
	?	2

4 ○ 3 ○ 2 ○ 1 ○

Name ______________________________

Regrouping 1 Ten for 10 Ones

Subtract 7 from 42.

Show 42. Regroup. Subtract 7 ones.

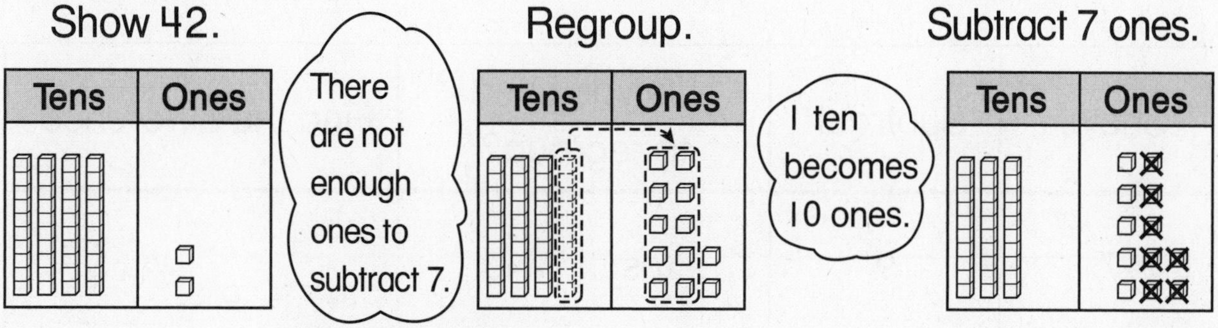

Do you need to regroup?

(Yes) No

$12 - 7 = 5$ ones

$42 - 7 =$ 35

Put cubes on your workmat.
Subtract. Regroup if needed.

1. Subtract 5 from 31.

Show 31. Regroup. Subtract 5 ones.

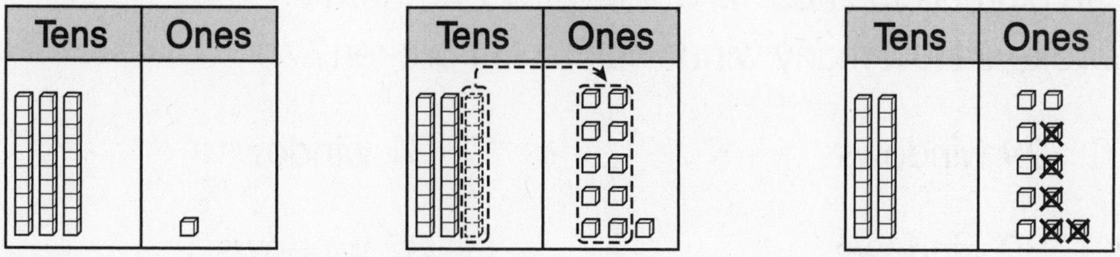

Do you need to regroup?

(Yes) No

$11 - 5 =$ 6 ones.

$31 - 5 =$ ______

Name ____________________

Practice 10-1

Regrouping 1 Ten for 10 Ones

Use a workmat and connecting cubes.
Subtract. Regroup if you need to.

Show.	Subtract.	Do you need to regroup?		Find the difference.
1. 47	9	Yes	No	47 − 9 = 38
2. 52	6	Yes	No	52 − 6 = ____
3. 38	5	Yes	No	38 − 5 = ____

4. Use a workmat and connecting cubes to solve the problem.

An old building has 48 windows. 19 of them are broken. How many windows are not broken?

- ○ 29 windows
- ○ 31 windows
- ○ 30 windows
- ○ 32 windows

5. **Spatial Thinking** The pole is 30 feet tall. The bug has crawled 14 feet. How much farther does the bug need to crawl to get to the top?

It needs to crawl

____ feet farther.

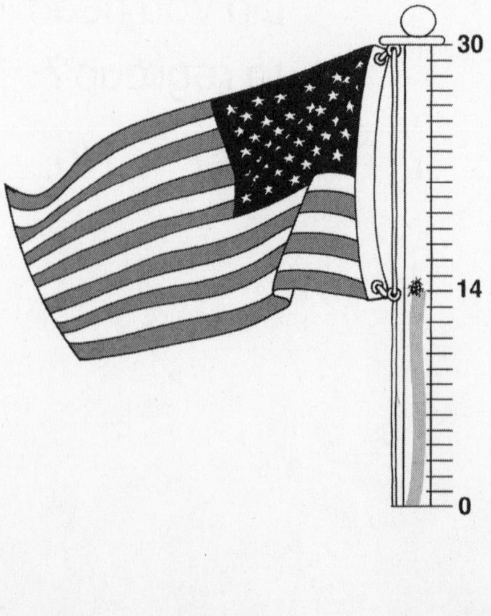

Name ______________________

Reteaching
10-2

Models to Subtract Two- and One-Digit Numbers

Subtract 8 from 52.

Step 1
Think: There are not enough ones to subtract 8.

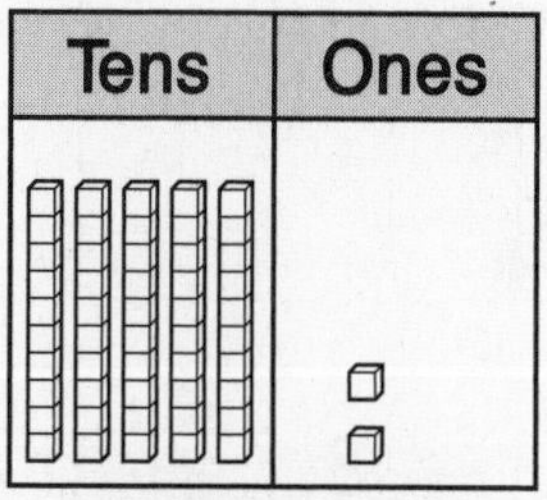

	Tens	Ones
	☐	☐
	5	2
−		8

Step 2
Regroup 1 ten as 10 ones.
Write 12 ones.
12 − 8 = 4 ones

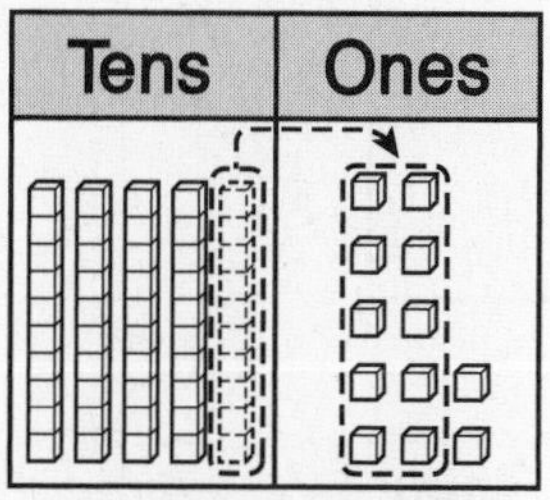

	Tens	Ones
	4	12
	~~5~~	~~2~~
−		8
		4

Step 3
Subtract the tens.
4 − 0 = 4 tens

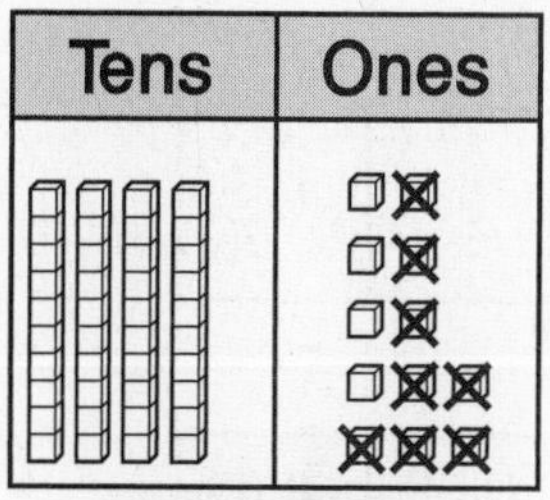

	Tens	Ones
	4	12
	~~5~~	~~2~~
−		8
	4	4

So, 52 − 8 = 44.

Put cubes on your workmat. Subtract.
Did you need to regroup? Circle **yes** or **no**.

1.

	Tens	Ones
	☐	☐
	4	3
−		9

yes no

	Tens	Ones
	☐	☐
	6	9
−		3

yes no

	Tens	Ones
	☐	☐
	3	5
−		8

yes no

	Tens	Ones
	☐	☐
	7	6
−		7

yes no

Name ________________________________

Practice
10-2

Models to Subtract Two- and One-Digit Numbers

Use a workmat and connecting cubes.
Subtract. Regroup if you need to.

1.

	Tens	Ones
	1	16
	2	6
−		7
	1	9

2.

	Tens	Ones
	☐	☐
	5	2
−		8

3.

	Tens	Ones
	☐	☐
	7	7
−		5

4.

	Tens	Ones
	☐	☐
	3	9
−		6

5.

	Tens	Ones
	☐	☐
	4	5
−		7

6.

	Tens	Ones
	☐	☐
	6	1
−		7

7.

	Tens	Ones
	☐	☐
	9	0
−		4

8.

	Tens	Ones
	☐	☐
	6	8
−		9

9. Solve. A bakery makes 64 muffins. They sell 29 muffins by noon. How many muffins are left?

○ 45 muffins ○ 35 muffins

○ 44 muffins ○ 34 muffins

10. Reasonableness There are 45 children in the gym. Some children leave. How many children could be in the gym now?

○ 37 children ○ 51 children

○ 45 children ○ 62 children

Name ____________________

Subtracting Two- and One-Digit Numbers

Remember the steps for subtracting.

Step 1
Think: Are there enough ones to subtract?

Step 2
Regroup the ones if you need to. Subtract.

Step 3
Subtract the tens.

Subtract.
Regroup if you need to.

Tens	Ones
☐	☐
2	7
−	3
2	4

Regroup? Yes (No)

Tens	Ones
3	12
~~4~~	~~2~~
−	6
3	6

Regroup? (Yes) No

Remember the steps for subtracting.
Subtract. Regroup if you need to.

1.

Tens	Ones
☐	☐
2	5
−	4

Tens	Ones
☐	☐
4	1
−	8

Tens	Ones
☐	☐
6	5
−	7

Tens	Ones
☐	☐
7	8
−	9

2. **Journal** Write a subtraction problem that needs regrouping.

Tens	Ones
☐	☐
−	

Name ______________________

Practice
10-3

Subtracting Two- and One-Digit Numbers

Subtract. Regroup if you need to.

1.

Tens	Ones
6	12
7	2
−	5
6	7

2.

Tens	Ones
6	1
−	7

3.

Tens	Ones
8	3
−	6

4.

Tens	Ones
3	8
−	3

5.

Tens	Ones
7	6
−	2

6.

Tens	Ones
9	3
−	4

7.

Tens	Ones
2	6
−	7

8.

Tens	Ones
8	7
−	8

9. Katara takes 21 kites to the park. She sells 17 of the kites. How many kites are left?

○ 3 kites
○ 14 kites
○ 4 kites
○ 17 kites

10. **Journal** Tell how you know when to regroup.

____

____

____

Name ______________________________

Models to Subtract Two-Digit Numbers

Subtract 16 from 43.

Step 1
Think: There are not enough ones to subtract 6.

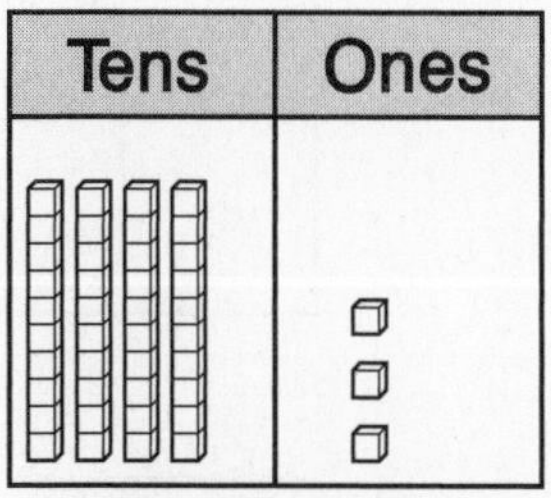

	Tens	Ones
	☐	☐
	4	3
−	1	6

Step 2
Think: Do I need to regroup?

13 − 6 = 7 ones

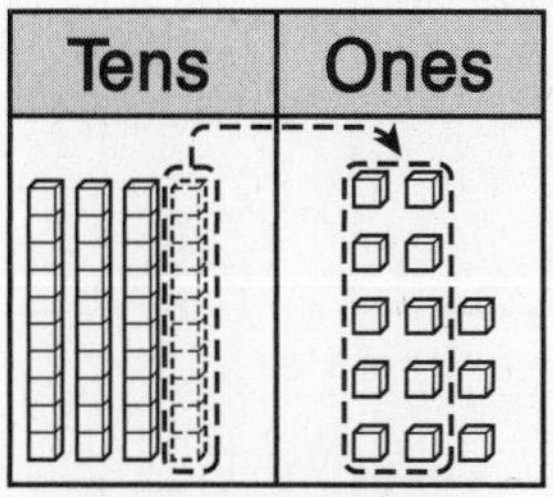

	Tens	Ones
	3	13
	~~4~~	~~3~~
−	1	6
		7

Step 3
Think: Subtract the tens.

3 − 1 = 2 tens

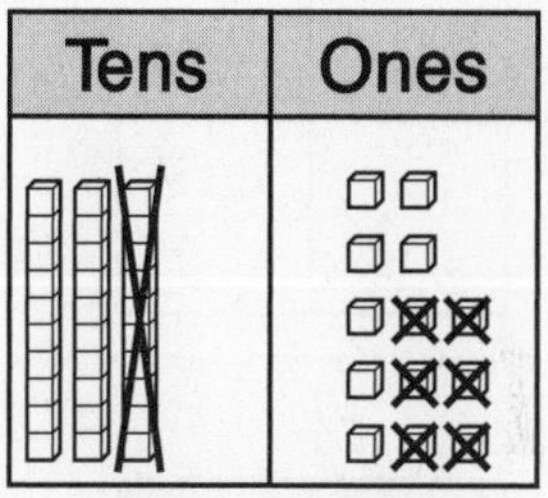

	Tens	Ones
	3	13
	~~4~~	~~3~~
−	1	6
	2	7

So, 43 − 16 = 27.

Put cubes on your workmat. Subtract.
Regroup if you need to.

1.

	Tens	Ones
	☐	☐
	3	7
−	1	5

	Tens	Ones
	☐	☐
	5	0
−	1	3

	Tens	Ones
	☐	☐
	7	6
−	2	8

	Tens	Ones
	☐	☐
	4	5
−	2	7

Name ______________________________

Models to Subtract Two-Digit Numbers

Use a workmat and connecting cubes.
Subtract. Regroup if you need to.

1.

	Tens	Ones
	7	16
	8	6
−	2	8
	5	8

2.

	Tens	Ones
	6	8
−	2	3

3.

	Tens	Ones
	5	4
−	1	5

4.

	Tens	Ones
	7	0
−	1	6

5.

	Tens	Ones
	4	3
−	2	7

6.

	Tens	Ones
	5	7
−	1	9

7.

	Tens	Ones
	6	7
−	3	4

8.

	Tens	Ones
	3	6
−	1	7

9. Reasoning Solve. Show your work.

Jamal has 54¢.
He wants to buy a toy that costs 70¢.
How much more money does he need?

○ 14¢ ○ 24¢

○ 16¢ ○ 26¢

	Tens	Ones
−		

Name ______________________________

Subtracting Two-Digit Numbers

Remember the steps for subtracting.

Step 1
Think: Are there enough ones to subtract?

Step 2
Regroup the ones if you need to. Subtract.

Step 3
Subtract the tens.

Write the problems in the frames. Find the difference.

38 − 13

	Tens	Ones
	☐	☐
	3	8
−	1	3
	2	5

Regroup? Yes (No)

54 − 17

	Tens	Ones
	4	14
	~~5~~	~~4~~
−	1	7
	3	7

Regroup? (Yes) No

Write the problems in the frames. Find the difference.

1. 37 − 14

	Tens	Ones
	☐	☐
−		

64 − 18

	Tens	Ones
	☐	☐
−		

45 − 26

	Tens	Ones
	☐	☐
−		

73 − 25

	Tens	Ones
	☐	☐
−		

2. **Number Sense** Write a number to make this a subtraction with regrouping problem.

	Tens	Ones
	☐	☐
−	2	3

Name ____________________

Practice **10-5**

Subtracting Two-Digit Numbers

Write the subtraction problem. Find the difference.

1. 64 − 39

	Tens	Ones
	5	14
	~~6~~	~~4~~
−	3	9
	2	5

2. 65 − 16

	Tens	Ones
−		

3. 72 − 31

	Tens	Ones
−		

4. 56 − 29

	Tens	Ones
−		

5. 84 − 25

	Tens	Ones
−		

6. 34 − 16

	Tens	Ones
−		

7. 96 − 48

	Tens	Ones
−		

8. 43 − 27

	Tens	Ones
−		

9. Norma has 48 buttons. Connie has 29 buttons. How many more buttons does Norma have than Connie?

○ 29 buttons ○ 19 buttons

○ 21 buttons ○ 11 buttons

10. Number Sense Use each number only once. Write and solve the subtraction problem with the greatest difference.

1 2 4 5

	Tens	Ones
−		

Name ______________________

Using Addition to Check Subtraction

When you subtract,
you start with the whole.
Then you take part away.
The other part is left.

	3 7	Whole
−	1 2	Part
	2 5	Part

To check your work,
add to put the parts
back together.
Your answer should
be the whole.

	2 5	Part
+	1 2	Part
	3 7	Whole

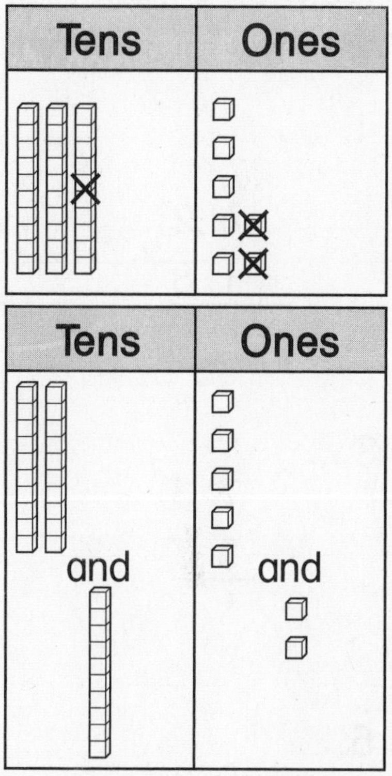

Subtract. Check your answer by adding.

1.

	Tens	Ones
	☐	☐
	3	3
−	2	1

2.

	Tens	Ones
	☐	☐
	8	6
−		9

3.

	Tens	Ones
	☐	☐
	5	4
−	1	9

4.

	Tens	Ones
	☐	☐
	6	3
−	3	7

Name ______________________

Practice
10-6

Using Addition to Check Subtraction

Subtract. Check your answer by adding.
Write the missing part.

1.

$$\begin{array}{r} \overset{5}{\cancel{6}}\overset{12}{\cancel{2}} \\ -\ 1\ 8 \\ \hline 4\ 4 \end{array} \qquad \begin{array}{r} \overset{1}{4\ 4} \\ +\ 1\ 8 \\ \hline 6\ 2 \end{array}$$

2.

$$\begin{array}{r} 8\ 3 \\ -\ 2\ 9 \\ \hline \end{array}$$

3.

$$\begin{array}{r} 7\ 3 \\ -\ 3\ 7 \\ \hline \end{array}$$

4.

$$\begin{array}{r} 4\ 8 \\ -\ 2\ 1 \\ \hline \end{array}$$

5.

$$\begin{array}{r} 9\ 4 \\ -\ 2\ 8 \\ \hline \end{array}$$

6.

$$\begin{array}{r} 7\ 5 \\ -\ 1\ 7 \\ \hline \end{array}$$

7. Lana has 39 moon stickers and 52 star stickers. How many more star stickers than moon stickers does she have?

○ 13 more ○ 17 more ○ 23 more ○ 27 more

8. Algebra Write the number that makes each number sentence true.

60 − 20 = 20 + ____ 70 − 30 = 10 + ____

50 − 40 = 10 + ____ 80 − 40 = 30 + ____

Name ______________________

Reteaching
10-7

Problem Solving: Two-Question Problems

Use the answer from the first question to answer the second question.

Tomas has 17 red toy cars and 8 blue toy cars.
How many toy cars does he have in all?

Follow Step 1 to answer this question.

Tomas gives 6 cars to his brother.
How many toy cars does Tomas have left?

Use the answer from the first question in Step 1 to answer this question. Follow Step 2.

Step 1

Add to find out how many toy cars Tomas has in all.

17 + 8 = 25

Step 2

Subtract the number of cars Tomas gives his brother.

25 − 6 = 19

Tomas has 19 cars left.

Use the answer from the first question to answer the second question.

1. Marta picked 12 red flowers and 9 pink flowers. How many flowers did Marta pick in all?

   She gives 5 flowers to her teacher. How many flowers does Marta have left?

Step 1
Add to find out how many flowers Marta picked in all.

_____ + _____ = _____

Step 2
Subtract to find out how many flowers Marta has left.

_____ − _____ = _____

Marta has _____ flowers left.

Name ______________________

Practice **10-7**

Problem Solving: Two-Question Problems

Solve. Use the answer from the first question to answer the second question.

1. Barb has 12 pink bows and 13 green bows. How many bows does she have in all? 25 bows

Barb gives 9 bows to her sister. How many bows does she have left? 16 bows

2. Amanda has 11 eggs in a carton. She has 16 eggs in a bowl. How many eggs does she have in all? _____ eggs

Amanda cooks 12 eggs for her family's breakfast. How many eggs does she have now? _____ eggs

3. Marcos had 20 quarters. He spent 7 quarters. Then he spent 5 quarters.

How many quarters does Marcos have now?

- ○ 8 quarters
- ○ 13 quarters
- ○ 12 quarters
- ○ 32 quarters

4. **Estimation** 21 people were at the lake. Then 42 more people joined them.

At 5:00, 30 people left. About how many people are still at the lake?

- ○ about 50 people
- ○ about 30 people
- ○ about 40 people
- ○ about 20 people

Name ______________________________

Understanding Measurement

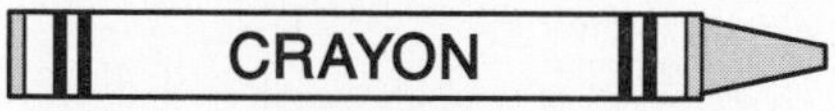

Look at the crayon.
About how many cubes long is the crayon?

When you **estimate** how long something is, you make a good guess.

Estimate.

I think the crayon is about _____ cubes long.

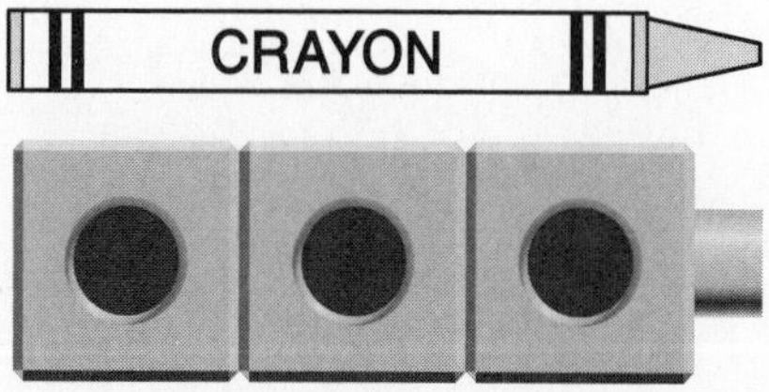

Then measure using cubes.

The crayon is about __3__ cubes long.

Estimate the length of each object.
Then measure using cubes.

1. I think the car is about _____ cubes long.

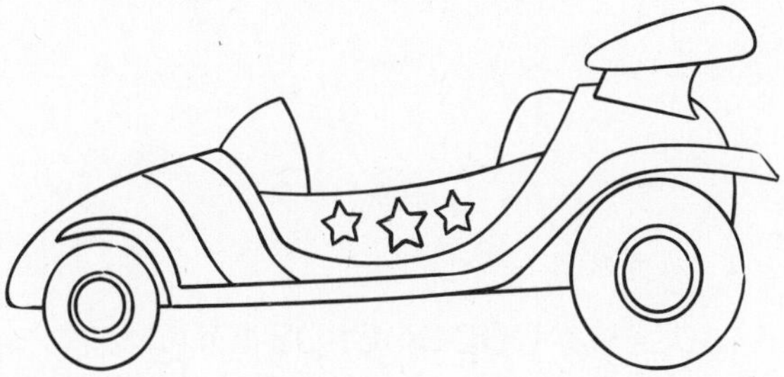

The car is about _____ cubes long.

2. I think the ribbon is about _____ cubes long.

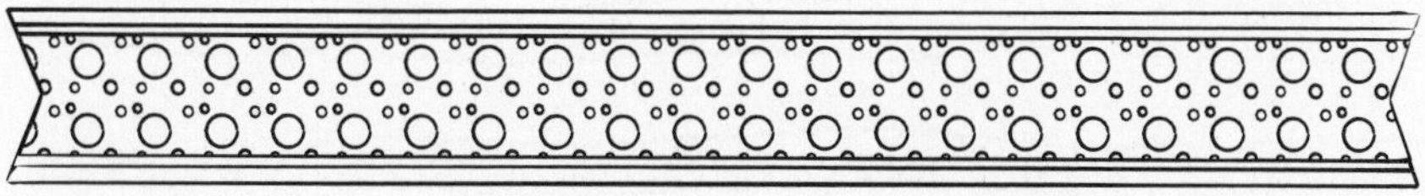

The ribbon is about _____ cubes long.

Name ______________________

Practice
11-1

Exploring Length

Estimate the length of each line.
Then use paper clips to measure.

1.

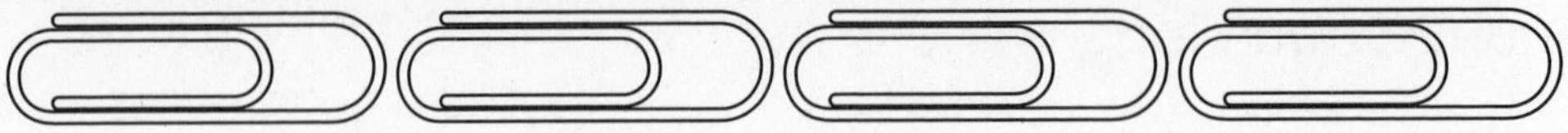

Estimate: about __4__ paper clips

Measure: about __4__ paper clips

2.

Estimate: about _____ paper clips

Measure: about _____ paper clips

Use paper clips to measure. How long is the frog?

3.

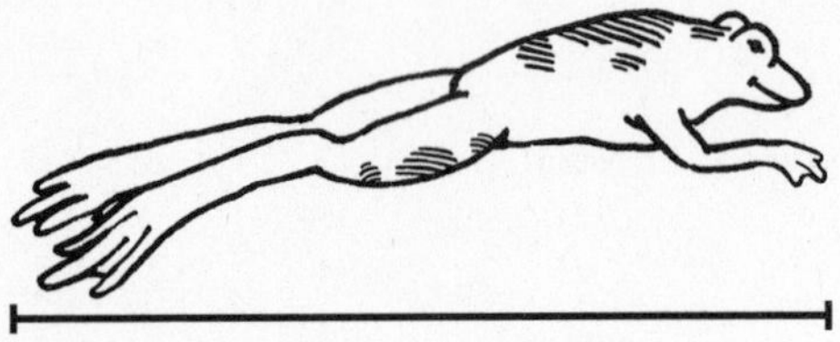

- ○ 4 paper clips long
- ○ 2 paper clips long
- ○ 3 paper clips long
- ○ 1 paper clip long

4. **Spatial Thinking** Circle the longest worm.

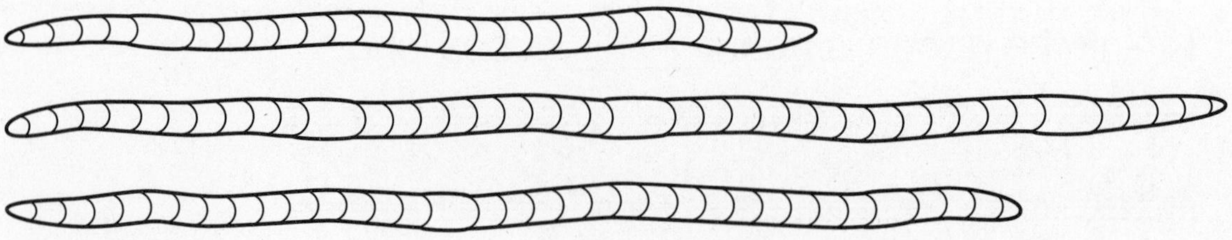

Name ______________________

Measuring Length Using Different Units

How tall is the domino?
You can measure using different units.

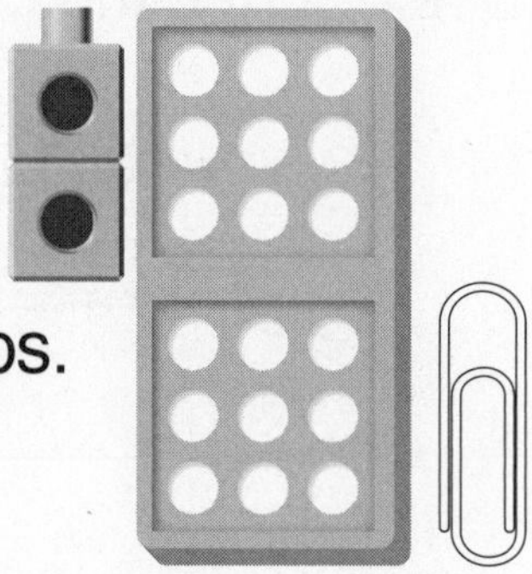

Use cubes.

It is about

2 cubes tall.

Use paper clips.

It is about

1 paper clips tall.

If you use smaller units, you need to use more.

Measure using cubes. Then measure using paper clips.

1. Use cubes.

It is about

_____ cubes tall.

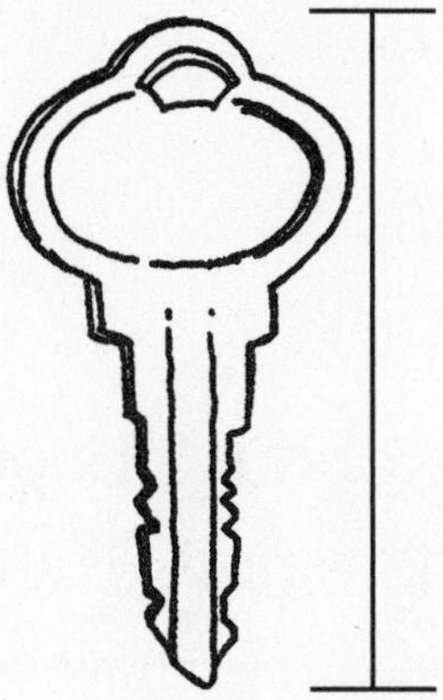

Use paper clips.

It is about

_____ paper clips tall.

2. Use cubes. It is about _____ cubes long.

Use paper clips. It is about _____ paper clips long.

Name ____________________

Practice
11-2

Measuring Length Using Different Units

Use connecting cubes and paper clips to measure each object.

1. 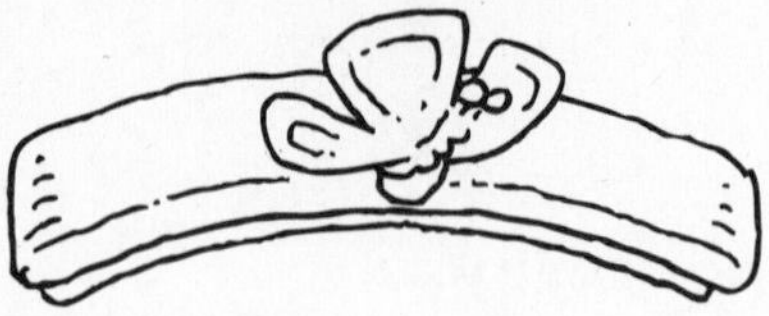

about __3__ cubes long

about __2__ paper clips long

2. 

about _____ cubes long

about _____ paper clip long

3. How tall is the nickel?

○ about 3 cubes

○ about 2 paper clips

○ about 1 cube

○ about 3 paper clips

4. Estimation The paintbrush is about 5 paper clips long. How long is it in cubes? Estimate first. Then measure.

Estimate:

about _____ cubes long

Measure:

about _____ cubes long

Name ____________________

Reteaching
11-3

Inches

Use a ruler to measure inches.

To measure to the nearest inch, look at the halfway mark between inches. If the object is longer, use the greater number. If the object is shorter, use the lesser number.

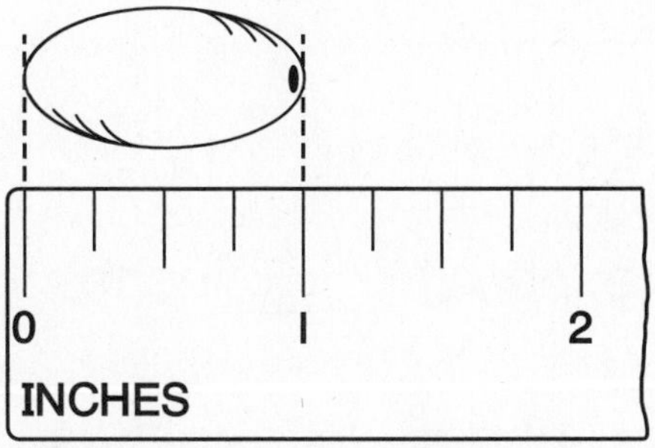

The bead is about

1 inch long.

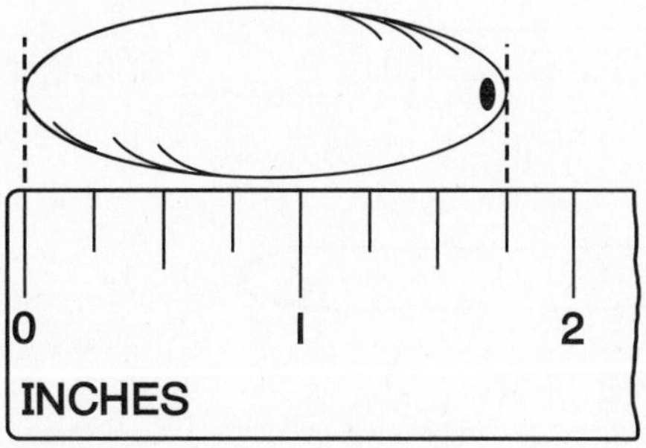

The bead is about

2 inches long.

1. Journal Find something in the classroom to measure in inches. Draw the object and write the measurement to the nearest inch.

Estimate the height or length.
Then use a ruler to measure.

2. height of a book

3. length of a pencil

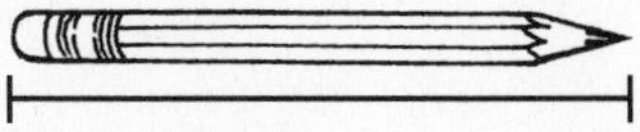

	Estimate	Measure
2.	about _____ inches	about _____ inches
3.	about _____ inches	about _____ inches

Name ______________________________

Inches

Estimate the length of each object.
Then use a ruler to measure.

1. 

Estimate: about _____ inches

Measure: about __4__ inches

2. 

Estimate: about _____ inches

Measure: about _____ inches

3. 

Estimate: about _____ inches

Measure: about _____ inches

4. **Reasonableness.** Measure the length of the straw in inches.
About how long is the straw?

○ about 5 inches

○ about 6 inches

○ about 7 inches

○ about 8 inches

Name ______________________

Centimeters

Use a ruler to measure centimeters.

To measure to the nearest centimeter, look at the halfway mark between centimeters. If the object is longer, use the greater number. If the object is shorter, use the lesser number.

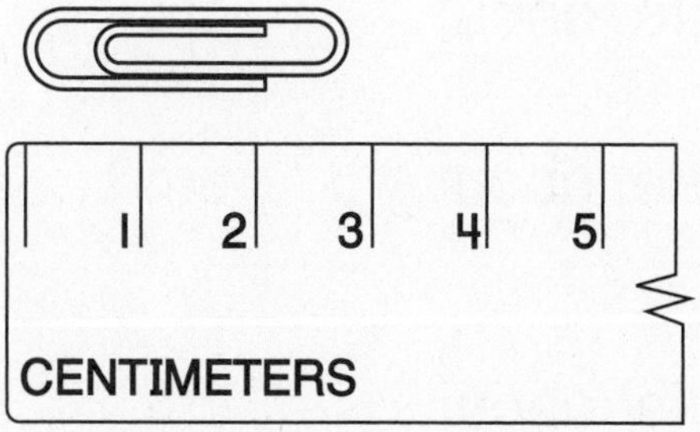

The paperclip is about

3 centimeters long.

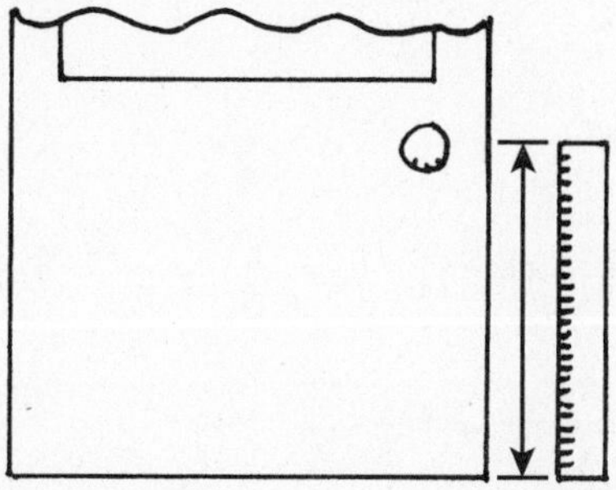

This part of the door is about

100 centimeters long.

1. Journal Find something in the classroom to measure in centimeters. Draw the object and write the measurement to the nearest centimeter.

Estimate the height or length.
Then use a ruler to measure.

2. length of a tape dispenser

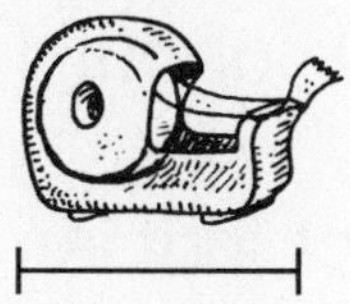

3. width of a book

	Estimate	Measure
2.	about _____ centimeters	about _____ centimeters
3.	about _____ centimeters	about _____ centimeters

Name ______________________

Centimeters

Estimate the length of each object.
Then use a ruler to measure.

1. 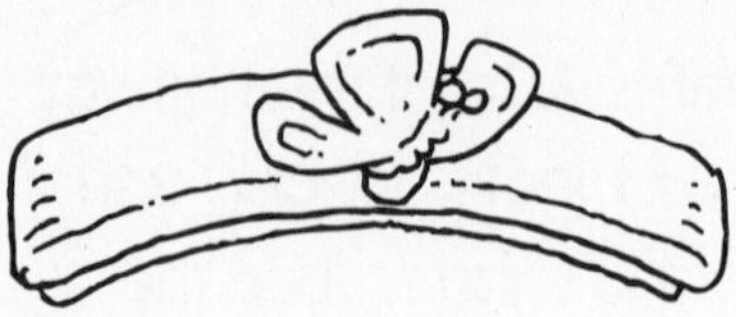

Estimate: about _____ cm

Measure: about __5__ cm

2. 

Estimate: about _____ cm

Measure: about _____ cm

3. 

Estimate: about _____ cm

Measure: about _____ cm

4. Look at the spoon. Measure the length of the spoon in centimeters. About how long is the spoon?

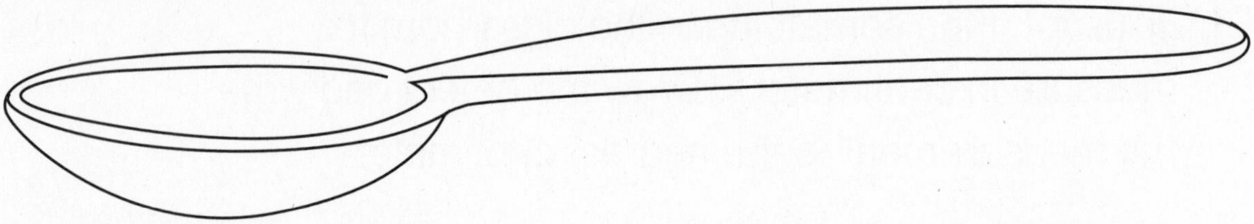

○ about 10 centimeters
○ about 16 centimeters
○ about 13 centimeters
○ about 18 centimeters

5. **Spatial Thinking** Choose the object that is about 1 centimeter long.

○ 
○ 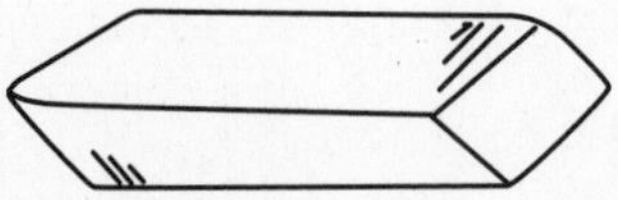
○ 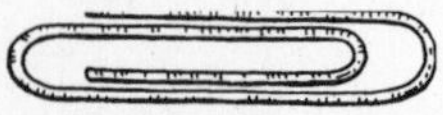
○ 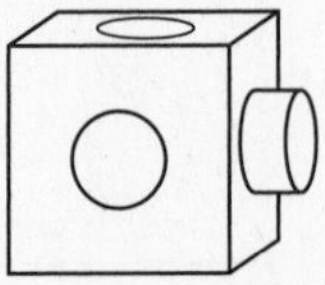

Name ______________________________

Estimating Measurements

To **estimate** means to make a good guess.
Estimate the length of the ribbon.

To estimate, think of something you have measured. You know a paper clip is about 1 inch long. Is the object you are measuring longer or shorter?

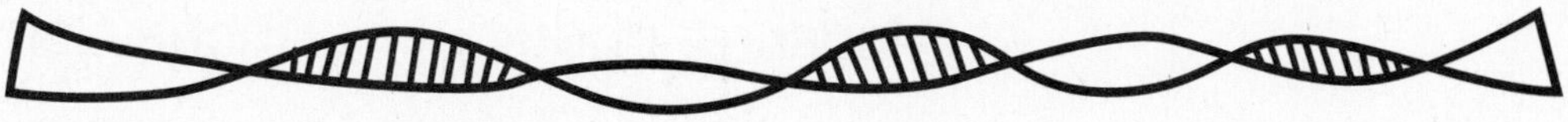

About _____ inches.
To check your estimate, measure to the nearest inch.

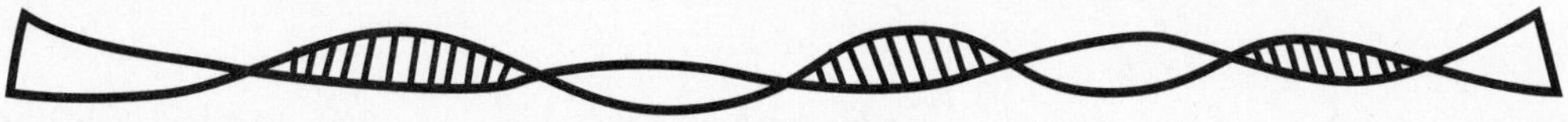

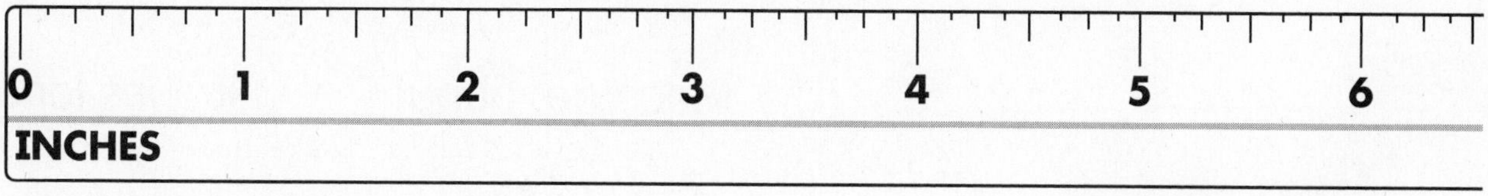

The ribbon is about __5__ inches long.
Did your estimate make sense?

Estimate. Check your estimate by measuring to the nearest inch.

2. width of a calculator

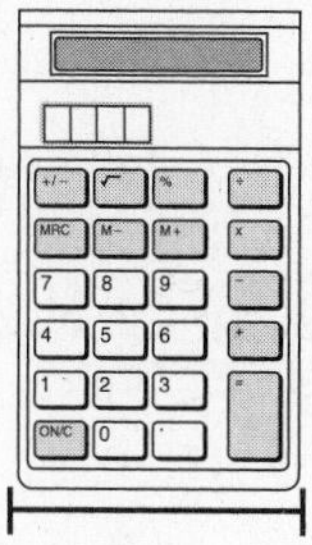

3. length of a pencil

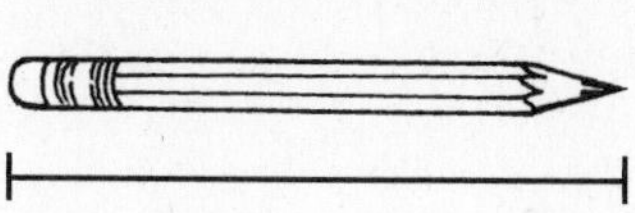

	Estimate	Measure
2.	about _____ inches	about _____ inches
3.	about _____ inches	about _____ inches

Name ____________________

Practice
11-5

Estimating Measurements

Estimate the length of each item. Then measure to the nearest inch. Write about how many inches long.

1. 

Estimate: about _____ inches long

Measure: about __6__ inches long

2. 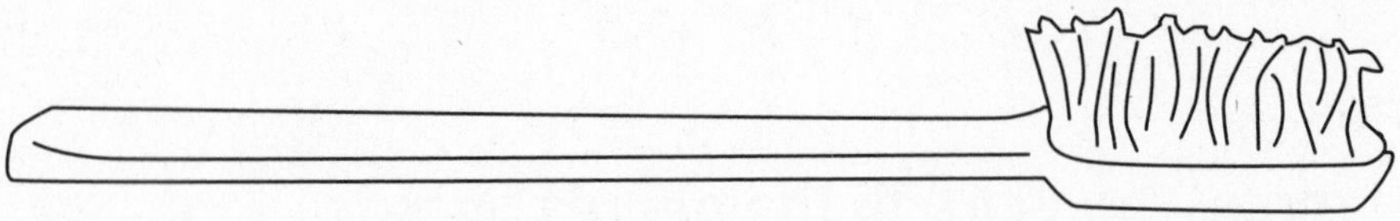

Estimate: about _____ inches long

Measure: about _____ inches long

3. 

Estimate: about _____ inches long

Measure: about _____ inches long

4. **Estimation** What is the best estimation for the length of the rope?

2 inches	5 inches	7 inches	9 inches
○	○	○	○

Name ______________________

Problem Solving: Use Objects

You can use a string to measure a path that is not straight.
First, place the string on top of the path.
Then, use a ruler to measure the string.

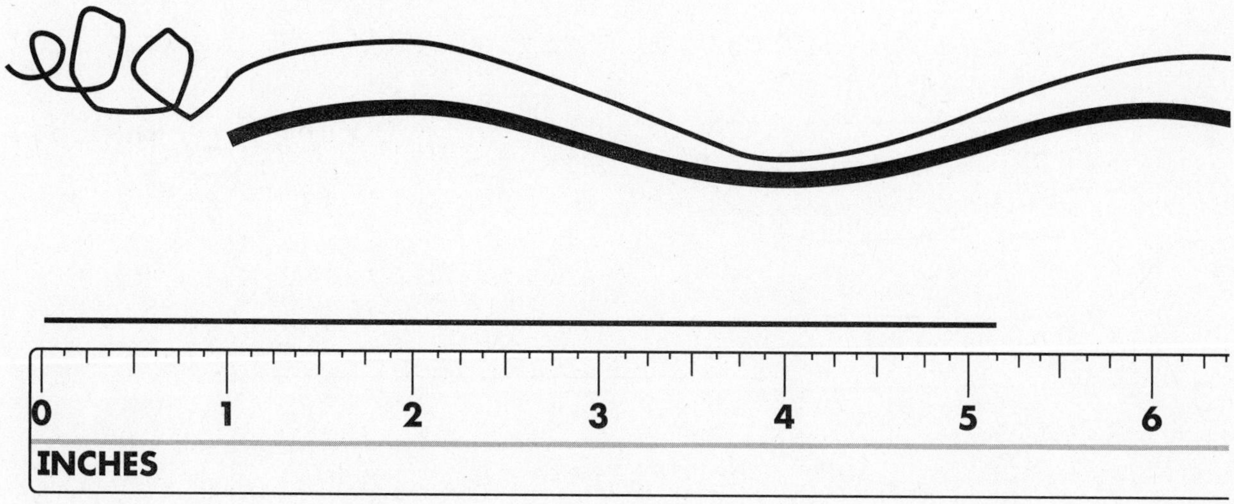

The path is about 5 inches long.

Use string to measure the path.
Then measure the string with a ruler.

1. The path is about _____ inches long.

2. The path is about _____ inches long.

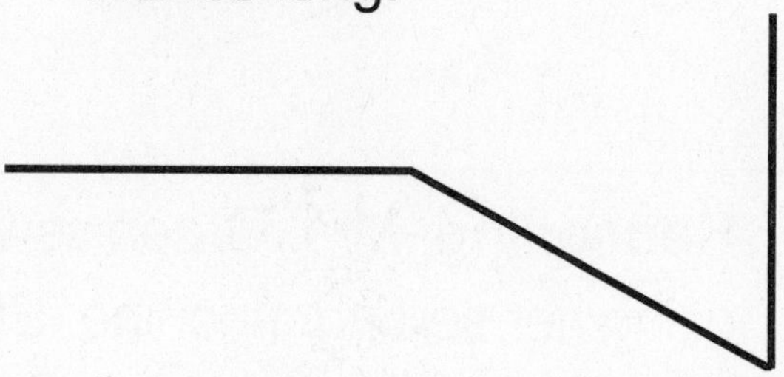

Name ______________________

Problem Solving: Use Objects

Measure.

1. 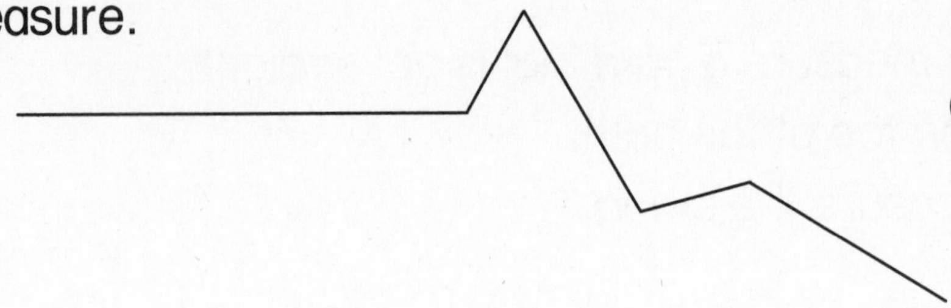

about __5__ inches

2. 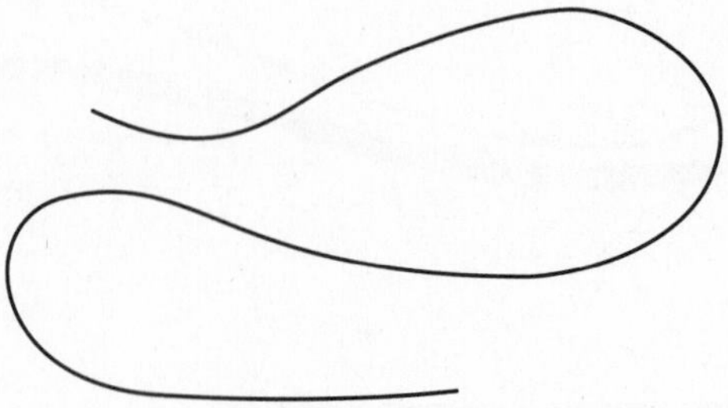

about _____ inches

3. 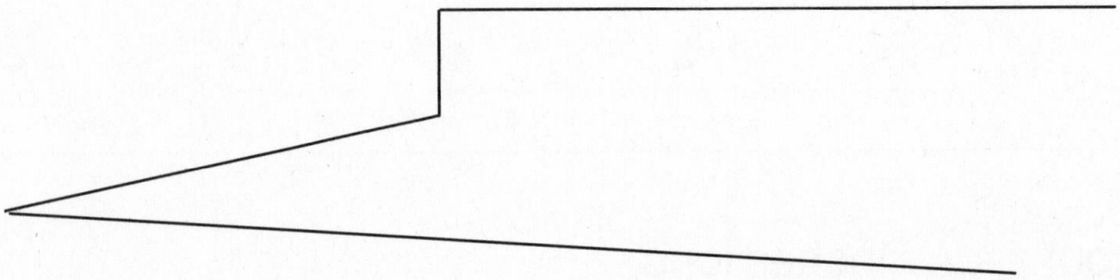

about _____ inches

4. 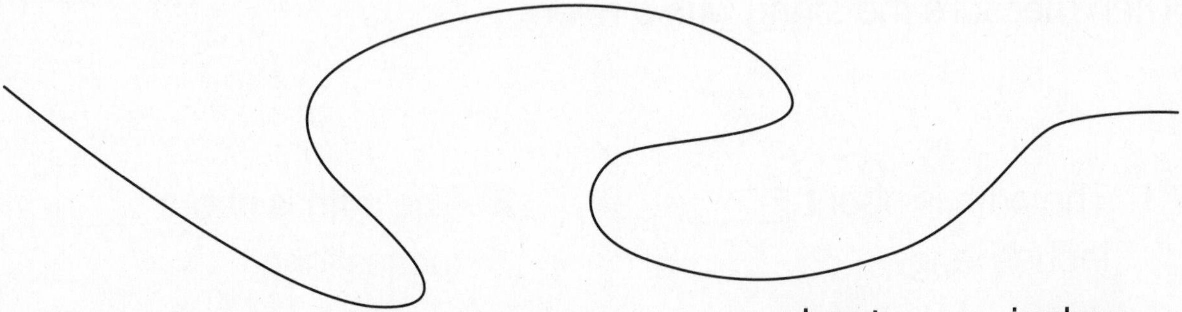

about _____ inches

5. **Reasoning** Mrs. Green sews these patterns on cloth with thread using her sewing machine. She needs to know how much thread to buy. Which pattern does she need to measure with string?

Name ____________________

Reteaching
12-1

Wholes and Equal Parts

Equal parts are the same shape and size.

2 equal parts

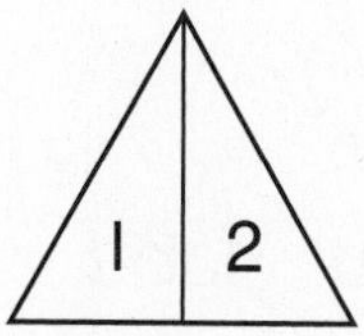

halves (circled)
thirds
fourths

3 equal parts

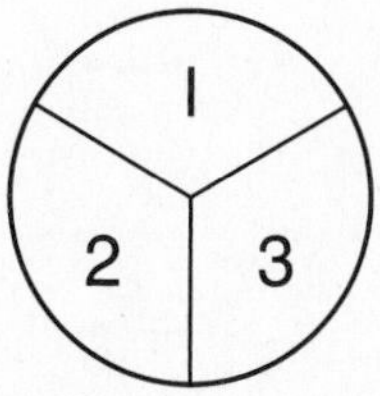

halves
thirds (circled)
fourths

4 equal parts

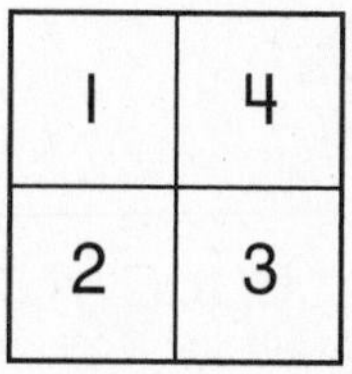

halves
thirds
fourths (circled)

How many equal parts? Write the number of parts.
Circle halves, thirds, or fourths.

1. _____ equal parts

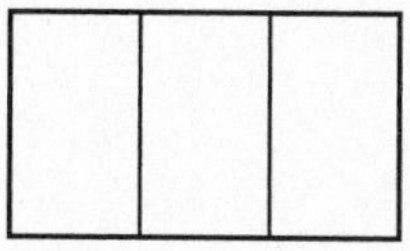

halves
thirds
fourths

2. _____ equal parts

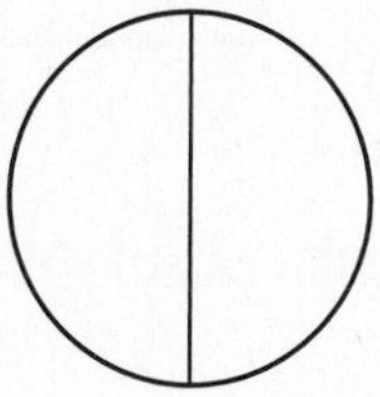

halves
thirds
fourths

3. _____ equal parts

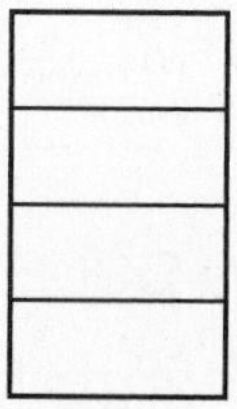

halves
thirds
fourths

4. _____ equal parts

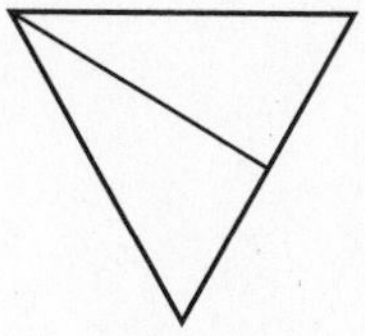

halves
thirds
fourths

5. _____ equal parts

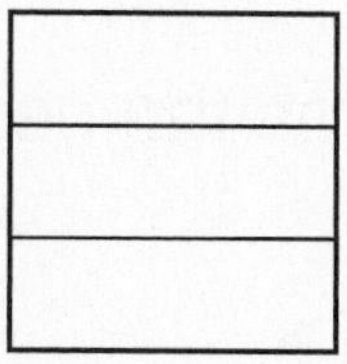

halves
thirds
fourths

6. _____ equal parts

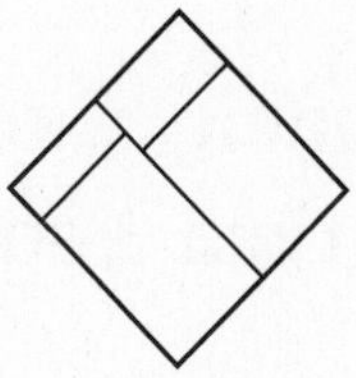

halves
thirds
fourths

Spatial Thinking Draw lines to show 2 equal parts.

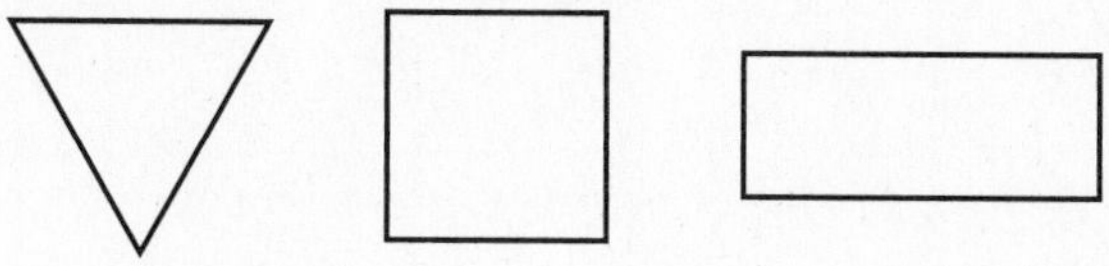

Name ______________________

Wholes and Equal Parts

Write the number of parts.
Circle **equal** or **unequal**.

1. 

2 (equal) unequal parts

2. 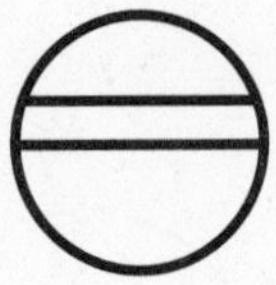

_____ equal unequal parts

Draw a line or lines to show equal parts.

3. fourths

4. thirds

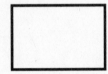

5. Sami has a paper heart. Which shows how she could cut it into halves?

6. **Reasoning** Circle **yes** or **no**. Can the heart be divided into 3 equal parts?

yes no

Name ______________________

Reteaching **12-2**

Unit Fractions and Regions

A fraction can name one of the equal parts of a whole shape.

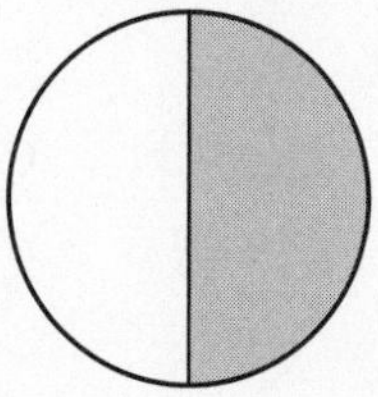

1 shaded part

2 equal parts

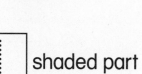

$\frac{1}{2}$ is shaded.

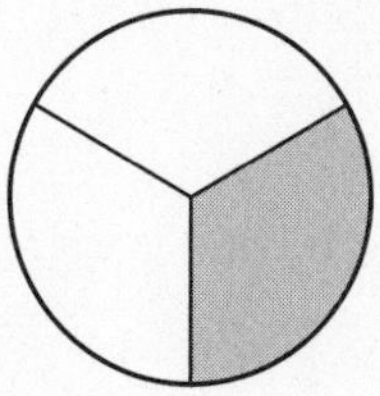

1 shaded part

3 equal parts

$\frac{1}{3}$ is shaded.

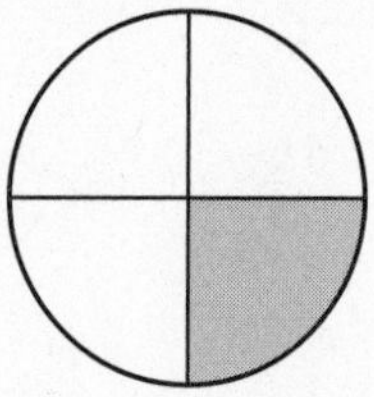

1 shaded part

4 equal parts

$\frac{1}{4}$ is shaded.

Color one part. Write how many shaded and equal parts. Write the fraction.

1.

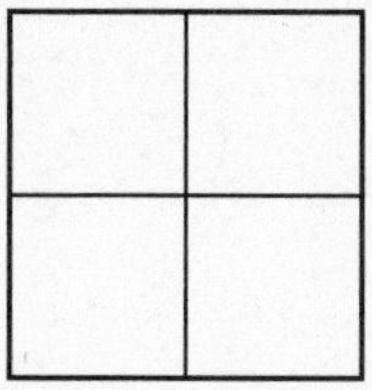

☐ shaded part

☐ equal parts

— is shaded.

2.

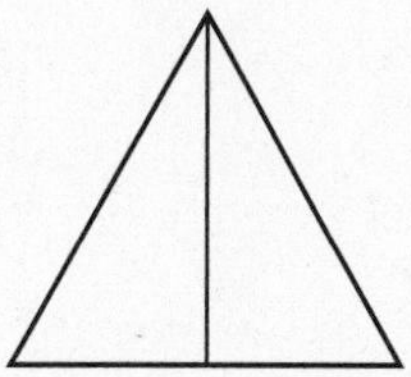

☐ shaded part

☐ equal parts

— is shaded.

Name ____________________

Unit Fractions and Regions

Write the fraction for the shaded part of the shape.

1. 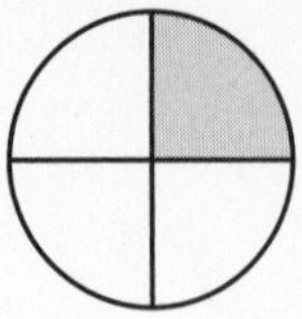

$\frac{1}{4}$

2. 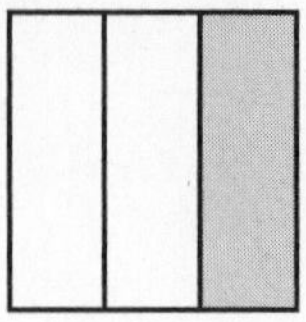

____

3. 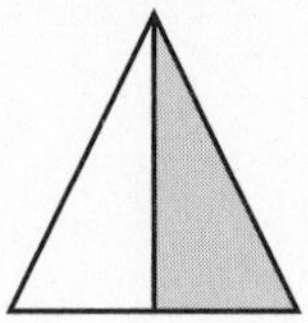

____

4. 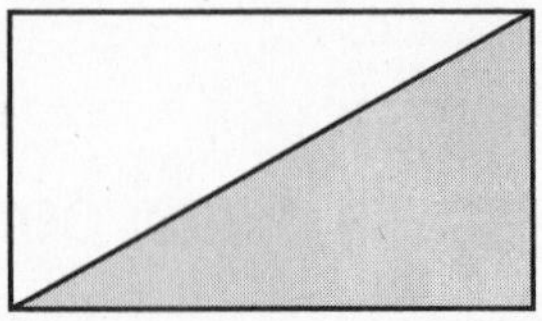

____

5. 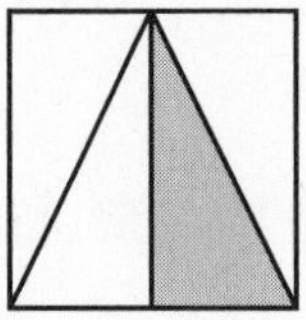

____

6. 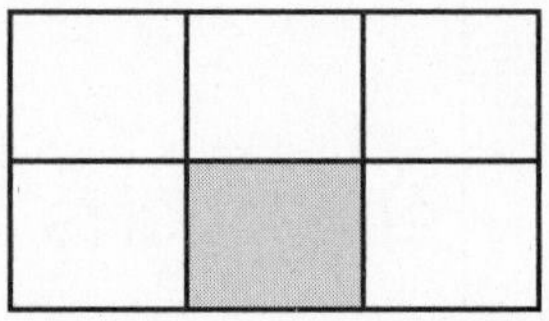

____

7. Vinnie colored one part of the circle. What fraction of the circle did he color?

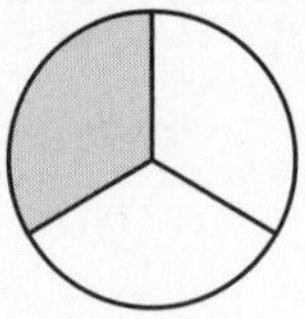

○ $\frac{1}{2}$ ○ $\frac{1}{3}$ ○ $\frac{1}{4}$ ○ $\frac{1}{6}$

8. Algebra Write the fractions. Look for a pattern. Which shape is missing?

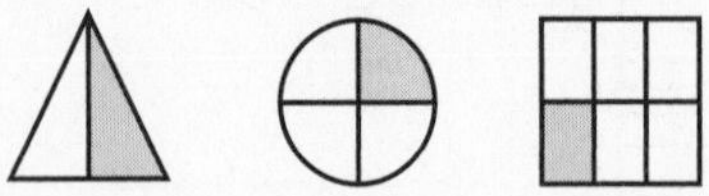

____ ____ ____ ____

○ 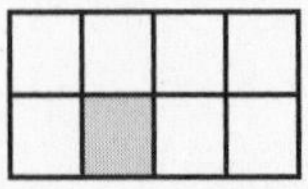 ○ 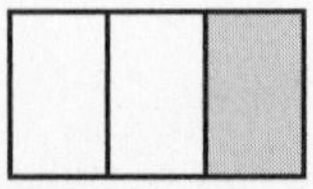

○ 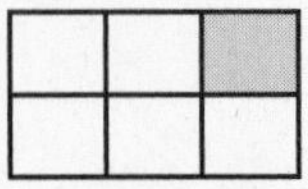 ○ 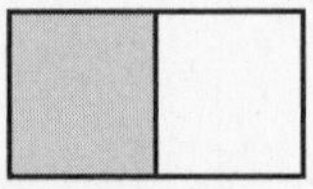

Name ______________________________

Non-Unit Fractions and Regions

A fraction can name two or more equal parts of a whole shape.

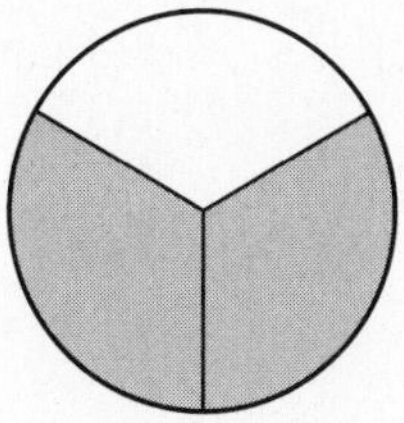

2 shaded parts

3 equal parts

$\frac{2}{3}$ is shaded.

Color the parts red.
Write the fraction for the shaded part.

1. Color 4 parts.

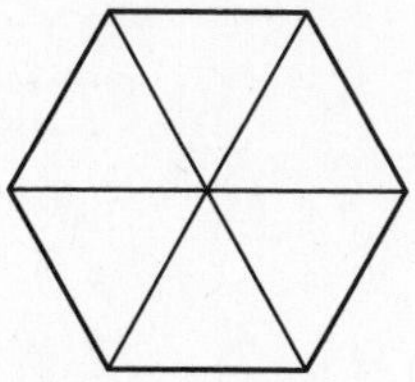

☐ parts are red.

☐ equal parts

____ is red.

2. Color 2 parts.

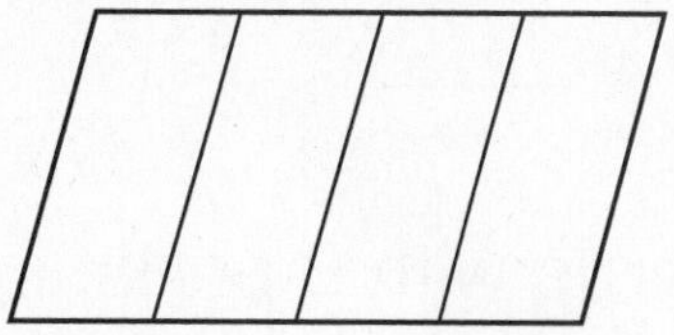

☐ parts are red.

☐ equal parts

____ is red.

3. Color 5 parts.

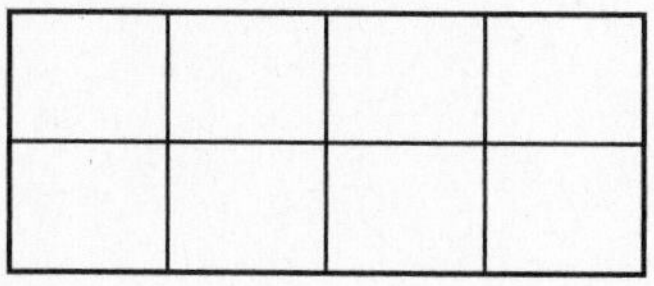

☐ parts are red.

☐ equal parts

____ is red.

4. Color 3 parts.

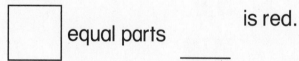

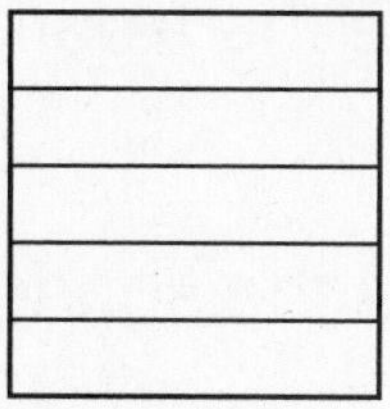

☐ parts are red.

☐ equal parts

____ is red.

Name ______________________________

Non-Unit Fractions and Regions

Write the fraction for the shaded part of the shape.

1. 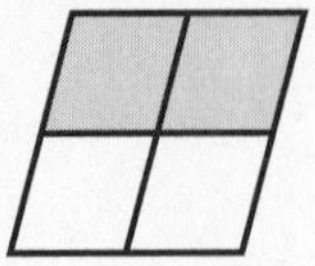

$\frac{2}{4}$

2. 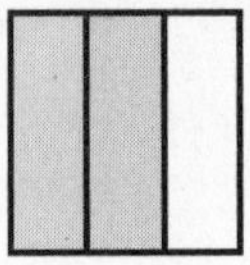

____

3. 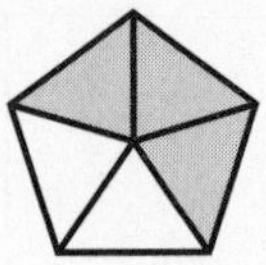

____

4. 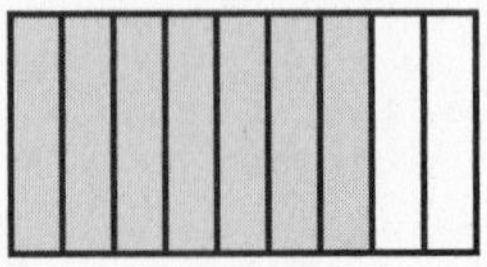

____

5. 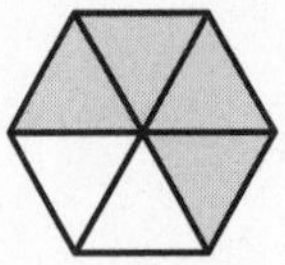

____

6. 

____

7. Jill has a rug with 8 parts. Four parts are white, and four parts are black. Which shows the rug?

○ 

○ 

○ 

○ 

8. **Geometry** Write the fraction for the shaded part of the rectangle.

What shape does the shaded part make?

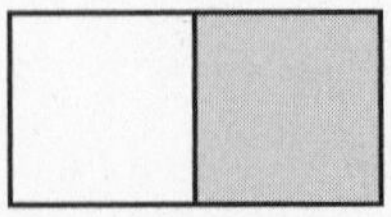

____

The shaded part is a ______________________.

Name ______________________

Fractions of a Set

A fraction can name parts of a set or a group.

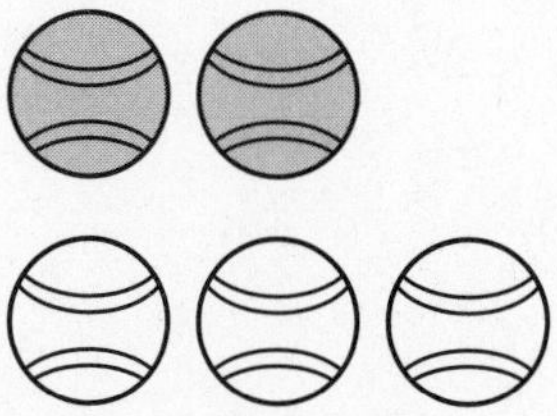

2 shaded balls

5 balls in all

$\frac{2}{5}$ of the balls are shaded.

Color the parts.
Write the fraction for the part you color.

1. Color 2 parts blue.

2 blue stars

6 stars in all

$\frac{2}{6}$ of the stars are blue.

2. Color 3 parts green.

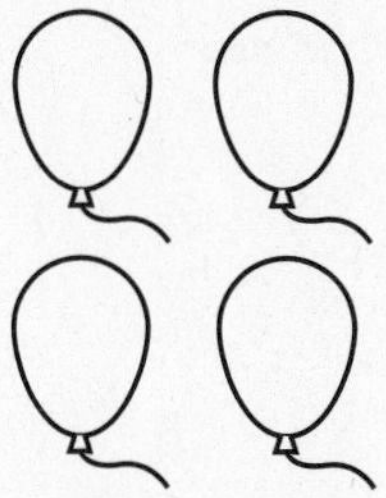

☐ green balloons

☐ balloons in all

____ of the balloons are green.

3. Color 5 parts red.

☐ red apples

☐ apples in all

____ of the apples are red.

Name ______________________________

Fractions of a Set

Color to show the fraction.

1. 

$\frac{4}{5}$ of the apples are red.

2. 

$\frac{3}{8}$ of the apples are red.

3. 

$\frac{2}{4}$ of the apples are red.

4. 

$\frac{2}{6}$ of the apples are red.

5. What fraction of the bananas are shaded?

○ $\frac{1}{2}$ ○ $\frac{3}{4}$

○ $\frac{4}{7}$ ○ $\frac{7}{4}$

6. What fraction of the cherries are shaded?

○ $\frac{12}{10}$ ○ $\frac{2}{12}$

○ $\frac{10}{12}$ ○ $\frac{1}{10}$

7. **Number Sense** Draw a picture to solve.

Sue has 9 baseball cards.
She gives 4 cards to Kris.
How many cards does Sue have left? _____

What fraction of the 9 cards does Sue have? _____

Name ______________________________

Understanding 1 as a Fraction

This whole pie is cut into 4 equal parts.
All the parts together equal **one whole,** or **1.**
$\frac{4}{4} = 1$

A whole can have different numbers of equal parts.
Complete these fractions that show 1 whole.

$\frac{3}{3} = 1$

$\frac{6}{6} = 1$

$\frac{8}{8} = 1$

Color to show 1 whole.
Write the fraction that equals 1 whole.

1.

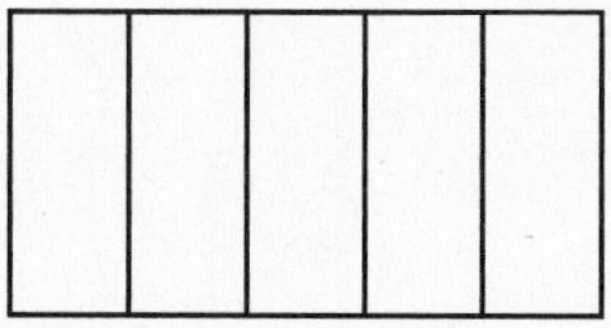

$\frac{\_\_\_}{\_\_\_} = 1$

2.

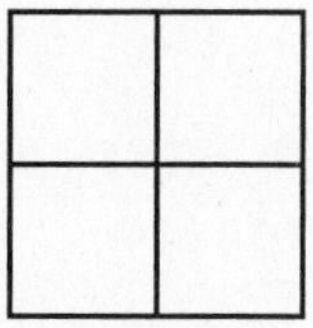

$\frac{\_\_\_}{\_\_\_} = 1$

3. Journal Draw a cookie that is divided into 2 equal parts. Write the fraction to go with your drawing.

Name ____________________

Understanding 1 as a Fraction

Color to show 1 whole.
Write the fraction that equals 1 whole.

1. 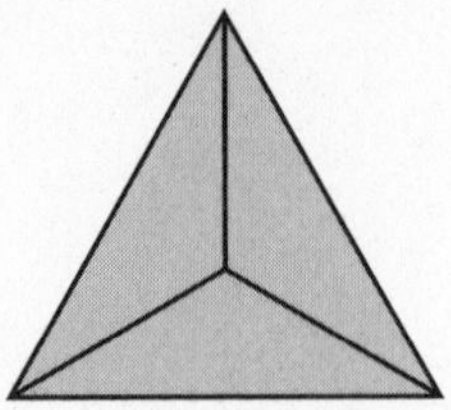 $\frac{3}{3} = 1$

2.  $\frac{\square}{\square} = 1$

3. Carlos cuts an orange in half. He eats both halves. Which fraction of the orange did Carlos eat?

○ $\frac{2}{2}$ ○ $\frac{1}{2}$

○ $\frac{4}{4}$ ○ $\frac{1}{4}$

4. Zeta folded a paper plate into fourths to make a spinner. Which fraction shows how much of the plate she used?

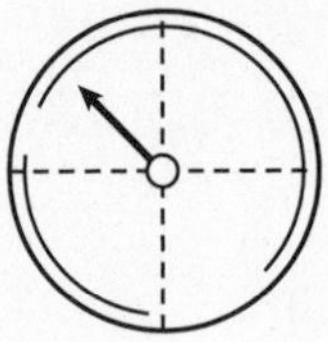

○ $\frac{3}{4}$ ○ $\frac{3}{3}$

○ $\frac{4}{4}$ ○ $\frac{6}{4}$

5. Spatial Thinking Which fraction is equal to 1 whole?

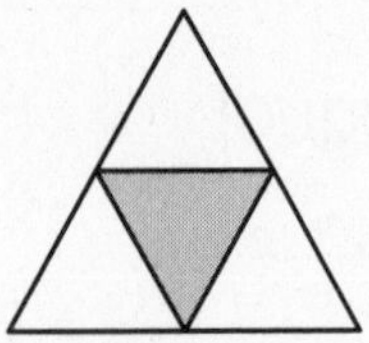 $\frac{1}{4}$ ○

 $\frac{2}{4}$ ○

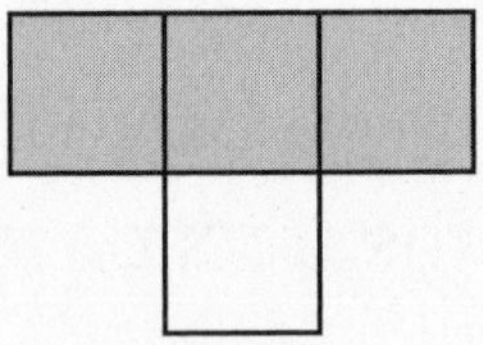 $\frac{3}{4}$ ○

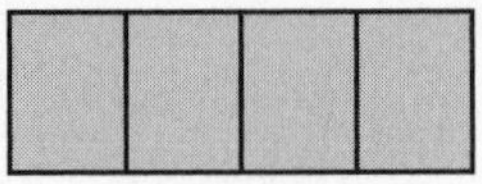 $\frac{4}{4}$ ○

Name ____________________

Reteaching **12-6**

Fractions and Decimals

How much is shaded?
You can name the shaded parts of a whole two ways.

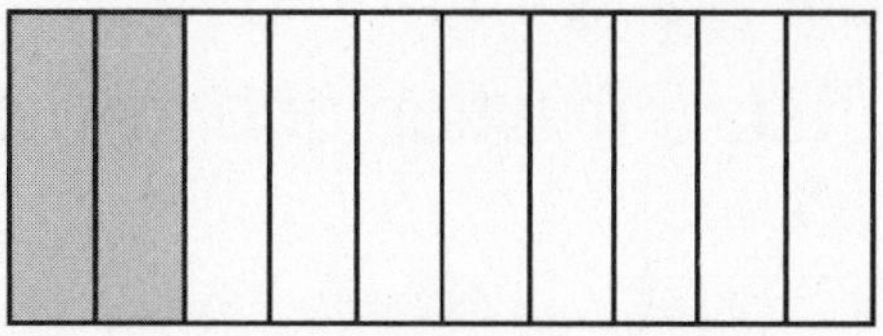

$\frac{2}{10}$ This **fraction** means **2 tenths,** or 2 of 10 parts.

0.2 This **decimal** means **2 tenths,** or 2 of 10 parts.

You can also name the parts of a whole set two ways.

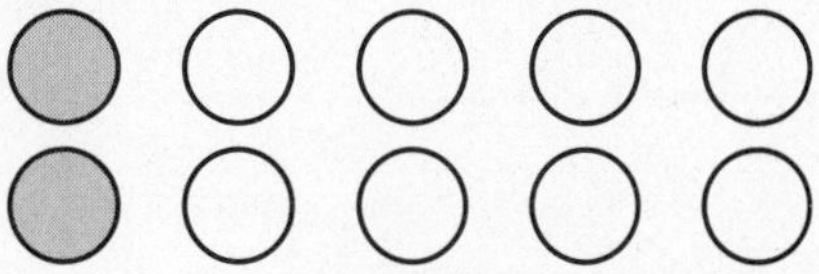

$\frac{2}{10}$ 0.2

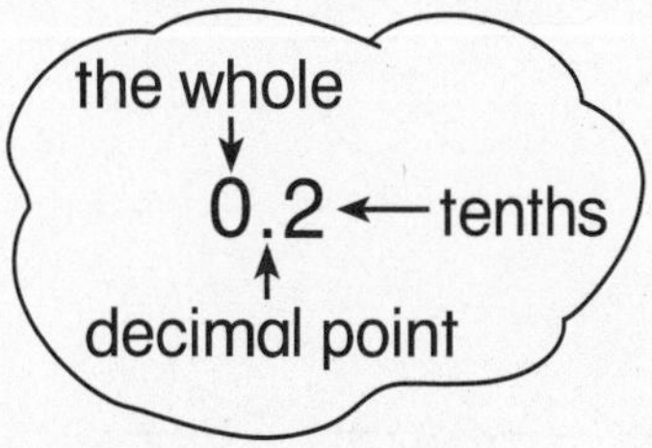

2 tenths of the circles are shaded.

Color 4 parts red. Write the fraction and the decimal.

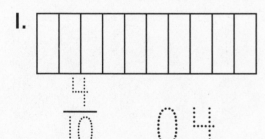

1.

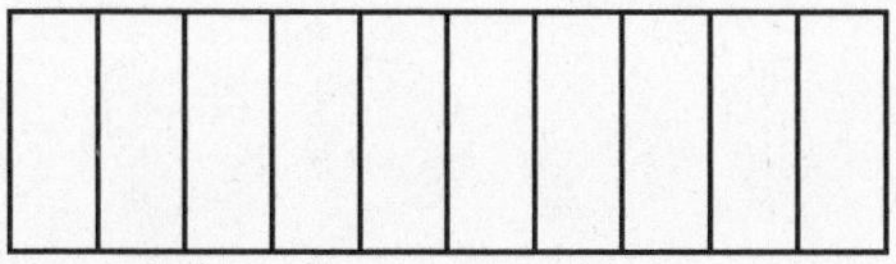

$\frac{4}{10}$ 0.4

2.

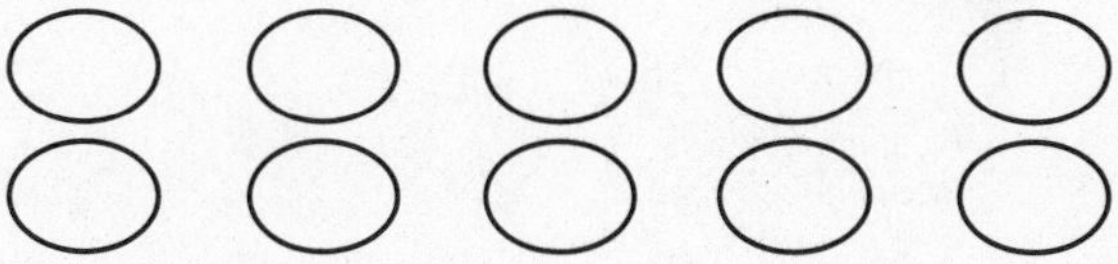

$\frac{4}{10}$ 0.4

Color 6 parts red. Write the fraction and the decimal.

3.

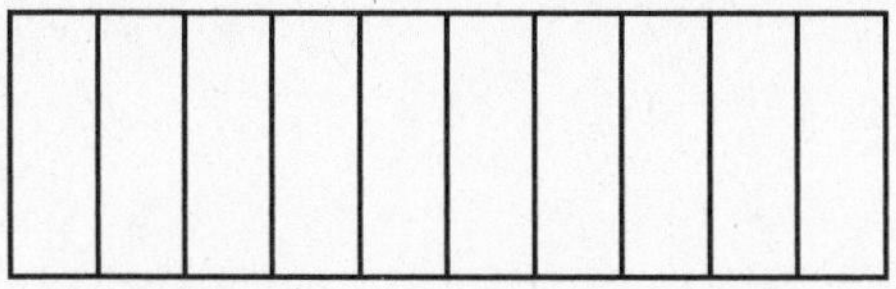

_______ _______

4.

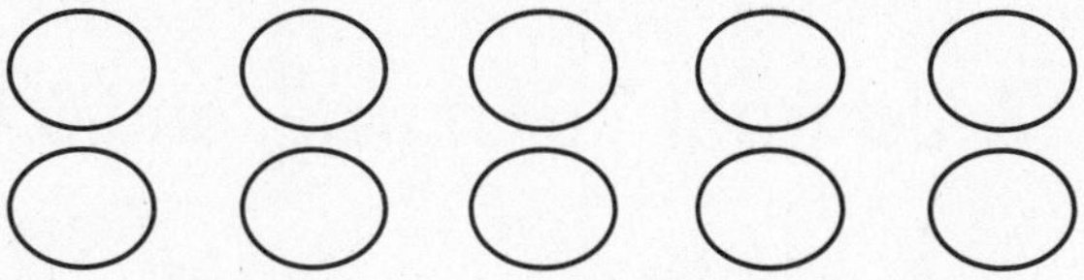

_______ _______

Name ____________________

Practice
12-6

Fractions and Decimals

Find the part that is shaded.
Write it as a fraction and as a decimal.

1. 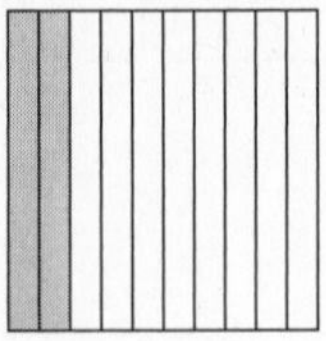

$\frac{2}{10}$ ____ 0.2 ____

2. 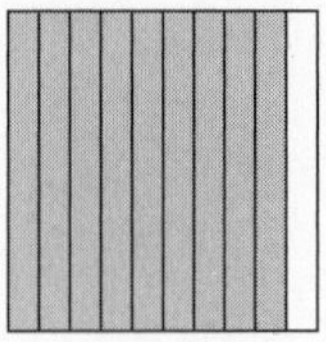

________ ________

3. 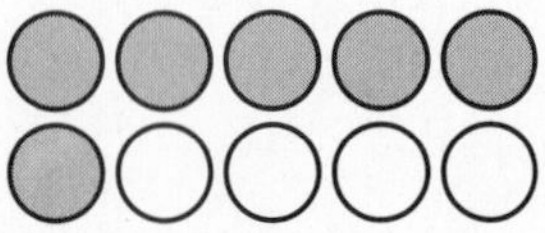

________ ________

4. 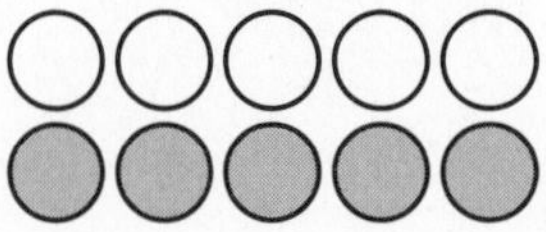

________ ________

5. Which decimal shows how much is shaded?

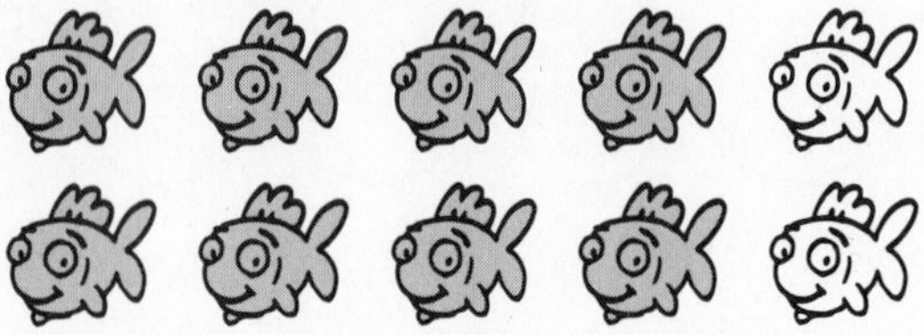

○ 0.3 ○ 0.8

○ 0.6 ○ 0.9

6. Which decimal shows how much is shaded?

○ 0.6 ○ 0.8

○ 0.7 ○ 0.9

7. **Journal** Tell how $\frac{4}{10}$ and 0.4 are alike.

____

____

Name ______________________

Reteaching
12-7

Problem Solving: Use Objects

There are 12 counters.

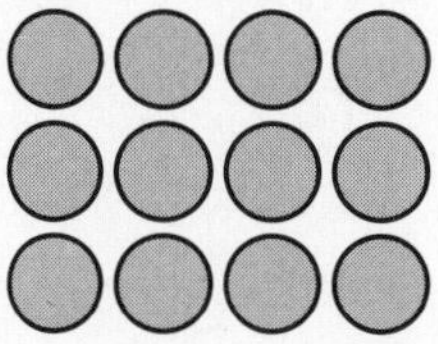

Find $\frac{1}{4}$ of a group of 12 counters.

Sort the 12 counters into 4 groups.

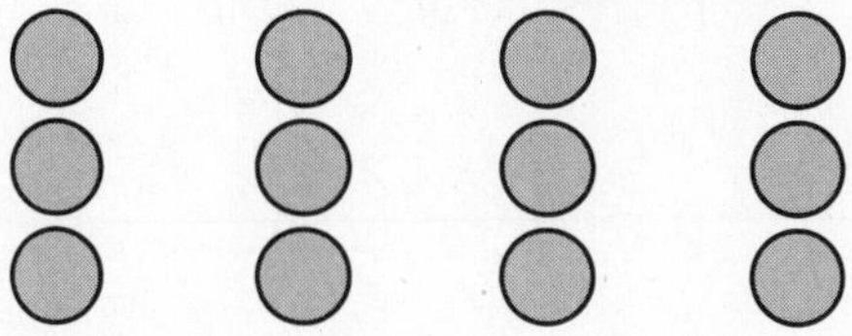

1 of the 4 groups has 3 counters,

so $\frac{1}{4}$ of 12 = 3

Use counters. Sort the counters into groups to solve the problems.

1. Kiyo has 9 balloons. $\frac{1}{3}$ of the balloons are red. How many balloons are red?

$\frac{1}{3}$ of _____ = _____

2. There are 10 apples in a bowl. $\frac{1}{2}$ of the apples are green. How many apples are green?

$\frac{1}{2}$ of _____ = _____

3. Josh has 16 fish. $\frac{3}{4}$ of the fish have stripes. How many fish have stripes?

$\frac{3}{4}$ of _____ = _____

4. There are 20 cars in a parking lot. $\frac{2}{5}$ of the cars are white. How many white cars are in the parking lot?

$\frac{2}{5}$ of _____ = _____

Name ______________________

Practice
12-7

Problem Solving: Use Objects

Solve the problems. Use counters to help.

1. Dennis has 16 balls.
$\frac{1}{2}$ of the balls are footballs.
How many balls are footballs?

$\frac{1}{2}$ of 16 = 8

2. A store has 25 bikes.
$\frac{2}{5}$ of the bikes are red.
How many bikes are red?

$\frac{2}{5}$ of 25 = _____

3. A park has 18 swings. $\frac{3}{9}$ of them are tire swings.
How many of the swings are tire swings?

- ○ 3 swings
- ○ 9 swings
- ○ 6 swings
- ○ 12 swings

4. Alice finds 12 shells. $\frac{1}{6}$ of the shells are black.
How many shells are black?

- ○ 2 shells
- ○ 6 shells
- ○ 4 shells
- ○ 8 shells

5. **Reasonableness** Draw counters to help solve the problem.

There are 12 girls on a gymnastics team.
Less than $\frac{1}{4}$ of the girls are in second grade.
How many girls on the gymnastics team could be in second grade?

_____ girls could be in second grade.

Name ______________________________

Telling Time to Five Minutes

To tell time to five minutes, count by 5s for every number.

The time is 4:25.

There are 30 minutes in a half hour and 60 minutes in an hour.

The time is 4:30.

The hour hand moves from number to number in 60 minutes.

The time is 5:15.

Count by 5s.
Write the time.

1.

2.

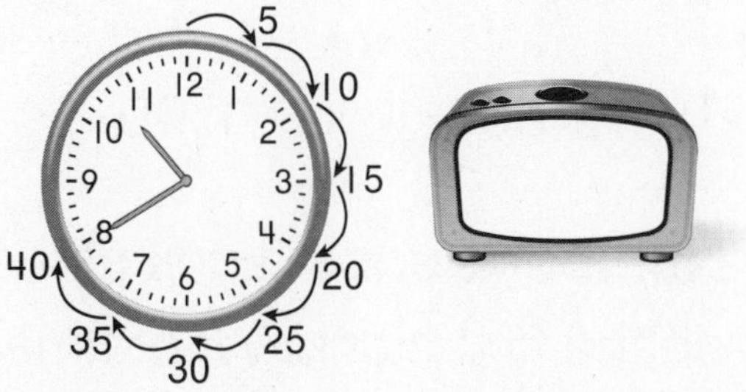

3.

4.

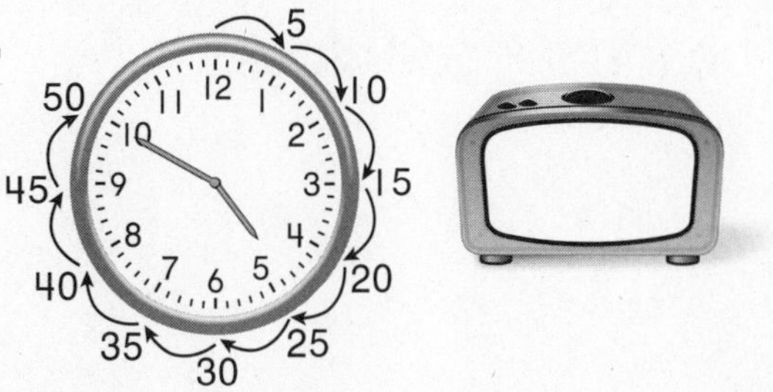

Name ______________________________

Telling Time to Five Minutes

Write the time.

1.

2.

3.

4.

5. The time is 6:05. What number would the minute hand be pointing to on a clock?

○ 6 ○ 5 ○ 2 ○ 1

6. Look at the clock. What time does it show?

○ 12:45 ○ 12:55

○ 12:50 ○ 1:00

7. Number Sense Look at the time on the first clock. What time will it be in five minutes? Show that time on the second clock.

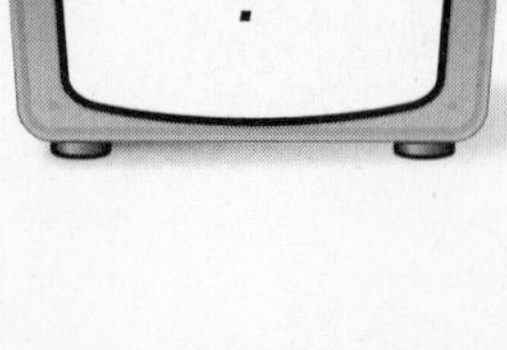

Name ______________________________

Telling Time to the Quarter Hour

Divide 1 hour into 4 equal parts, or quarters.
Start at 1:00. Color each quarter of the hour. Then read the time.

quarter past 1 | half past 1 | quarter to 2 | 2 o'clock

You also can tell the time by adding minutes.
Each quarter adds 15 minutes.

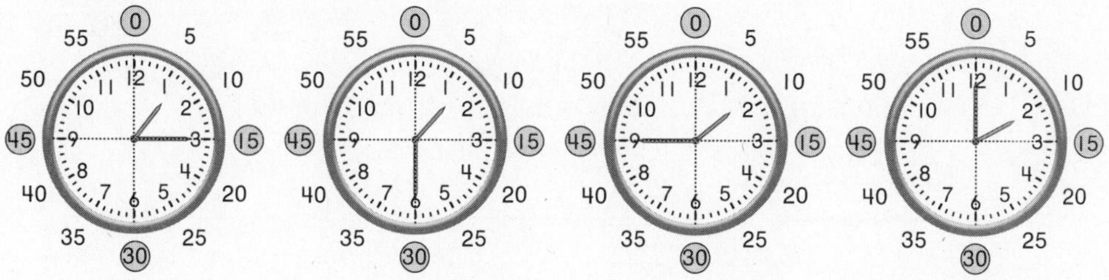

1:15 | 1: 30 | 1: 45 | 2:00

Draw the missing hand to show the time.

1.

quarter past 11

2.

quarter to 4

3.

2:30

4.

4:45

Name ____________________

Practice
13-2

Telling Time to the Quarter Hour

Look for a pattern. Write the time for each clock.
Draw the missing hands.

1.

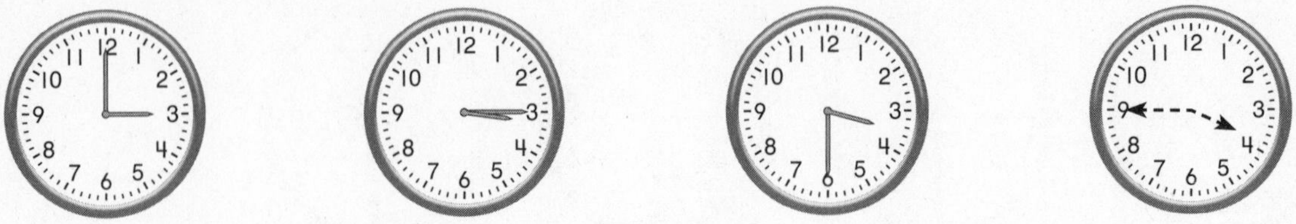

3:00   3:15   ________   ________

2.

________   ________   ________   ________

---

3. Draw the hands on the clock to solve.
Travis has to catch the bus in 15 minutes.
It is 12:30. What time will the bus come?

---

4. Algebra Look for a pattern. Which clock comes next?

?

____

○   ○   ○   ○

Name ______________________________

Reteaching
13-3

Telling Time Before and After the Hour

There are different ways to say time before and after the hour.

6:15

15 minutes after 6 or **quarter past** 6

6:30

30 minutes after 6 or **half past** 6

6:45

45 minutes after 6 or **quarter to** 7

2:35

25 minutes **before** 3 or 35 minutes after 2

Count by 5s to tell the time. Write the time.

1.

____

30 minutes after _____

or **half past** _____

2.

____

15 minutes after _____

or **quarter past** _____

3. Reasoning The time is 6:10. Is the hour hand closer to 6 or 7? Why?

____

____

Name ________________________

Practice
13-3

Telling Time Before and After the Hour

Write the time or draw the hands to show the time.
Then write the time before or after the hour.

1.

quarter to 11

2.

half past ____

3. Joyce gets up at ten minutes before 7.
Which clock shows this time?

○

○

○

○

4. Journal Write two ways to say the time shown.

____

____

Name ______________________________

Reteaching
13-4

Estimating Time

About how long does it take to wash your face?

about 1 second — No, 1 second is too short.

about 1 minute (circled) — Yes, 1 minute is reasonable. It makes sense.

about 1 hour — No, 1 hour is too long.

about 1 day — No, 1 day is too long.

Circle the amount of time each activity would take.

1. Drinking milk

about 1 minute

about 1 hour

about 1 day

2. Watching a TV show

about 1 second

about 1 hour

about 1 day

3. Going on a picnic

about 2 minutes

about 2 hours

about 2 days

4. Going on a trip

about 5 minutes

about 5 hours

about 5 days

Name ______________________________

Practice **13-4**

Estimating Time

Choose the amount of time each activity would take.

1. making a sandwich

○ about 5 seconds ○ about 5 hours

○ about 5 minutes ○ about 5 days

2. visiting a friend

○ about 3 seconds ○ about 3 hours

○ about 3 minutes ○ about 3 days

3. going on vacation

○ about 10 seconds ○ about 10 hours

○ about 10 minutes ○ about 10 days

4. touching your nose

○ about 1 second ○ about 1 hour

○ about 1 minute ○ about 1 day

5. Bill mows the lawn.
Megan rings the doorbell.
Whose activity takes
about 2 seconds?

____

6. Estimation You and a friend play "Pass the Potato."
How many times do you think you can pass the potato in one minute?

3 times 30 times

Name ______________________________

Reteaching
13-5

Elapsed Time

Count the number of hours to find out how much time has passed.

Find the hour hand. Count from the start time to the end time.

Start Time	End Time	Start Time	End Time

3:00	5:00	7:30	10:30
2 hours		3 hours	

Write the times. Then write how many hours have passed.

1.

Start Time	End Time

________	________
____ hour	

2.

Start Time	End Time

________	________
____ hours	

Name ______________________________

Practice **13-5**

Elapsed Time

Draw the clock hands and write the end time for each activity. Use a clock if you need to.

	Starts	Lasts	Ends	
1.  reading class		1 hour		9:00
2.  play soccer		2 hours		______
3.  field trip		3 hours		______

4. Paula starts her homework at the time shown on the clock. She works for 30 minutes. What time does she finish her homework?

4:00	4:30	5:00	5:30
○	○	○	○

5. Reasonableness The school fair started at 7:00. It was over at 9:00. Chen said that the school fair lasted 3 hours. Is he correct? Explain.

____

Name ______________________

Reteaching
13-6

Using a Calendar

This calendar shows the month of March.
The list shows the months of the year in order.

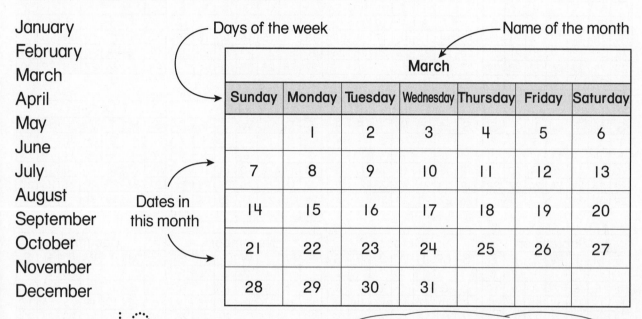

January
February
March
April
May
June
July
August
September
October
November
December

Days of the week — Name of the month — Dates in this month

March						
Sunday	Monday	Tuesday	Wednesday	Thursday	Friday	Saturday
	1	2	3	4	5	6
7	8	9	10	11	12	13
14	15	16	17	18	19	20
21	22	23	24	25	26	27
28	29	30	31			

Look at the last date in the month to find how many days in March.

There are 12 months.

March is the 3rd month of the year.

There are 31 days in March.

Use the calendar and list to answer the questions.

1. There are 52 weeks in a year. There are 5 weeks in March.

2. What is the day after Wednesday? ______________

3. What day is the 16th of March? ______________

4. What is the date of the last Sunday in March? ________

5. What is the last month of the year? ______________

Name ______________________

Practice
13-6

Using a Calendar

Use the calendar to answer the questions.

January

S	M	T	W	T	F	S
						1
2	3	4	5	6	7	8
9	10	11	12	13	14	15
16	17	18	19	20	21	22
23	24	25	26	27	28	29
30	31					

February

S	M	T	W	T	F	S
		1	2	3	4	5
6	7	8	9	10	11	12
13	14	15	16	17	18	19
20	21	22	23	24	25	26
27	28					

March

S	M	T	W	T	F	S
		1	2	3	4	5
6	7	8	9	10	11	12
13	14	15	16	17	18	19
20	21	22	23	24	25	26
27	28	29	30	31		

April

S	M	T	W	T	F	S
					1	2
3	4	5	6	7	8	9
10	11	12	13	14	15	16
17	18	19	20	21	22	23
24	25	26	27	28	29	30

May

S	M	T	W	T	F	S
1	2	3	4	5	6	7
8	9	10	11	12	13	14
15	16	17	18	19	20	21
22	23	24	25	26	27	28
29	30	31				

June

S	M	T	W	T	F	S
			1	2	3	4
5	6	7	8	9	10	11
12	13	14	15	16	17	18
19	20	21	22	23	24	25
26	27	28	29	30		

July

S	M	T	W	T	F	S
					1	2
3	4	5	6	7	8	9
10	11	12	13	14	15	16
17	18	19	20	21	22	23
24	25	26	27	28	29	30
31						

August

S	M	T	W	T	F	S
	1	2	3	4	5	6
7	8	9	10	11	12	13
14	15	16	17	18	19	20
21	22	23	24	25	26	27
28	29	30	31			

September

S	M	T	W	T	F	S
				1	2	3
4	5	6	7	8	9	10
11	12	13	14	15	16	17
18	19	20	21	22	23	24
25	26	27	28	29	30	

October

S	M	T	W	T	F	S
						1
2	3	4	5	6	7	8
9	10	11	12	13	14	15
16	17	18	19	20	21	22
23	24	25	26	27	28	29
30	31					

November

S	M	T	W	T	F	S
		1	2	3	4	5
6	7	8	9	10	11	12
13	14	15	16	17	18	19
20	21	22	23	24	25	26
27	28	29	30			

December

S	M	T	W	T	F	S
				1	2	3
4	5	6	7	8	9	10
11	12	13	14	15	16	17
18	19	20	21	22	23	24
25	26	27	28	29	30	31

Spatial Thinking

1. What month comes just before May? April

2. What month comes just after August? ______________

3. What day of the week is December 3? ______________

4. Sara's birthday is in a month that has 5 Thursdays.
Her birthday is on a Thursday, and is the 23rd of the month.
What month is her birthday on this calendar?

○ June ○ August

○ September ○ December

Name ______________________________

Equivalent Times

"Equivalent" is another way to say "the same" or "equal to."
There are different ways to name the same amount of time.

30 minutes is the same as 1 half hour.

I day is equal to 24 hours.

March						
S	M	T	W	T	F	S
	1	2	3	4	5	6
7	8	9	10	11	12	13
14	15	16	17	18	19	20
21	22	23	24	25	26	27
28	29	30	31			

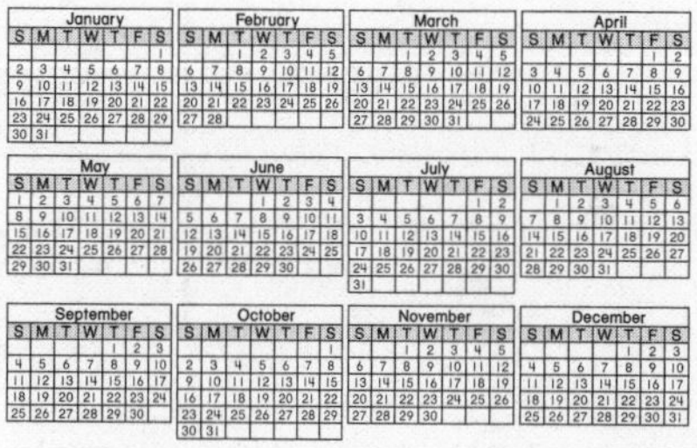

I year is equivalent to 12 months

Circle the equivalent times.

1. Mario reads for 1 quarter hour.

30 minutes   60 minutes   15 minutes

2. Erin was on vacation for 7 days.

1 week   1 month   1 year

3. Journal Write the time that lunch starts and ends.
Write the equivalent times in minutes and hours.

Name ______________________

Practice **13-7**

Equivalent Times

Use the schedule to answer the questions.

Afternoon Schedule	
12:15 – 12:45	Music
12:45 – 1:45	Science
1:45 – 2:00	Recess
2:00 – 2:15	Story Time
2:15 – 2:45	Social Studies
2:45 – 3:00	Clean Up

Equivalent Times	
one quarter hour	15 minutes
one half hour	30 minutes
one hour	60 minutes
1 day	24 hours
1 week	7 days
1 year	12 months

1. Which two activities are each one half hour long?

   Music, Social Studies

2. How many hours long is science? ______________

3. Name two other activities that are as long as Recess.

   ____

4. Melanie went swimming for an hour.
   How many minutes did she swim?

   ○ 15 minutes　　○ 30 minutes

   ○ 24 minutes　　○ 60 minutes

Name ______________________________

Reteaching **13-8**

Problem Solving: Multiple-Step Problems

Read the problem. Follow the steps to solve.

Think: You need to figure out the number of extra minutes Pat has.

Pat has 60 minutes before the bus comes.
It takes 20 minutes to dress for school.
It takes 20 minutes to eat breakfast.
How many extra minutes does Pat have?

Step 1 Add the time Pat uses to dress and to eat:

20 + 20 = 40

Step 2 Subtract the time used from the time Pat has:

60 − 40 = 20

Think: Does the answer make sense?

Pat has 20 extra minutes.

Use two steps to solve.

1. Andy has 30 minutes before the soccer game. It takes 15 minutes to dress. It takes 10 minutes to get to the park. How much extra time does Andy have before the game?

Step 1

15 + _____ = _____

Step 2

_____ − _____ = _____

Andy has _____ extra minutes.

Name ____________________

Practice
13-8

Problem Solving: Multiple-Step Problems

Solve. Write a number sentence for each part of the problem. Use base-ten blocks if you need to.

1. Kit spent 30 minutes on the slide. He spent 20 minutes on the swings. How much time did he spend at the playground? Kit also spent 40 minutes in the picnic area. How much time did he spend at the park in all?

   30 + 20 = 50 minutes

   50 + 40 = 90 minutes

2. **Algebra** This week Tracey played baseball for 5 hours and soccer for 7 hours. How much time did she spend on both sports? Tracey spent 15 hours on sports. How much time did she spend at the swimming pool if the rest of her time was spent swimming?

   ____________ hours

   ____________ hours

3. Rita read a book for 50 minutes. She watched TV for 30 minutes. If Rita has 100 minutes before bedtime, how much time does she have to take a bath?

   ○ 35 minutes ○ 25 minutes

   ○ 30 minutes ○ 20 minutes

Name ______________________

Reteaching
14-1

Organizing Data

Use this data to make a bar graph.

Children at Grand School sold tickets to their school play.

Grade 1 sold 8 tickets.
Grade 2 sold 15 tickets.
Grade 3 sold 12 tickets.

Color the boxes to show the number of tickets each grade sold.

Tickets Sold to School Play

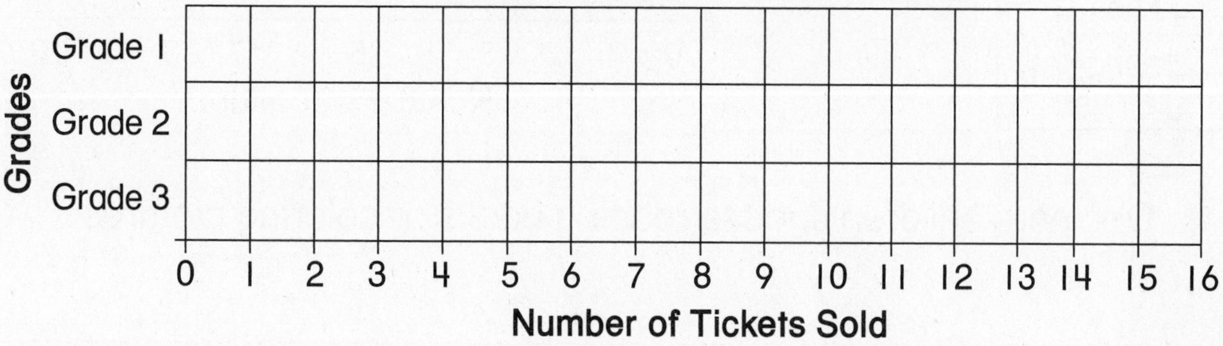

Use the bar graph to compare data.

1. How many tickets did Grade 3 sell? 12
2. How many tickets did Grade 1 sell? __________
3. Which grade sold the fewest tickets? __________
4. Which grade sold the most tickets? __________
5. How many more tickets did Grade 3 sell than Grade 1? _____
6. Which grade sold more than 13 tickets? __________

Name ______________________

Practice
14-1

Organizing Data

Use the table to make the bar graph.
Then use the bar graph to solve the problems.

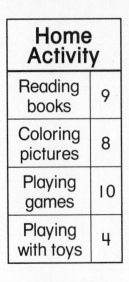

Home Activity	
Reading books	9
Coloring pictures	8
Playing games	10
Playing with toys	4

Favorite Home Activity

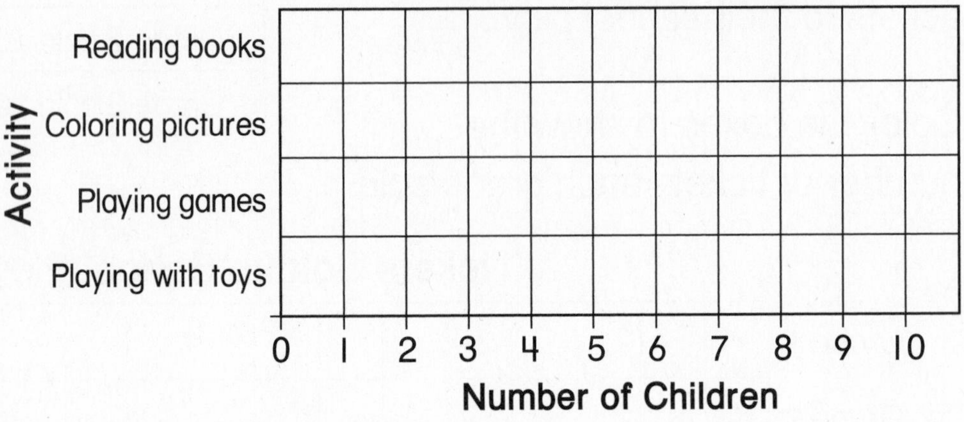

1. Did more children choose reading books or coloring pictures?

____

2. Which activity is the favorite of the greatest number of children?

____

3. Which activity is the favorite of the fewest number of children?

____

4. Estimation About how many children were asked to vote for their favorite home activity?

○ about 10 children ○ about 30 children

○ about 20 children ○ about 40 children

Name ______________________

Reteaching
14-2

Range and Mode

This bar graph shows the ages of children in a neighborhood. Use the graph to find the range and the mode.

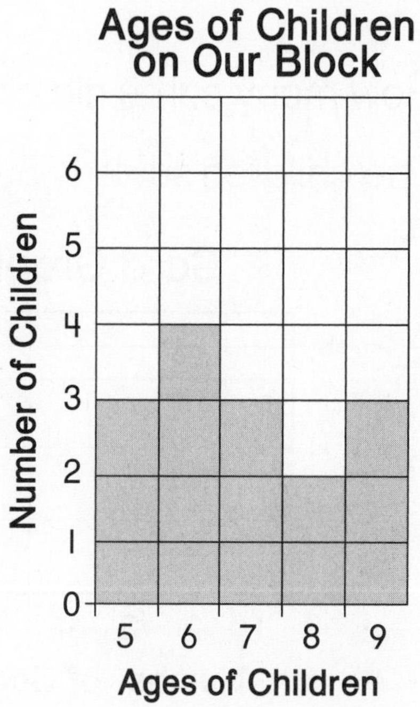

The **range** is the difference between the greatest and the least numbers.

9 – 5 or 4

The **mode** is the number that shows up most often.
What is the mode? 6

Use the bar graph to answer the questions.

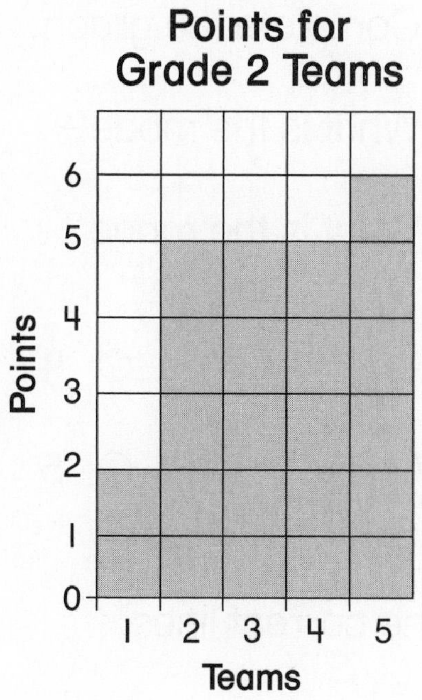

1. What is the greatest number of points a team scored? _____
2. What is the least number of points a team scored? _____
3. What is the range? _____
4. What number of points was scored most often? _____
5. What is the mode? _____

Name ____________________

Range and Mode

Use the data to answer the questions.

How many cards did children send?

The children said: 1, 5, 3, 3, 4, 2, 1, 3, 2, 6

Card Graph

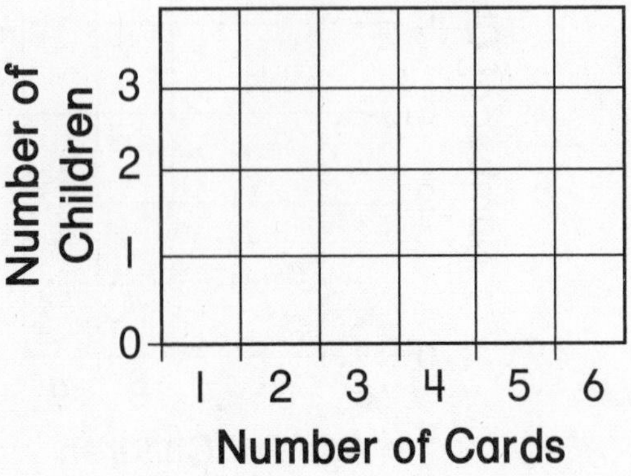

1. Complete the graph.
2. What is the mode? 3
3. What is the range?

6 – 1, or ____

How many brothers and sisters do we have?

The children said: 2, 2, 0, 3, 2, 5, 4, 4, 3, 0, 2, 1

Brothers and Sisters

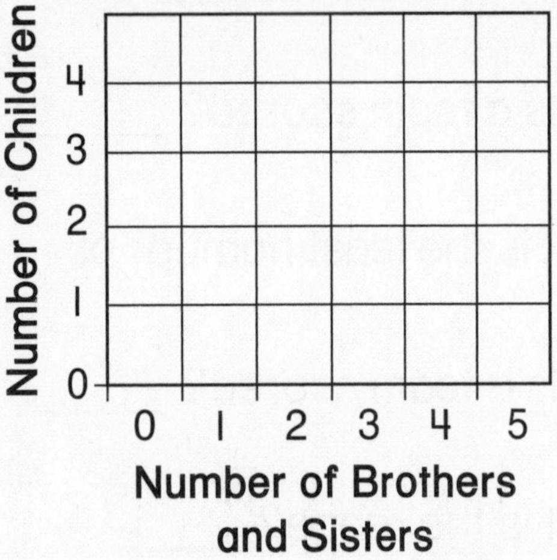

4. Complete the graph.
5. What is the mode? ____
6. What is the range?

○ 2 ○ 4

○ 3 ○ 5

7. **Journal** Write **range** and **mode** on the correct lines.

________ the number that shows up the most in a data set

________ the difference between the greatest and least numbers in a data set

Name ______________________________

Pictographs

A pictograph uses pictures or symbols to show information.
Write how many children chose each snack.

> There are 9 symbols for popcorn. So 9 children chose popcorn.

Each ☺ = 1 child

Favorite Snacks

Popcorn	☺☺☺☺☺☺☺☺☺	9
Fruit Cups	☺☺☺☺	____
Yogurt	☺☺☺☺☺☺☺	____
Cheese and Crackers	☺☺☺☺☺☺☺☺☺☺	____

Use the graph to answer the questions.

1. How many children like cheese and crackers best? _____ children

2. How many children like yogurt the best? _____ children

3. Which snack is the least favorite? __________________

4. Which snack is favored by most children? __________________

5. How many more children like yogurt than fruit cups? _____ children

6. How many more children like cheese and crackers than yogurt? _____ children

Name ____________________

Practice 14-3

Pictographs

Use the tally chart to complete the pictograph.
Then use the pictograph to solve the problems.

Shapes	
Circle	~~////~~
Square	////
Triangle	~~////~~ ///

Our Favorite Shapes	
1. Circle	
2. Square	
3. Triangle	

4. How many children chose squares? _4_ children

5. **Geometry** Which shape is favored the least?

○ triangle　○ rectangle　○ square　○ circle

6. Look at the tally chart.
It shows favorite snacks.
Which graph matches
the tally chart?

Our Favorite Snacks	
Banana	/
Crackers	///
Yogurt	//

○

Our Favorite Snacks	
Banana	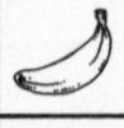
Crackers	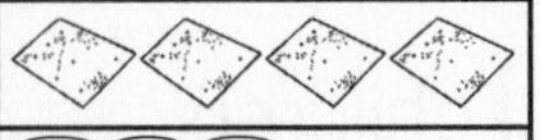
Yogurt	

○

Our Favorite Snacks	
Banana	
Crackers	
Yogurt	

○

Our Favorite Snacks	
Banana	
Crackers	
Yogurt	

○

Our Favorite Snacks	
Banana	
Crackers	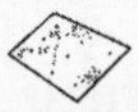
Yogurt	

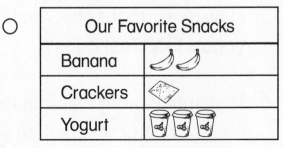

Name ____________________

Reteaching
14-4

Bar Graphs

The tally chart shows how children voted to name the class goldfish.

Use the data from the tally chart to make a bar graph.

Goldfish Names	
Flash	卌 II
Goldie	卌
Rocky	卌 III
Bubbles	卌 卌

Goldfish Names

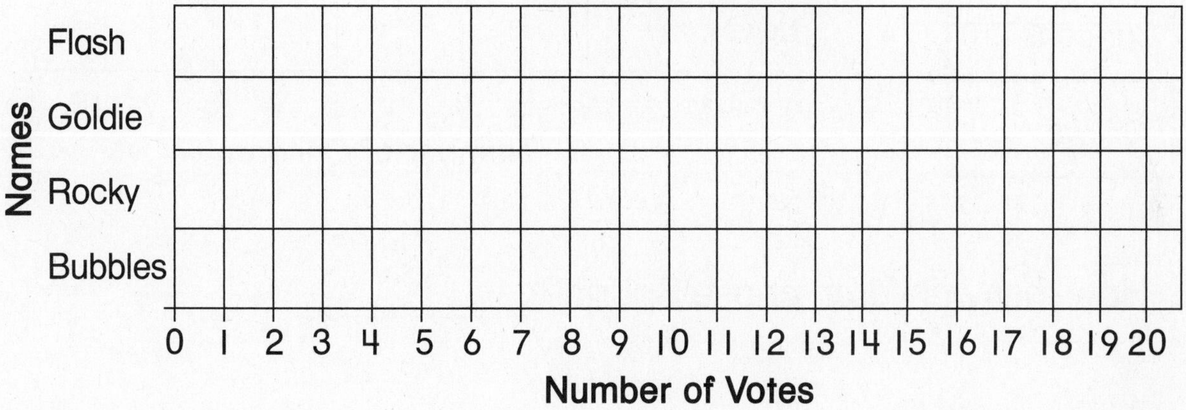

Use the bar graph to answer the questions.

1. How many children voted for the name Goldie? _____

2. How many children voted for the name Flash? _____

3. Which name did most children choose? __________

4. Which name did the fewest children choose? __________

5. Did more children prefer the name Rocky or Flash? __________

6. **Journal** Ask classmates to vote for their favorite goldfish name. Make a tally chart to show how they voted.

Name ____________________

Practice
14-4

Bar Graphs

Use the tally chart to complete the bar graph.
Then use the bar graph to answer the questions.

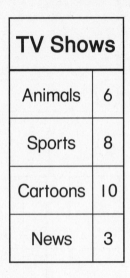

TV Shows	
Animals	6
Sports	8
Cartoons	10
News	3

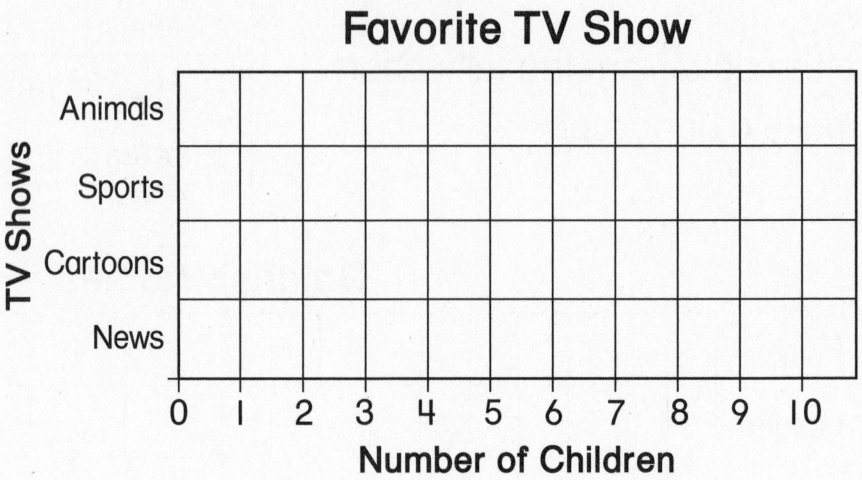

1. How many children chose Sports? ___8___

2. Which TV show did most children choose? ____________

3. Did more children choose News or Animals? ____________

4. Which TV show did the fewest children choose?

   Animals ○ Sports ○ Cartoons ○ News ○

5. **Reasoning** How would the bar graph change if two more children voted for Animals?

____

____

Name ______________________________

Problem Solving: Use a Graph

You can use the data on the graph to solve the problem.
How many more votes did the Tigers get than the Lions?

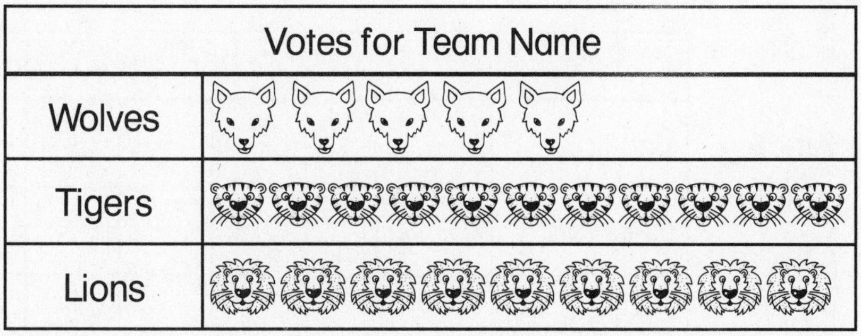

Count the Tigers and Lions on the graph.
Then subtract.

11 – 9 = 2

There are 2 more votes for Tigers than Lions.

Use the graph to solve the problem.
How many more children chose soccer than T-ball?

Game Choices

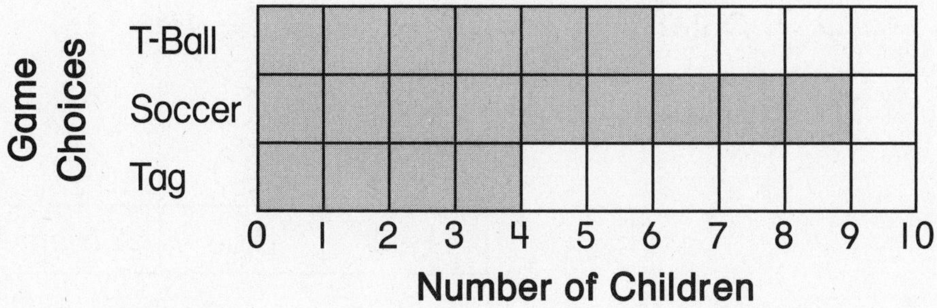

1. How many children chose soccer? 9

2. How many children chose T-ball? _____

3. Subtract. _____ – _____ = _____ children

Name ____________________

Practice
14-5

Problem Solving: Use a Graph

Use the bar graph to answer the questions.

1. Which ice cream got the most votes? chocolate

2. Which ice cream is least favored? ____________________

3. How many children voted? _____ children

4. Use the picture graph.
How many children like blue best?

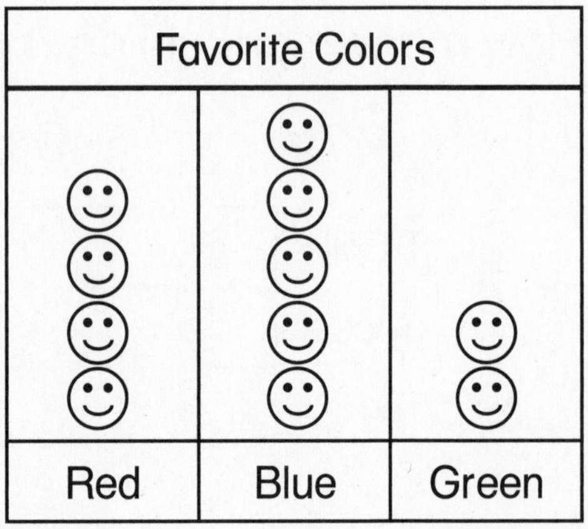

○ 2 children   ○ 4 children

○ 3 children   ○ 5 children

5. Journal What does the picture graph show?

____

____

____

Name ____________________

Reteaching
15-1

Reading and Writing Numbers to 1,000

Expanded form uses plus signs to show hundreds, tens, and ones.

200 + 60 + 4

You can draw models to show expanded form.

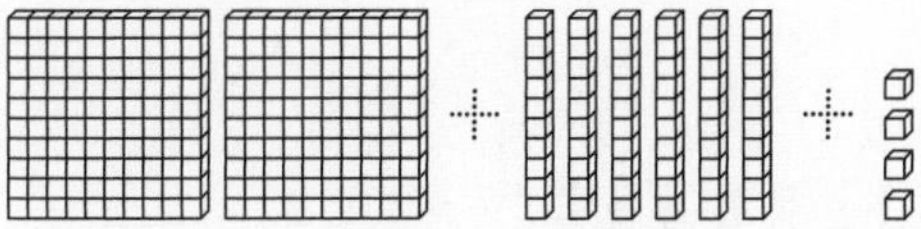

The **number word** is two hundred sixty-four.

The **standard form** is 264.

Draw models to show the expanded form.
Write the number in standard form.

1. 400 + 30 + 8 four hundred thirty-eight

____

2. 300 + 70 + 2 three hundred seventy-two

____

3. Write the number in expanded and standard form. five hundred fourteen

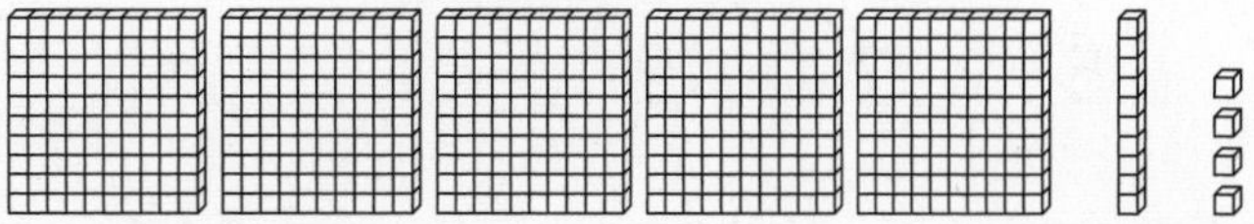

_______ + _______ + _______ _______

Name ____________________

Practice
15-1

Reading and Writing Numbers to 1,000

Circle the models to match the expanded form.
Then write the standard form.

1. 200 + 70 + 5

two hundred
seventy-five

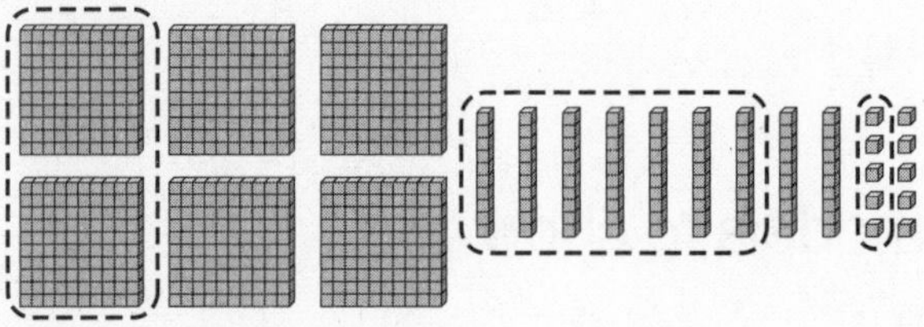

275

2. 100 + 40 + 0

one hundred
forty

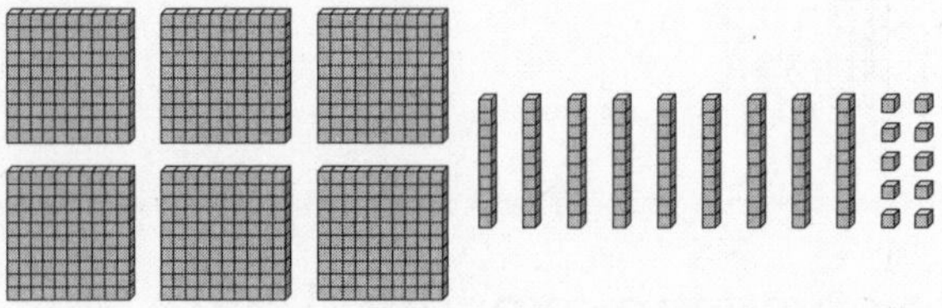

______

3. 300 + 60 + 2

three hundred
sixty-two

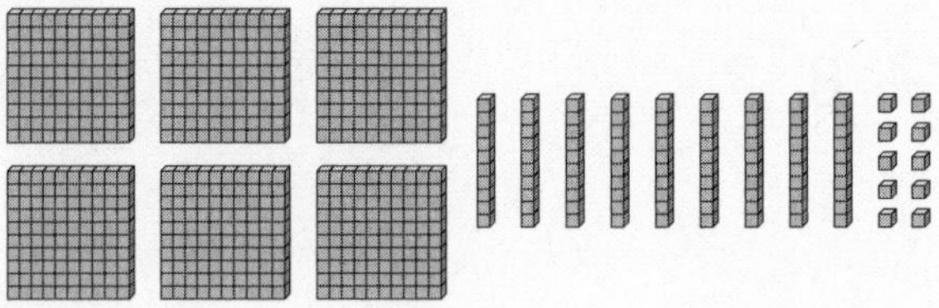

______

4. 329 cars are parked in a parking lot.

What is the expanded form of 329?

○ 200 + 90 + 3 ○ 300 + 20 + 9

○ 200 + 20 + 9 ○ 300 + 90 + 2

5. Reasoning What is the greatest number you can make using these digits?

5 7 2

257	572	725	752
○	○	○	○

Name ______________________

Changing Numbers by Hundreds and Tens

When you change a number by adding or subtracting tens, the tens digit changes.

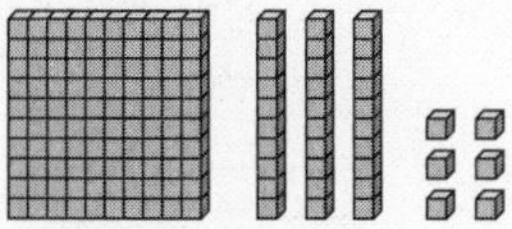

100 + 30 + 6 = 136

Use mental math to think: 10 more.

136 + 10 = 146

Use mental math to think: 20 less.

136 − 20 = 116

When you change a number by adding or subtracting hundreds, the hundreds digit changes.

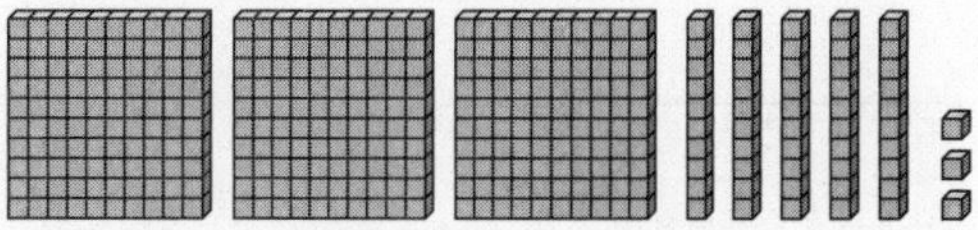

300 + 50 + 3 = 353

Use mental math to think: 100 more.

353 + 100 = 453

Use mental math to think: 200 less.

353 − 200 = 153

1. Use models and mental math to solve.

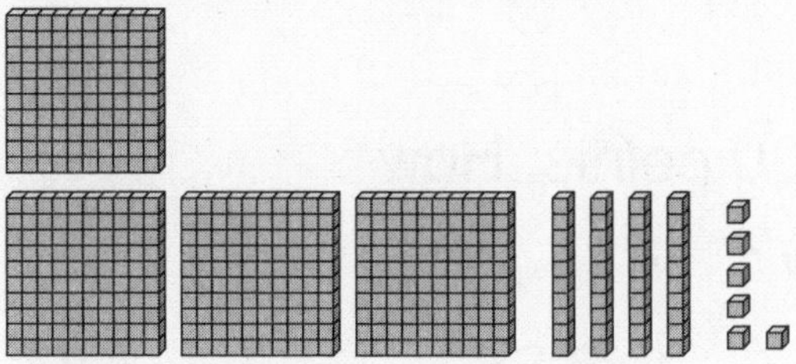

400 + 40 + 6 = 446

446 + 20 = ______

446 + 200 = ______

2. **Journal** Draw hundreds, tens, and ones models for 254. Show 10 more. Solve.

254 + 10 = ______

Name ______________________

Practice
15-2

Changing Numbers by Hundreds and Tens

Use models, drawings, or mental math to solve.
Write the numbers.

1. Start with 148.

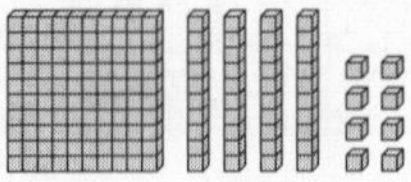

148 + 40 = 188

148 + 400 = 548

2. Start with 594.

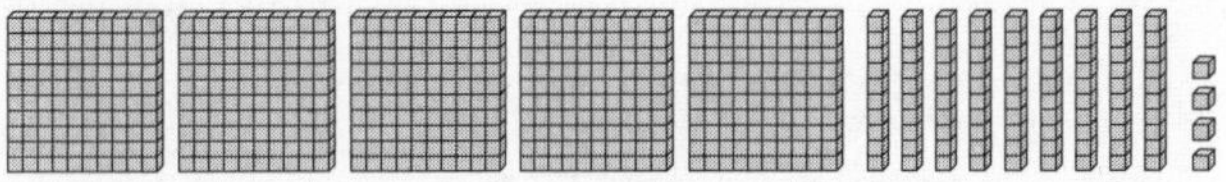

594 − 30 = ______

594 − 300 = ______

3. Suki has 350 points. She gets 30 more points.

How many points does Suki have now?

○ 320 ○ 353 ○ 360 ○ 380

4. Abdul has 687 points. He loses 100 points. How many points does Abdul have now?

○ 787 ○ 687 ○ 686 ○ 587

5. **Algebra** Write the number.
How many more hundreds do you need to make 500?

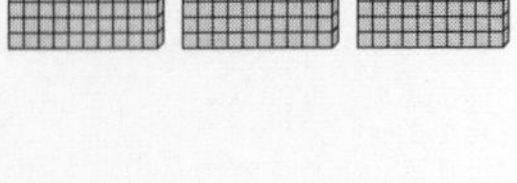 + ______ = 500

Name ____________________

Reteaching
15-3

Patterns with Numbers on a Hundred Chart

Pick a row on the top chart. Read the numbers across the row.

11	12	13	14	15	16	17	18	19	20
21	22	23	24	25	26	27	28	29	30
31	32	33	34	35	36	37	38	39	40

The ones go up by ___

Pick a column and read the numbers from top to bottom.

110	111	112	113	114	115	116	117	118	119	120
210	211	212	213	214	215	216	217	218	219	220
310	311	312	313	314	315	316	317	318	319	320
410	411	412	413	414	415	416	417	418	419	420

The tens go up by ___

In the bottom chart, the hundreds digits from top to bottom go up by ___.

Look at the digits. Look for a pattern.
Write the missing numbers.

1.

	33	34
42	43	
52	53	54

	77	78
86	87	
96		98

2.

43		45
53		55
		65

430		450
530		550
		650

3. **Number Sense** What is the rule?

60 ⟶ 70 670 ⟶ 680

Name ______________________________

Practice
15-3

Patterns with Numbers on Hundreds Charts

Write the missing numbers.

1.

52	53	54
62	63	64
72	73	74

520	530	
620		
		740

2.

		69
77	78	
		89

	680	
770		790
	880	

3.

15		
	26	
		37

	160	
250		
350		370

4. Which best describes the pattern of the numbers on the mailboxes?

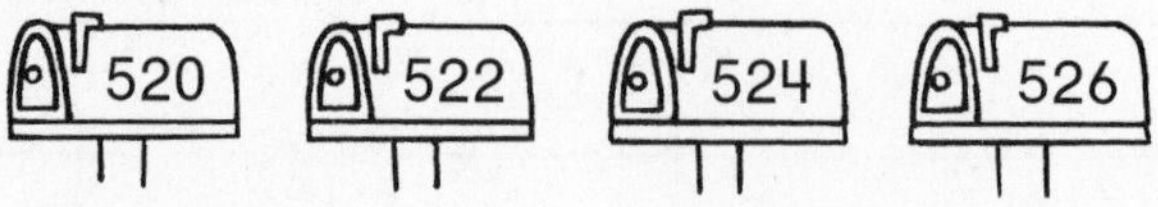

10 more ○ 10 less ○ 2 more ○ 2 less ○

5. Number Sense Look for a pattern. What is the rule?

740 730 720 710

100 more ○ 100 less ○ 10 more ○ 10 less ○

Name ______________________

Comparing Numbers

Compare the digits with the greatest place value first.

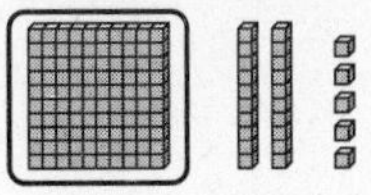

125

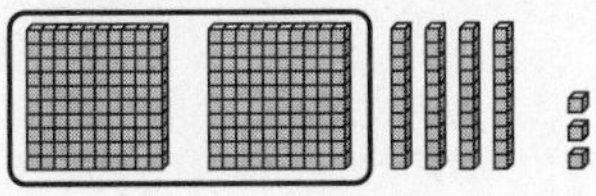

243

100 is less than 200. So, 125 < 243.

If the hundreds are equal, compare the tens.

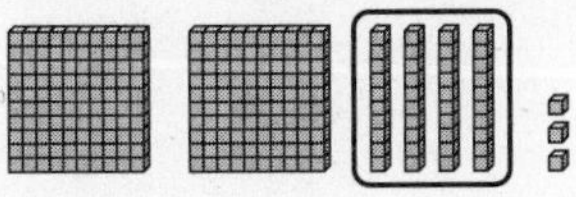

243

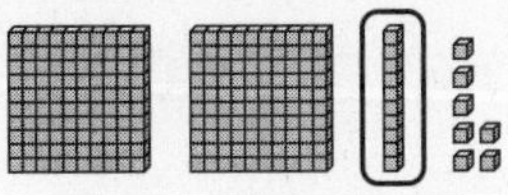

217

40 is more than 10. So, 243 > 217.

If the tens are equal, compare the ones.

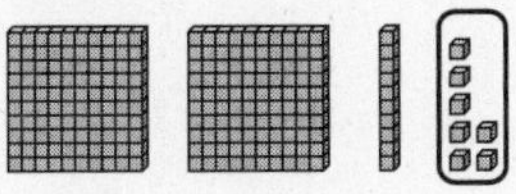

217

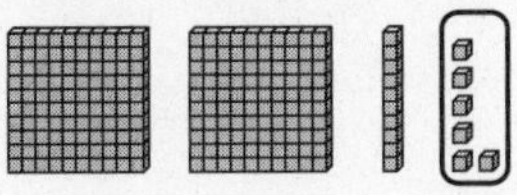

216

7 is more than 6. So, 217 > 216.

Compare.
Write <, >, or =.

1. 341 ◯ 432

2. 890 ◯ 880

3. 621 ◯ 639

4. 546 ◯ 546

Name ______________________

Practice
15-4

Comparing Numbers

Compare. Write **greater than**, **less than**, or **equal to**.
Then write >, <, or =.

1. 157 is less than 214. 157 ◯< 214

2. 600 is ______________ 598. 600 ◯ 598

3. 771 is ______________ 771. 771 ◯ 771

4. This week, 261 fans watched a soccer game.
Last week, 216 fans watched a soccer game.
Which comparison is correct?

○ 216 = 261 ○ 261 < 216

○ 216 > 261 ○ 216 < 261

5. **Spatial Thinking** Circle hundreds, tens, and ones to show your answer.

This number is less than 200. The ones digit is 5 less than 10. The tens digit is 2 more than the ones digit. What is the number?

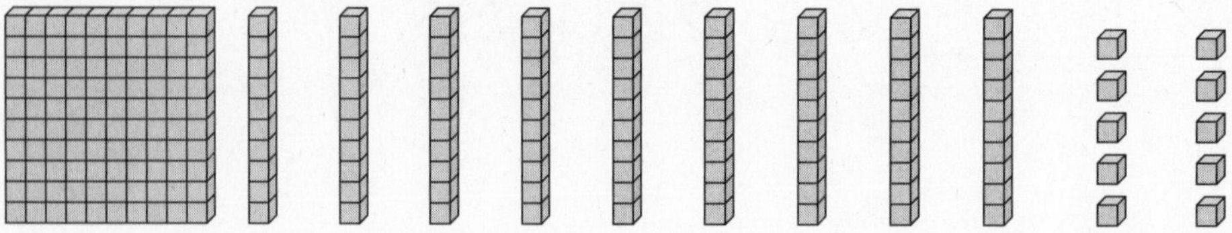

______

Name ______________________

Reteaching
15-5

Before, After, and Between

Think about the order of numbers.

150	151	152	153	154	155	156	157	158	159
160	161	162	163	164	165	166	167	168	169

Use the words **before**, **after**, and **between** to describe numbers.

152 is **before** 153

168 is **after** 167

161 is **between** 160 and 162

Use the number chart to help you write the missing numbers.

300	301	302	303	304	305	306	307	308	309
310	311	312	313	314	315	316	317	318	319

Write the number that is one **before**.

1. ________, 304 ________, 314 ________, 319

Write the number that is one **after**.

2. 301, ________ 307, ________ 316, ________

Write the number that is **between**.

3. 300, ________, 302 314, ________, 316

4. Journal Write a riddle about a number. Use the words **before**, **after**, or **between** to give clues.

Name ______________________

Practice 15-5

Before, After, and Between

Write the number that is one before.

1. 438, 439   2. ________, 624   3. ________, 201

4. ________, 516   5. ________, 840   6. ________, 111

Write the number that is one after.

7. 333, ________   8. 701, ________   9. 899, ________

10. 250, ________   11. 669, ________   12. 807, ________

Write the number that is between.

13. 518, ________, 520   14. 299, ________, 301

15. 393, ________, 395   16. 747, ________, 749

17. Monty picked a number card. The number is between 282 and 284.

What is the number?

281 ○   283 ○   285 ○   823 ○

18. **Reasoning** Which two numbers come after 297?

213, 298 ○   751, 157 ○   307, 299 ○   200, 300 ○

Name ____________________

Reteaching
15-6

Ordering Numbers

Put the numbers in order from least to greatest.

273	250	499

Step 1. Compare the hundreds digits to find the greatest number.
273 **2**50 **4**99

4 hundreds is greater than 2 hundreds.
499 is the greatest number.

Step 2. Then compare the tens digits.
2**7**3 2**5**0

7 tens is greater than 5 tens.
So, 250 is the least number.

250, 273, 499
least greatest

Write the numbers in order from least to greatest.

1. | 187 | 126 | 219 | ______, ______, ______ least greatest

2. | 489 | 352 | 327 | ______, ______, ______ least greatest

3. | 734 | 632 | 638 | ______, ______, ______ least greatest

4. **Number Sense** Write three numbers in order from least to greatest.

______, ______, ______
least greatest

Name ____________________

Practice **15-6**

Ordering Numbers

Write the numbers in order from least to greatest.

1. 276 267 207

207, 267, 276
least greatest

2. 16 600 60

____, ____, ____
least greatest

Write the numbers in order from greatest to least.

3. 986 789 892

____, ____, ____
greatest least

4. 377 737 773

____, ____, ____
greatest least

5. Which number is the least?

529	531	560	528
○	○	○	○

6. Which number is the greatest?

120	102	110	100
○	○	○	○

7. Journal Tell how you would decide which number is the greatest. Then circle it.

572, 570, 576

____

____

Name ______________________________

Reteaching
15-7

Problem Solving: Look for a Pattern

Put these numbers in order from least to greatest.

How do the numbers change each time? Look for a pattern.

240 210 230 250 220

210, 220, 230, 240, 250

The pattern rule is +10

Look for a number pattern to solve.

1. 

Put the room number signs in order from least to greatest.

300, 305, ________, ________

The pattern rule is ________

What room number would come next? ________

2. 

Put the taxis in order by number from least to greatest.

________, ________, ________, ________

The pattern rule is ________

What taxi number would come next? ________

Name ______________________________

Problem Solving: Look for a Pattern

Look for a number pattern to solve.

1.

Put the numbers on the bears in order from least to greatest.

616, 636,

656, ______

What is the pattern rule?

+20

What is the next number?

696

2.

Put the numbers on the geese in order from least to greatest.

______, ______,

______, ______

What is the pattern rule?

______

What is the next number?

______

3.

What is the next mailbox number?

751	791	841	881
○	○	○	○

4. Algebra Look at the pattern. What is the missing number?
400, 425, ____, 475

470	465	450	435
○	○	○	○

over

Name ______________________

Dime, Nickel, and Penny

dime
10 cents
10¢

nickel
5 cents
5¢

penny
1 cent
1¢

Count dimes by tens.

10¢ 20¢

Count nickels by fives.

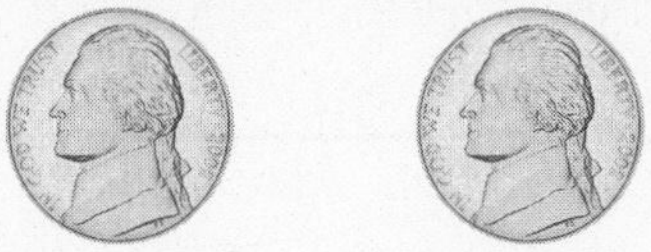

5¢ 10¢

Count pennies by ones.

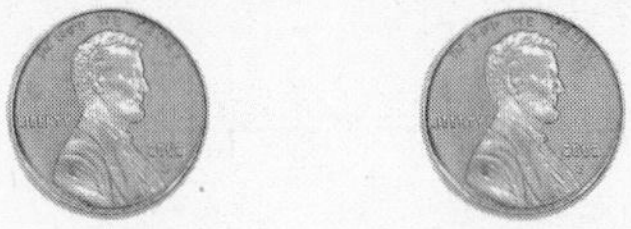

1¢ 2¢

Count on to find the total amount. Use coins if you need to.

1. Start with 5¢. Count on by ones.

5¢ ____ ____ ____ ____

Total Amount

2. Start with 10¢. Count on by fives.

____ ____ ____ ____ ____

Total Amount

3. Number Sense You have 5 coins that total 23¢.
Label the coins D, N, or P for dimes, nickels, or pennies.

○ ○ ○ ○ ○

Name ______________________________

Practice
16-1

Dime, Nickel, and Penny

Count on to find the total amount.

1. 

10¢ 15¢ 16¢ ______ ______

Total Amount
18¢

2. 

______ ______ ______ ______ ______

Total Amount

3. 

3¢ ○ 15¢ ○ 30¢ ○ 50¢ ○

4. 

4¢ ○ 12¢ ○ 22¢ ○ 40¢ ○

5. Reasoning Draw a picture to solve.
Dara has 5 coins in her purse.
The coins total 40¢.
Draw the coins that Dara has.

Name ____________________

Reteaching
16-2

Quarter and Half-Dollar

quarter
25 cents
25¢

half-dollar
50 cents
50¢

Start with 25¢. Count on by fives.

Think: 25¢ 5¢ more 5¢ more

25¢ 30¢ 35¢

Start with 50¢. Count on by tens.

Think: 50¢ 10¢ more 10¢ more

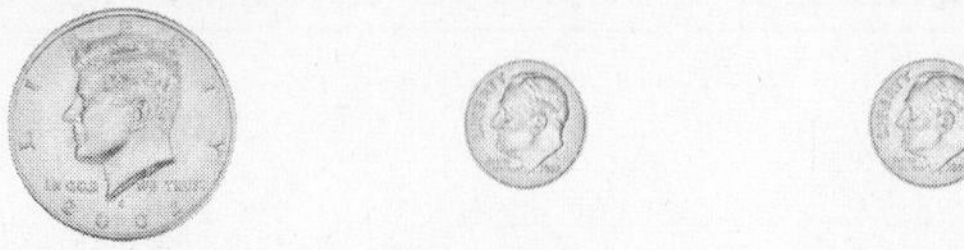

50¢ 60¢ 70¢

Count on to find the total amount.
Use coins if you need to.

1. Start with 25¢. Count on by tens.

25¢ ______ ______ ______ ______

Total Amount
______

2. Start with 50¢. Count on by tens and ones.

______ ______ ______ ______ ______

Total Amount
______

3. Number Sense Draw coins so the hand holds 40¢.

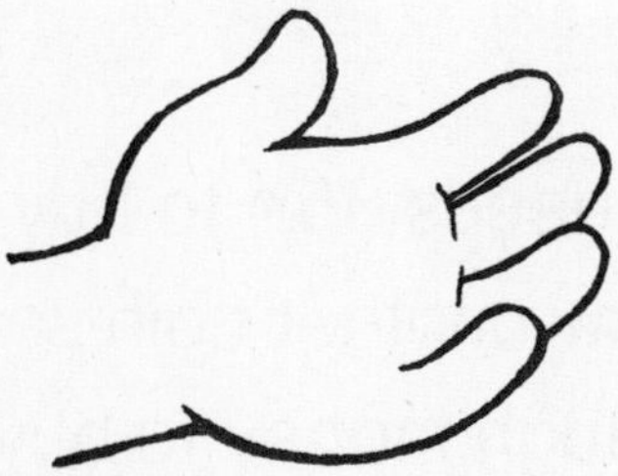

Name ______________________

Practice
16-2

Quarter and Half-Dollar

Count on to find the total amount.

1. 

25¢ 50¢ 60¢ ____ ____

Total Amount
70¢

2. 

____ ____ ____ ____ ____

Total Amount

3. Which group of coins has a value of 90¢?

○ 

○ 

○ 

○ 

4. Reasoning Jamal has these coins:

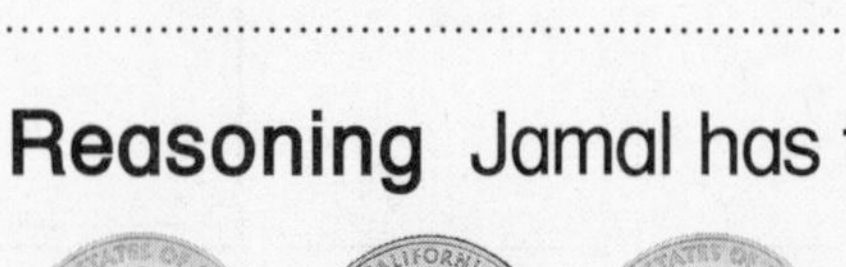

He needs 85¢ to buy a toy car.
Draw another coin so that Jamal has
enough money to buy the toy car.

Name ______________________

Counting Collections of Coins

To count coins, start with the coin that has the greatest value.
Count on coins from the greatest to the least value.

Find the total amount.
Draw an X on the coin with the greatest value.

Think: 50¢ | 60¢ | 70¢ | 75¢

Start with 50¢. 50¢ 60¢ 70¢ 75¢

Draw an X on the coin with the greatest value.
Count on to find the total amount.

1.

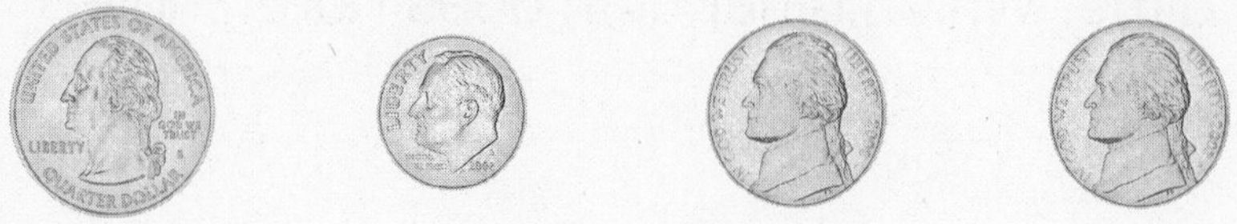

Start with ______. ______ ______ ______ ______

2.

Start with ______. ______ ______ ______ ______

Name ______________________

Practice
16-3

Counting Collections of Coins

Draw the coins from the greatest to the least value.
Count on to find the total amount. You can use coins.

1. 

(25¢) (10¢)

25¢ 35¢ ______ ______

The total amount is 46¢.

2. 

______ ______ ______ ______

The total amount is ______.

3. Karen has 85 cents. She has a half dollar and a dime. Which other coin does Karen have?

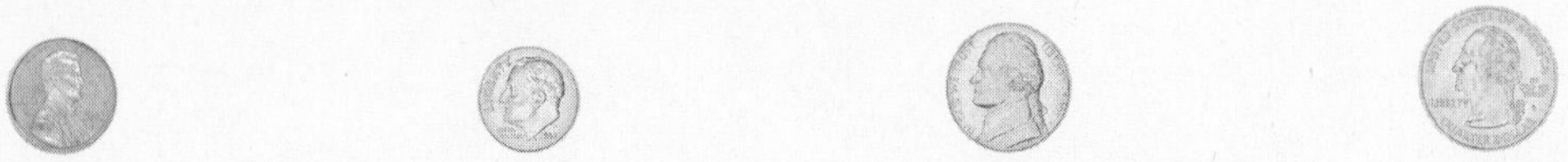

○ ○ ○ ○

4. **Estimation** Kobe has about 50¢. Circle the coins he might have.

Name ______________________

Reteaching
16-4

Comparing Collections of Coins

Which pocket has more money?
Count the coins in each pocket.
Compare the amounts.

> means "is greater than"
< means "is less than"
= means "is equal to"

25¢ 30¢ 31¢ (>) 10¢ 20¢ 21¢
31¢ < 21¢
=

Count the coins. Compare the amounts. Circle >, <, or =.

I.

_____ _____ _____ > _____ _____
<
_____ = _____

2.

_____ _____ _____ > _____ _____ _____
<
_____ = _____

Name ______________________________

Comparing Collections of Coins

Write the total amounts and compare them.
Write >, <, or =.

1.  

65¢ ◯ ______

Choose the correct symbol.

2.  ◯ 

>	<	=	¢
○	○	○	○

3.  ◯ 

>	<	=	¢
○	○	○	○

4. Journal Which stack of coins is the greater amount of money? Explain.

____

____

____

____

Name ______________________________

Ways to Show the Same Amount

A **dollar bill** is equal to 100¢.

Remember to use a **dollar sign** and **decimal point** when you write $1.00.

100 pennies = **1 dollar**

100¢ = $1.00

Circle coins to show $1.00.
Write the number of coins.

1. 

_____ dimes = 1 dollar

2. 

_____ quarters = 1 dollar

3. 

_____ half-dollars = 1 dollar

4. **Algebra** What 2 coins will make the statement true?

 (____) (____) = $1.00

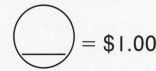

Name ____________________

Ways to Show the Same Amount

Write each total amount.

Circle sets of coins that equal $1.00.

1. 

Total Amount
$1.00

2. 

Total Amount

3. Ed has these coins.

How much money does he need to make a dollar?

1¢	5¢	10¢	25¢
○	○	○	○

4. **Number Sense** Pam has 4 coins. The coins total 100¢. Circle the coins that Pam has.

Name ____________________

One Dollar

How much money?
Start counting with the dollar bill.
Then count the coins from the greatest to least value.
Write numbers to show the counting order.

3	2	1	4

Count on to find the total amount.

	+25	+10	+1	\$1.36
\$1.00	\$1.25	\$1.35	\$1.36	Total Amount

How much money? Count on to find the total amount.

1.

				Total Amount
\$1.00	\$2.00	______	______	______

2.

				Total Amount
______	______	______	______	______

Name ____________________

Practice
16-6

One Dollar

Count on to find the total amount.

1. 

$2 $3 $3.50   Total Amount $3.50

2. 

_____ _____ _____ _____ Total Amount _____

3. 

_____ _____ _____ Total Amount _____

4. Algebra Abby needs 5 dollars to go to the movie. She has the money shown at the right in her purse. How much money does she need to make 5 dollars?

○ 

○ 

○ 

○ 

Name ______________________

Reteaching
16-7

Problem Solving: Make an Organized List

How many ways can you make 25¢?
Two ways are shown in the chart.

Use coins to help you find another way.
Show 1 dime. Make 1 tally mark.

How many nickels do you need to make 25¢?
3
Make 3 tally marks.

Ways to Show 25¢			
Quarter	Dime	Nickel	Total Amount
/			25¢
	/ /	/	25¢
	/	/ / /	25¢

Show 3 ways to make 45¢?
Use tally marks (/) to record the coins.

Ways to Show 45¢			
Quarter	Dime	Nickel	Total Amount
			45¢
			45¢
			45¢

Name ______________________________

Practice
16-7

Problem Solving: Make an Organized List

Use coins. Finish the list.

1. Adrian wants to buy a plum for 80¢. He has half-dollars, quarters, and dimes. Find all the ways he can make 80¢.

Half-Dollar	Quarter	Dime	Total Amount
/		///	80¢
			80¢
			80¢

2. How many ways can Adrian make 80¢?

○ 1 way ○ 3 ways ○ 2 ways ○ 4 ways

3. Beth wants to buy some crackers for 13¢. She has dimes, nickels, and pennies. Find all the ways she can make 13¢.

Dime	Nickel	Penny	Total Amount
			13¢
			13¢
			13¢
			13¢

4. How many ways can Beth make 13¢?

○ 4 ways ○ 3 ways ○ 2 ways ○ 1 way

5. **Reasonableness** Circle **yes** or **no.**
Can you make 38¢ with these coins? Explain.

yes no

____

____

Name ___________________________

Mental Math

Use mental math to add these three-digit numbers: 315 + 200.

You just need to add the hundreds.

Only the hundreds digit will change.

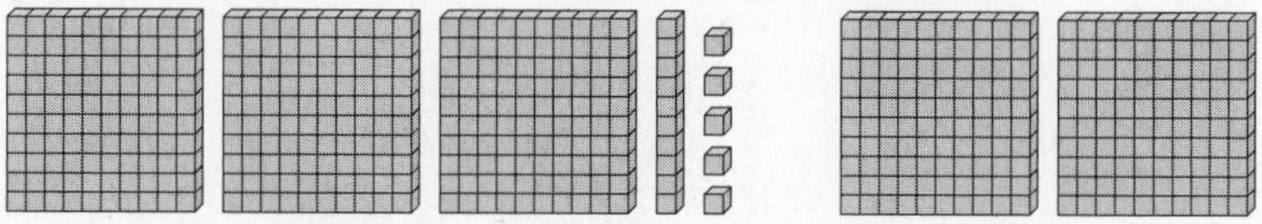

315 + 200 = 5 15

Add using mental math. Complete the addition sentence.

1. 323 + 200

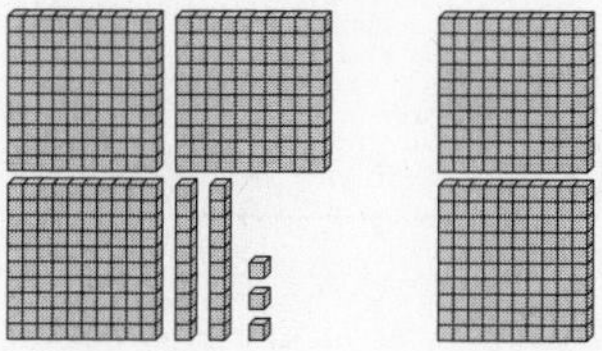

323 + 200 = 523

2. 281 + 400

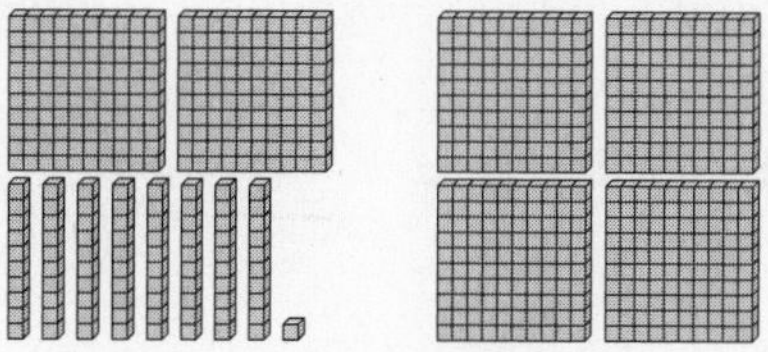

_______ + 400 = _______

3. 193 + 500

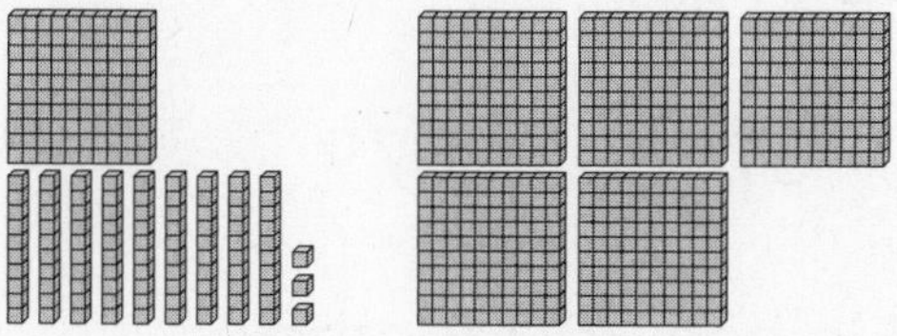

_______ + 500 = _______

4. 487 + 300

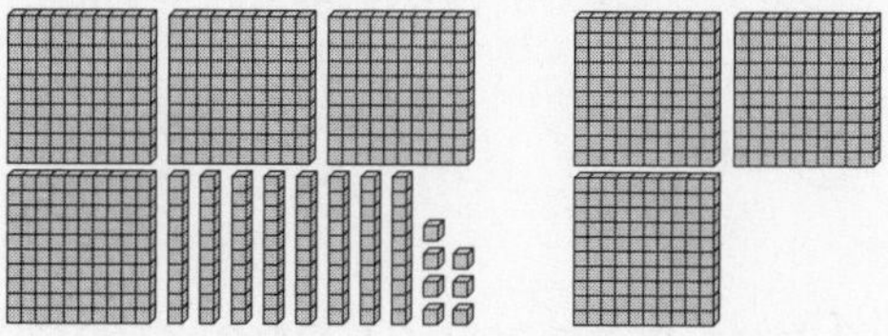

_______ + 300 = _______

5. Add using mental math. Use models if needed.

560 + 300 = _______

Name ______________________

Practice
17-1

Mental Math

Add using mental math. Use models if you need to.

1.  **and 300**

413 + 300 = 713

2. 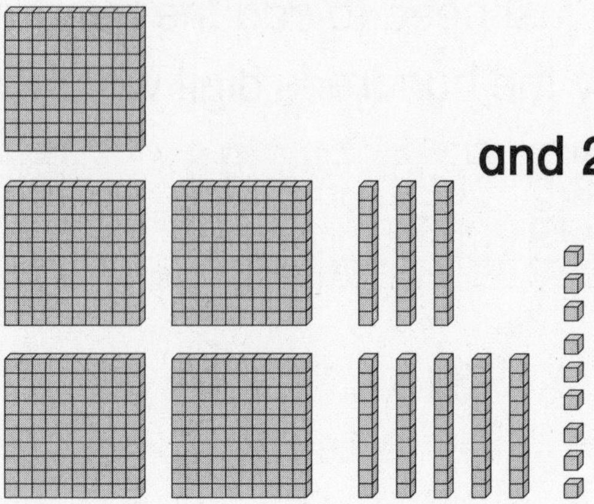 **and 200**

______ + ______ = ______

3. 718 + 200 = ______

4. 605 + 300 = ______

5. 400 + 234 = ______

6. 600 + 241 = ______

7. Tanner has 500 star stickers. She has 179 rainbow stickers. How many stickers does Tanner have in all?

○ 479 ○ 500 ○ 579 ○ 679

8. Darrin has 274 basketball stickers. He has 300 football stickers. How many stickers does Darrin have in all?

○ 163 ○ 279 ○ 574 ○ 682

9. **Algebra** Write the missing numbers that make these number sentences true.

400 + 500 = 600 + ______ ______ = 899 + 100

Name ____________________

Reteaching
17-2

Estimating Sums

You can estimate the sum of 135 + 337.
Is it greater than or less than 500?

One way to estimate:
Step 1: Add 300 to 135.

135 + 300 = 435.

Step 2: Look at the tens and ones in 3**37**.

So, 435 + **37** is less than 500.

Another way to estimate:
Step 1: Add the hundreds in both numbers.

135 + **3**37 = 400.

Step 2: Look at the tens in both numbers.
30 + 30 = 60
So, 400 + 60 is less than 500.

Follow the steps to estimate.

Is 179 + 267 greater than or less than 600?

1. Add 200 to 179. 179 + 200 = ______

2. Look at the tens and ones in 2**67**. Then circle greater than or less than.

379 + 67 greater than / less than 600.

Choose a way to estimate. Circle greater than or less than.

3. 237 + 417 is greater than / less than 600.

Name ______________________________

Practice
17-2

Estimating Sums

Do the two buckets have more cherries or fewer cherries than the tub can hold? Circle more or fewer.

1. 

more fewer

2. 

more fewer

3. 

more fewer

4. There are 314 apples in baskets. There are 281 apples still on the trees. Are there 600 apples in all? Explain.

____

5. One week, a group of chimpanzees ate 437 bananas. The next week, they ate 465 bananas. Did they eat more than 900 bananas during both weeks? Explain.

____

6. **Estimation** Which problem has a sum that is less than 400?

329 + 161	216 + 251	245 + 198	262 + 126
○	○	○	○

Name ______________________

Reteaching
17-3

Models for Adding with Three-Digit Numbers

135 + 248 = ______

Step 1: Add the ones. Regroup if you need to.
Step 2: Add the tens. Regroup if you need to.
Step 3: Add the hundreds.

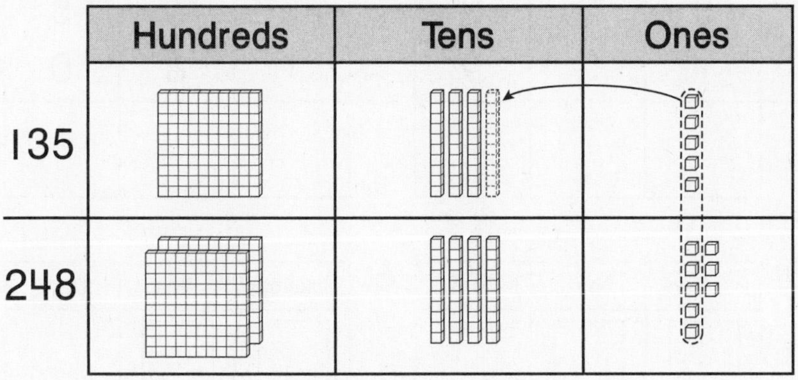

5 + 8 = 13 ones.
Regroup 10 ones
for 1 ten.

135 + 248 = 383

Add to find the sum.
Use models and your workmat.

1.

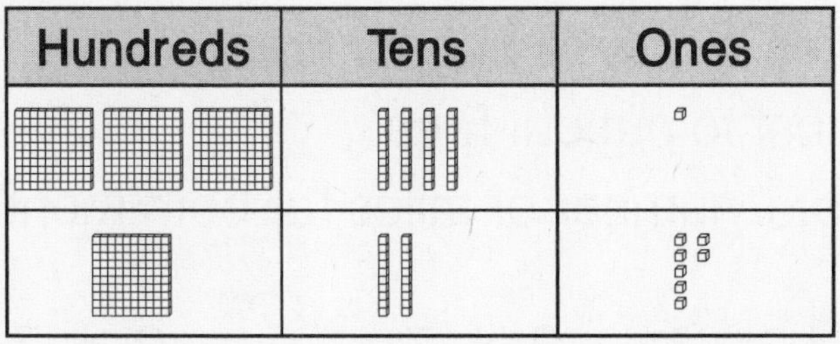

341 + 127 = ______

2.

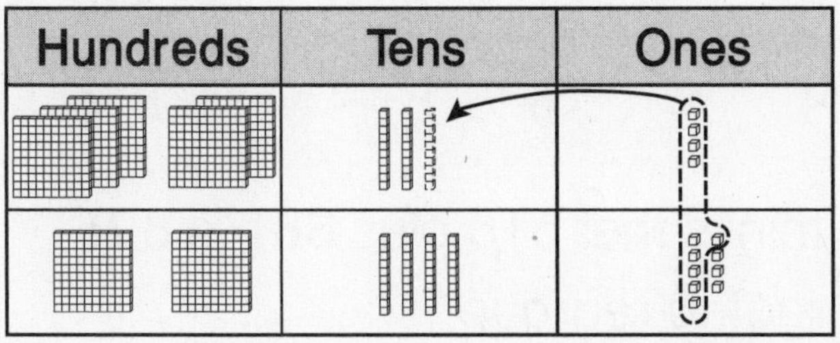

524 + 249 = ______

Name ______________________

Practice
17-3

Models for Adding with Three-Digit Numbers

Add. Regroup if needed.

1.

	Hundreds	Tens	Ones
	☐	1	
	6	3	4
+	2	1	8
	8	5	2

2.

	Hundreds	Tens	Ones
	☐	☐	
	5	9	3
+	1	3	9

3.

	Hundreds	Tens	Ones
	☐	☐	
	7	6	5
+	1	8	0

4.

	Hundreds	Tens	Ones
	☐	☐	
	3	5	6
+	4	3	4

5.

	Hundreds	Tens	Ones
	☐	☐	
	2	7	6
+	5	9	3

6.

	Hundreds	Tens	Ones
	☐	☐	
	4	4	1
+	1	9	9

7. A fire truck traveled 267 miles in July to put out fires.
It traveled 398 miles in August to put out fires.
Which problem shows the total number of miles for both months?

○
$$\begin{array}{r} {\scriptstyle 1\,1\,\,} \\ 267 \\ +\,398 \\ \hline 665 \end{array}$$

○
$$\begin{array}{r} {\scriptstyle 1\,1\,\,} \\ 276 \\ +\,398 \\ \hline 674 \end{array}$$

○
$$\begin{array}{r} {\scriptstyle 1\,\,\,\,\,} \\ 267 \\ +\,398 \\ \hline 655 \end{array}$$

○
$$\begin{array}{r} {\scriptstyle 1\,\,\,} \\ 267 \\ +\,398 \\ \hline 565 \end{array}$$

8. **Reasonableness** George thinks that 515 plus 381 is 896.
Markita says that George forgot to regroup.
Do you have to regroup to add 515 and 381? Explain.

____

Name ______________________

Adding Three-Digit Numbers

Step 1: Add the ones. Regroup if you need to.
Step 2: Add the tens. Regroup if you need to.
Step 3: Add the hundreds.

Think:
Regroup 10 tens
for 1 hundred.

163 + 174 = __?__

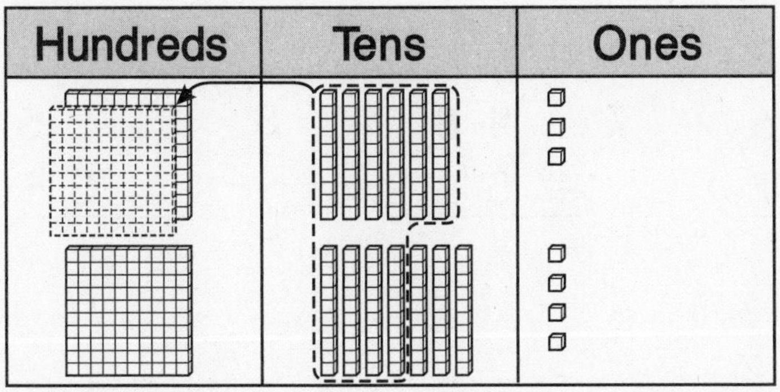

	Hundreds	Tens	Ones
	☐ (1)	☐	
	1	6	3
+	1	7	4
	3	3	7

Draw to regroup. Add.

1. 218 + 136 = __?__

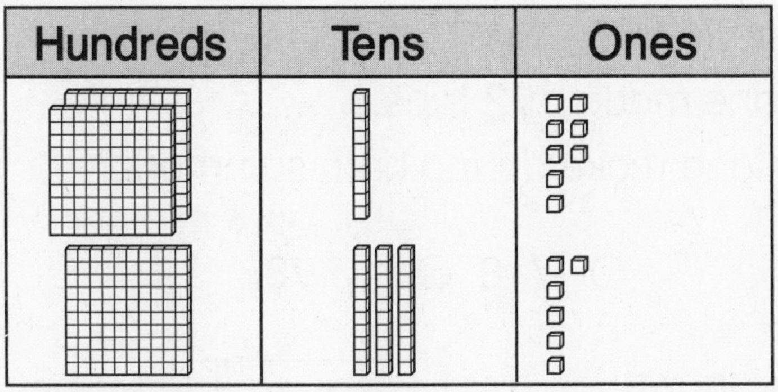

	Hundreds	Tens	Ones
	☐	☐	
	2	1	8
+	1	3	6

Add. Use models and your workmat.

2.

	Hundreds	Tens	Ones
	☐	☐	
	1	2	5
+	2	4	2

3.

	Hundreds	Tens	Ones
	☐	☐	
	4	1	9
+	2	5	6

Name ______________________________

Adding Three-Digit Numbers

Add. Use models if needed.

1. $\begin{array}{r} 472 \\ +\ 347 \\ \hline \end{array}$ 2. $\begin{array}{r} 609 \\ +\ 166 \\ \hline \end{array}$ 3. $\begin{array}{r} 267 \\ +\ 228 \\ \hline \end{array}$ 4. $\begin{array}{r} 473 \\ +\ 338 \\ \hline \end{array}$

5. $\begin{array}{r} 314 \\ +\ 599 \\ \hline \end{array}$ 6. $\begin{array}{r} 186 \\ +\ 357 \\ \hline \end{array}$ 7. $\begin{array}{r} 487 \\ +\ 512 \\ \hline \end{array}$ 8. $\begin{array}{r} 225 \\ +\ 135 \\ \hline \end{array}$

9. $\begin{array}{r} 235 \\ +\ 146 \\ \hline \end{array}$ 10. $\begin{array}{r} 465 \\ +\ 264 \\ \hline \end{array}$ 11. $\begin{array}{r} 308 \\ +\ 238 \\ \hline \end{array}$ 12. $\begin{array}{r} 356 \\ +\ 29 \\ \hline \end{array}$

13. One summer, an airplane made 326 trips.
The next summer, the airplane made 392 trips.
How many trips did the airplane make during both summers?

○ 192 ○ 618 ○ 718 ○ 798

14. **Reasoning** Caitlin's paper shows how she added 345 and 271. What mistake did she make?

$\begin{array}{r} 345 \\ +\ 271 \\ \hline 516 \end{array}$

____

____

Name ____________________

Reteaching
17-5

Mental Math: Ways to Find Missing Parts

Count on by hundreds and tens to find the parts of the whole.

260 + ______ = 700

First, count on by hundreds. __4__ hundreds

260, 360, 460, 560, 660

100 200 300 400

Next, count on by tens. __4__ tens

660, 670, 680, 690, 700

10 20 30 40

4 hundreds and 4 tens is 440.

So, 260 + __440__ = 700

700	
260	440

1. 350 + __?__ = 600

Count on by hundreds. _____ hundreds

350, ______, ______

Count on by tens. _____ tens

550, ______, ______, ______, ______, ______

_____ hundreds and _____ tens is ______.

So, 350 + ______ = 600

Name ____________________

Practice
17-5

Mental Math: Ways to Find Missing Parts

Count on or count back to find the missing part.
Write the number.

1. 420 + 540 = 960

2. ______ + 190 = 630

3. Clyde and Javier counted a total of 450 sheep. Javier counted 225 sheep. How many sheep did Clyde count?

225 ○ 250 ○ 325 ○ 450 ○

4. **Geometry** Which weight is needed to balance the scale?

○ ○ ○ ○

Name ____________________

Reteaching
17-6

Estimating Differences

Estimate the difference: 596 − 221.

First, find the nearest hundred.
Is 596 closer to 500 or 600? 600

Is 221 closer to 200 or 300? 200

Then, subtract.

600 − 200 = 400

So, 596 − 221 is about 400.

Estimate each difference. First, find the nearest hundred.
Then circle the estimate that matches the problem.

1. 502 − 105 is about 200 300 (400)

500 − 100 = ?

2. 609 − 403 is about 200 300 400

_______ − _______ = ?

3. 511 − 298 is about 100 200 300

_______ − _______ = ?

4. Number Sense 881 − 500 is about _______

Name ______________________

Practice
17-6

Estimating Differences

Circle the problem that matches the estimate.

1. about 200 — 820 − 205 or 421 − 196

2. about 400 — 637 − 231 or 794 − 512

3. about 300 — 679 − 199 or 916 − 593

4. about 600 — 909 − 287 or 726 − 204

5. Marcus has to put about 100 cans on a shelf to finish his job. Circle the box of cans he should put on the shelf.

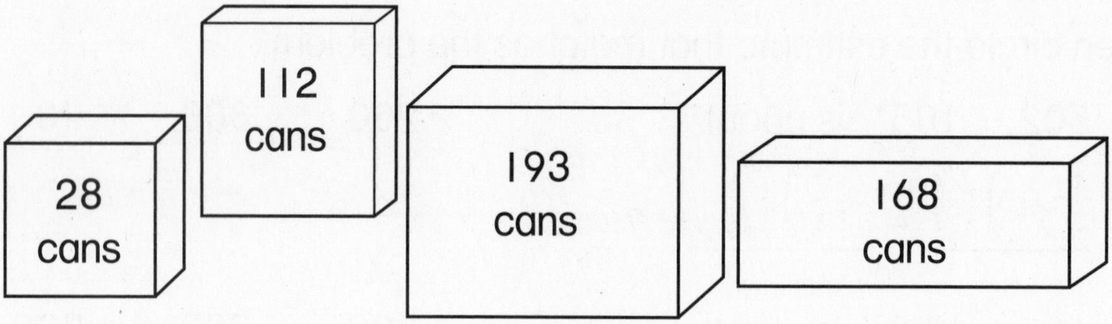

○ 28 ○ 112 ○ 168 ○ 193

6. **Estimation** Cowhand Dusty put 203 cows inside of the fences. There are 694 cows in the herd. About how many more cows does Dusty need to put inside of the fences?

○ about 300 cows ○ about 500 cows

○ about 400 cows ○ about 600 cows

Name ____________________

Reteaching
17-7

Models for Subtracting with Three-Digit Numbers

327 − 164 = __?__

Step 1: Subtract the ones. Regroup if you need to.
Step 2: Subtract the tens. Regroup if you need to.
Step 3: Subtract the hundreds.

Regroup 1 hundred for 10 tens

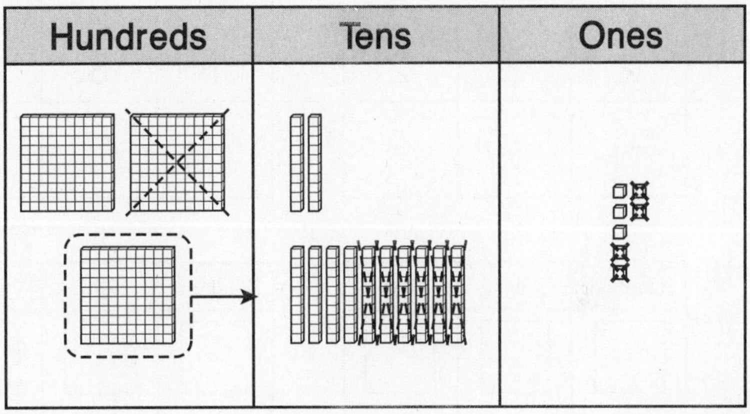

327 − 164 = __163__

Subtract to find the difference.
Use models and your workmat.

1.

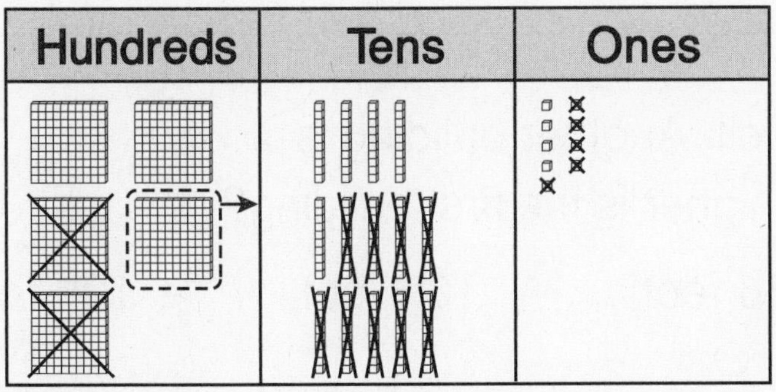

549 − 295 = ________

2.

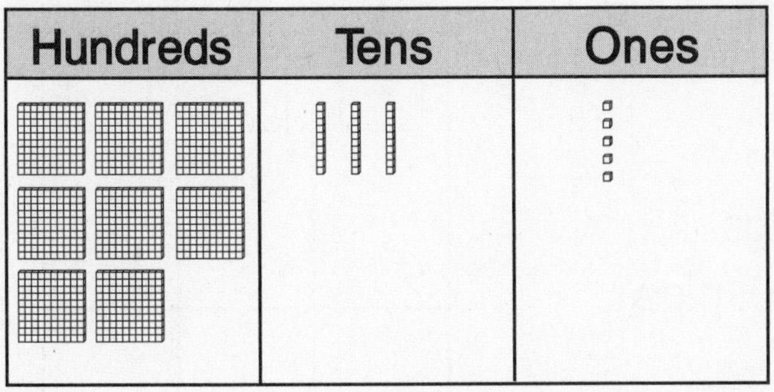

835 − 516 = ________

Name ______________________

Practice **17-7**

Models for Subtracting with Three-Digit Numbers

Use models and your workmat. Subtract. Regroup if needed.

1.

Hundreds	Tens	Ones
6	15	
~~7~~	~~5~~	5
− 2	8	2
4	7	3

2.

Hundreds	Tens	Ones
4	8	5
− 1	3	9

3.

Hundreds	Tens	Ones
5	7	8
− 2	9	7

4.

Hundreds	Tens	Ones
6	5	7
− 1	2	8

5.

Hundreds	Tens	Ones
7	3	2
− 4	5	8

6.

Hundreds	Tens	Ones
9	2	7
− 3	0	4

7. One building is 332 feet tall. Another building is 208 feet tall. How much higher is the first building?

○ 540 feet ○ 136 feet ○ 134 feet ○ 124 feet

8. **Spatial Thinking** Use the model to help you subtract.

A farm has 319 animals.
136 of the animals are pigs.
How many animals are not pigs?

______ animals are not pigs.

Hundreds	Tens	Ones
−		

Name ______________________________

Subtracting Three-Digit Numbers

Step 1: Subtract the ones. Regroup if you need to.
Step 2: Subtract the tens. Regroup if you need to.
Step 3: Subtract the hundreds.

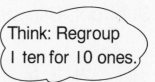

Think: Regroup 1 ten for 10 ones.

362 − 125 = __?__

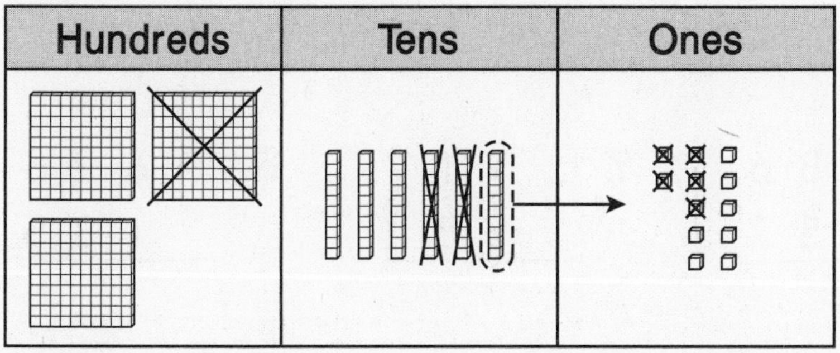

	Hundreds	Tens	Ones
	☐	5	12
	3	~~6~~	~~2~~
−	1	2	5
	2	3	7

Draw to regroup. Subtract.

1. 429 − 174 = __?__

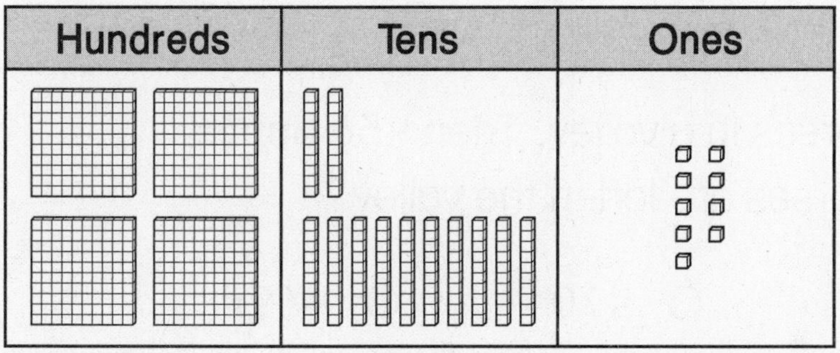

	Hundreds	Tens	Ones
	☐	☐	☐
	4	2	9
−	1	7	4

Subtract. Use models and your workmat if needed.

2.

	Hundreds	Tens	Ones
	☐	☐	☐
	5	7	4
−	2	1	3

3.

	Hundreds	Tens	Ones
	☐	☐	☐
	7	8	8
−	2	6	9

Name ____________________

Practice
17-8

Subtracting Three-Digit Numbers

Subtract. Use models if needed.

1. $426 - 271$

2. $659 - 372$

3. $953 - 209$

4. $390 - 126$

5. $622 - 189$

6. $486 - 357$

7. $917 - 582$

8. $625 - 135$

9. $589 - 193$

10. $707 - 264$

11. $611 - 196$

12. $356 - 29$

13. There were 926 wild horses in a valley. Then 456 horses ran away. How many horses are left in the valley?

○ 530 ○ 582 ○ 470 ○ 469

14. Number Sense Use these numbers only once to finish the two subtraction problems. Then subtract.

2 5 7 1 4 6

Make the greatest difference.

$950 - \square\square\square = \square\square\square$

Make the least difference.

$950 - \square\square\square = \square\square\square$

Name ______________________

Problem Solving: Make a Graph

Grade 2 collected 100 pop tops on Tuesday and 300 on Wednesday. Add this data to the table.

Pop Tops Collected			
	Monday	Tuesday	Wednesday
Grade 1	150	100	200
Grade 2	200	100	300

Show the data on a bar graph.
First, add the pop tops collected on Monday.

150 + 200 = 350

Then, color the Monday column to show 350 pop tops were collected. Next, do the same for Tuesday and Wednesday.

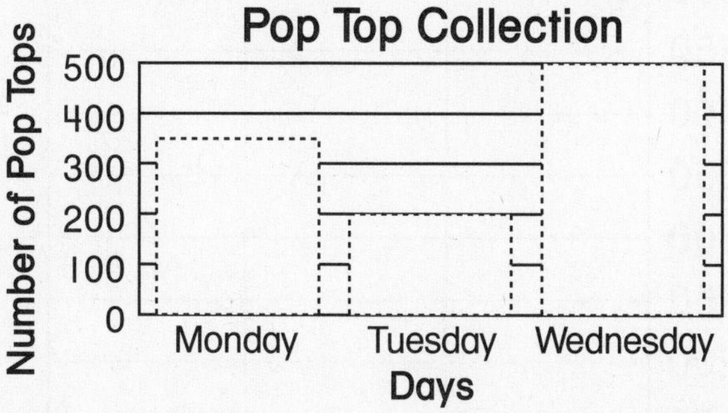

Use the graph to answer the questions.

1. How many pop tops were collected on Tuesday? ________

2. How many pop tops were collected on Wednesday? ________

3. **Number Sense** If Grade 2 collected 200 pop tops on Tuesday, how would the graph change?

____

Name ______________________________

Problem Solving: Make a Graph

Use the chart to answer the questions.

Art Supplies			
	Crayons	Paints	Brushes
Art Room 1	350	200	300
Art Room 2	400	150	250

1. How many crayons are there in all?

   750 crayons

2. How many paints are there in all?

   __________ paints

3. How many brushes are there in all?

   __________ brushes

4. Use your answers from Exercises 1-3 to complete the graph. Show how many crayons, paints, and brushes there are in both rooms.

Art Supplies

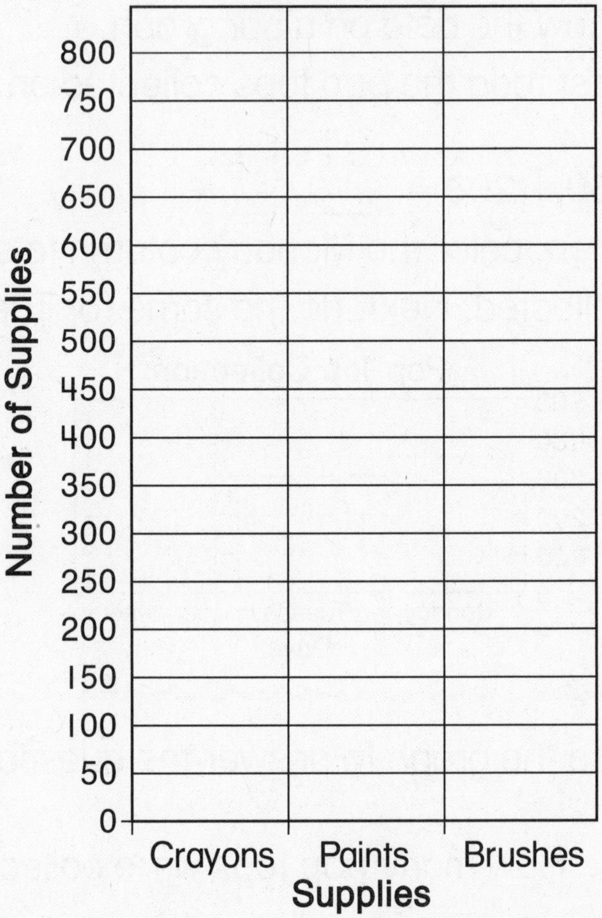

5. Together, which art supply do the two art rooms have the most of?

   ○ clay ○ crayons ○ paints ○ brushes

6. **Journal** How is a bar graph different from a chart?

   ____

   ____

Name ______________________

Repeated Addition and Multiplication

Add equal groups to find how many in all.
Multiply equal groups to find how many in all.

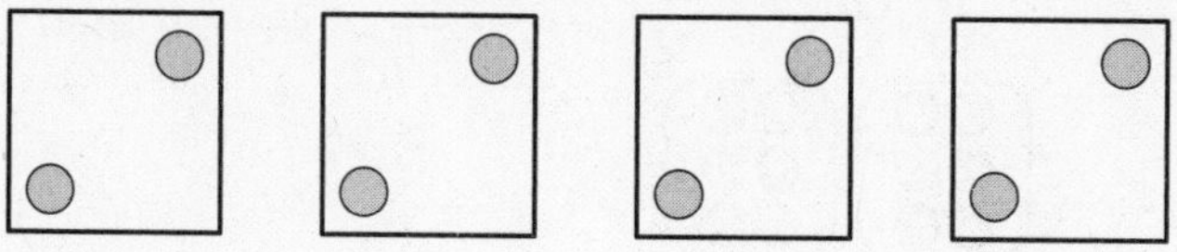

2 + 2 + 2 + 2 = a **sum** of 8

4 × 2 = a **product** of 8

4 × 2 means
4 times 2

1. Number Sense Draw dots to show equal groups.
Find the sum and the product.

3 + 3 + 3 = ____

3 × 3 = ____

Find the sum and the product.

2.

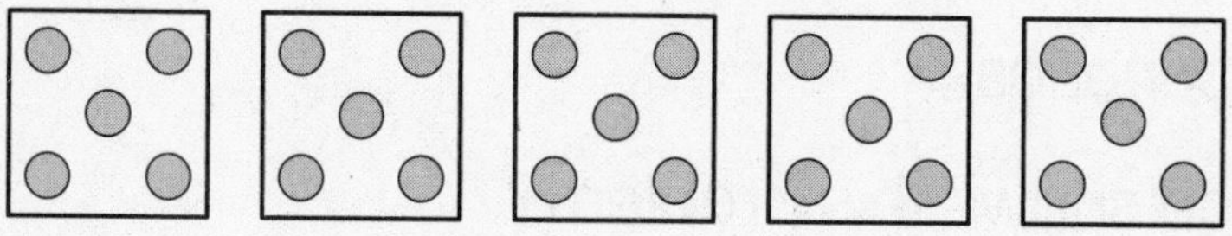

5 + 5 + 5 + 5 + 5 = ____ 5 × 5 = ____

3.

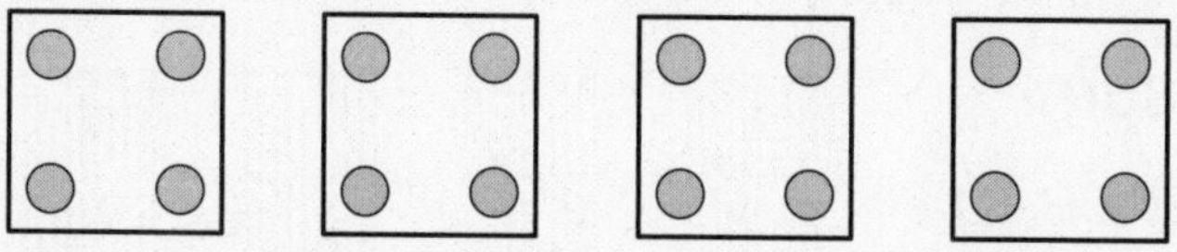

4 + 4 + 4 + 4 = ____ 4 × 4 = ____

Name ______________________

Practice
18-1

Repeated Addition and Multiplication

Use the model.
Complete each sentence.

1. ? in all

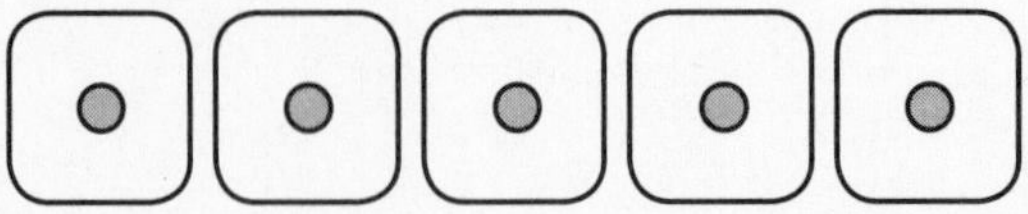

$1 + 1 + 1 + 1 + 1 =$ 5

$5 \times 1 =$ 5

2. ? in all

$6 + 6 =$ ____

$2 \times 6 =$ ____

3. ? in all

$3 + 3 + 3 =$ ____

$3 \times 3 =$ ____

4. ? in all

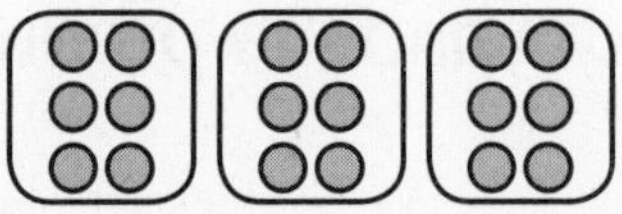

$6 + 6 + 6 =$ ____

$3 \times 6 =$ ____

5. 2 monkeys climb a tree.
Each monkey picks 3 bananas.

Which number sentence shows this problem?

○ $2 + 3$ ○ 2×2 ○ 2×3 ○ 3×3

6. Number Sense Find the sum.
Write a multiplication sentence to show the same amount.

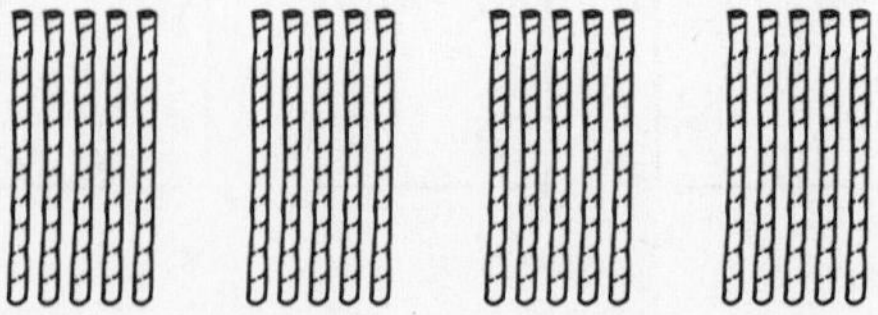

$5 + 5 + 5 + 5 =$ ____

____ $\times$ ____ $=$ ____

Name ______________________________

Building Arrays

A collection of objects arranged in equal rows and columns is an **array.** You can use an **array** to show equal groups.

Array

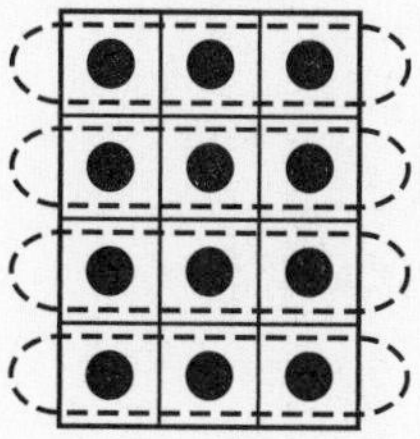

Circle each row. Count the number of rows.

There are __4__ rows.

Count the number of dots in each row.

There are __3__ dots in each row.

Write the multiplication sentence.

__4__ × __3__ = __12__

row   in each row   product

Circle each row. Count the number of rows.
Count the number of dots in each row.
Write the multiplication sentence.

1.

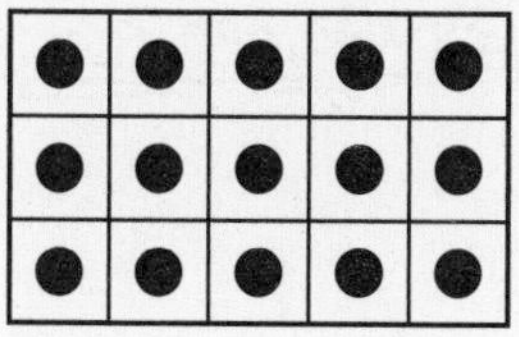

There are _____ rows.

There are _____ dots in each row.

_____ × _____ = _____

row   in each row   product

2.

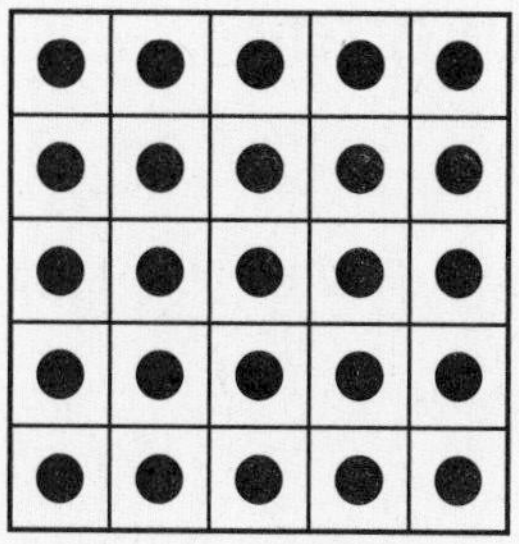

There are _____ rows.

There are _____ dots in each row.

_____ × _____ = _____

row   in each row   product

Name ____________________

Practice
18-2

Building Arrays

Write the multiplication sentence.

1. 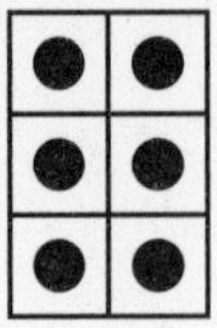

3 × 2 = 6
rows columns product

2. 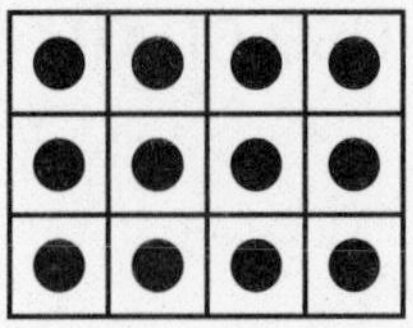

____ × ____ = ____
rows columns product

3. 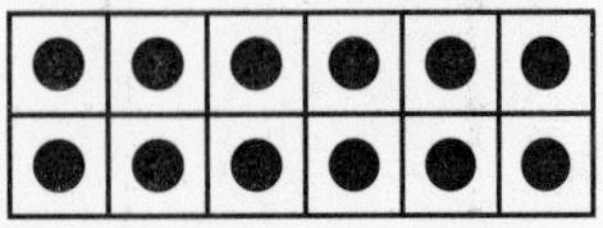

____ × ____ = ____
rows columns product

4. 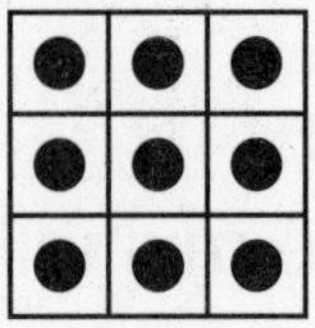

____ × ____ = ____
rows columns product

5. Mrs. Rose takes cookies out of the oven. They are in 4 rows and 5 columns.
Which multiplication sentence shows how many cookies in all?

○ 4 × 4 ○ 4 × 6

○ 4 × 5 ○ 5 × 5

6. **Spatial Thinking** Draw an array with 2 rows and 4 columns. Then write a number sentence for your array.

____ × ____ = ____
rows columns product

Name ____________________

Writing Multiplication Stories

You can draw a picture and write a story to show 2 × 3.

Draw 2 fish tanks.

Draw 3 fish in each tank.

Solve the story.

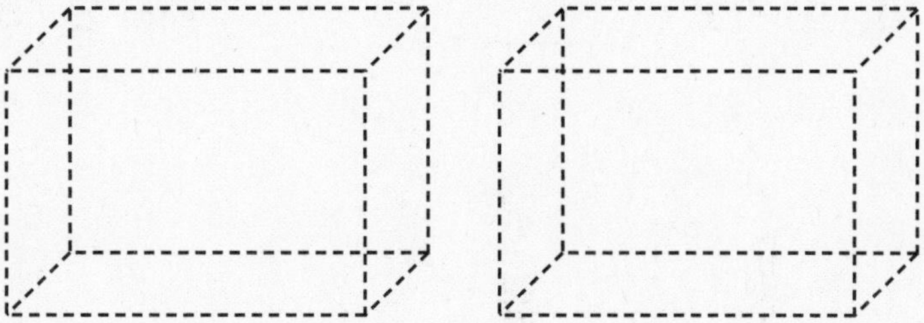

There are 2 tanks.

There are 3 fish in each tank.

How many fish in all? 2 × 3 = 6

Finish the picture and the story for 6 × 3.

1.

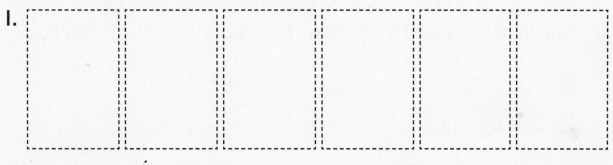

There are 6 boxes.

There are ____________________ in each box.

How many ____________________ in all? 6 × 3 = ____

2. Journal Draw a picture and write a story about 4 × 2.

Name ______________________

Practice
18-3

Writing Multiplication Stories

Draw a picture. Write a story and solve.

1. $4 \times 2 =$ 8

____

____

____

2. $5 \times 3 =$ _____

____

____

____

3. Margot has 4 pencil holders. Each one holds 3 pencils. Which number sentence shows how many pencils Margot has?

○ $3 \times 3 = 9$ ○ $4 \times 3 = 12$

○ $4 \times 4 = 16$ ○ $3 \times 5 = 15$

4. **Journal** Jeb drew this picture to show 3×8. Write a story about the picture. Solve.

____

____

____

$3 \times 8 =$ _____

Name ______________________

Vertical Form

You can write multiplication sentences in two ways.

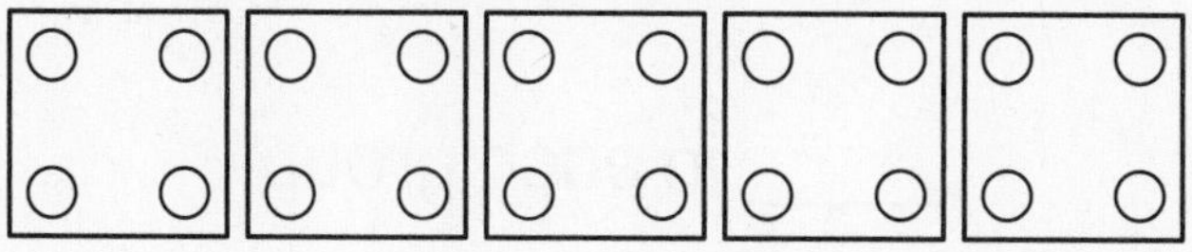

Across is called **horizontal** form.
Down is called **vertical** form.

Across 5 × 4 = 20
(groups × in each group = product)

Down

4 in each group
× 5 groups
20 product

Fill in the factors. Then write the product.

1.

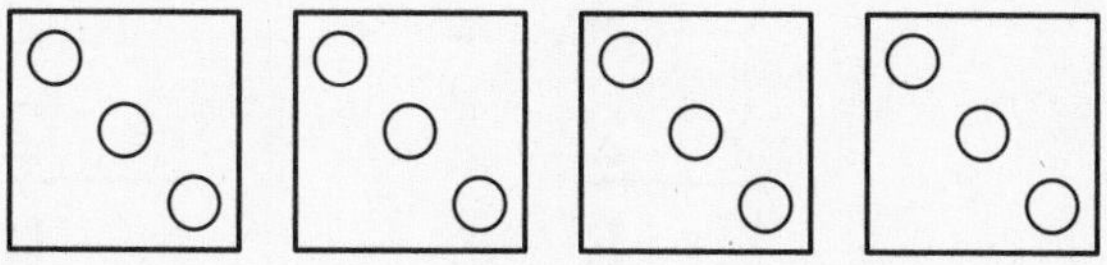

____ × ____ = ____
(groups × in each group = product)

☐ in each group
× ☐ groups
☐ product

2.

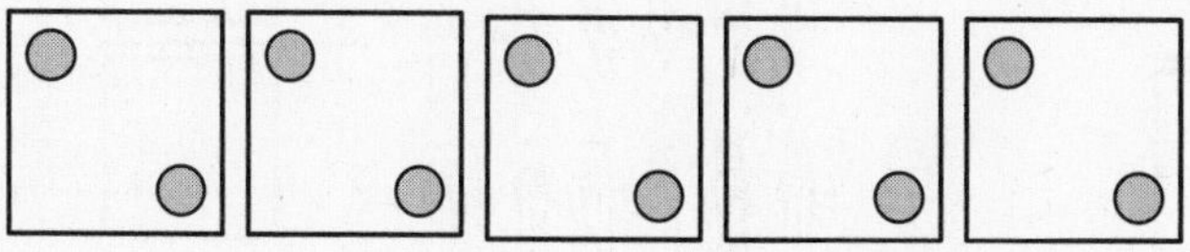

____ × ____ = ____
(groups × in each group = product)

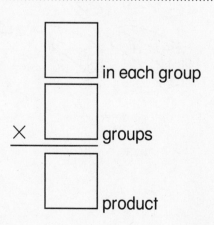

☐ in each group
× ☐ groups
☐ product

Name ______________________

Practice
18-4

Vertical Form

Fill in the factors.
Then write the product.

I. 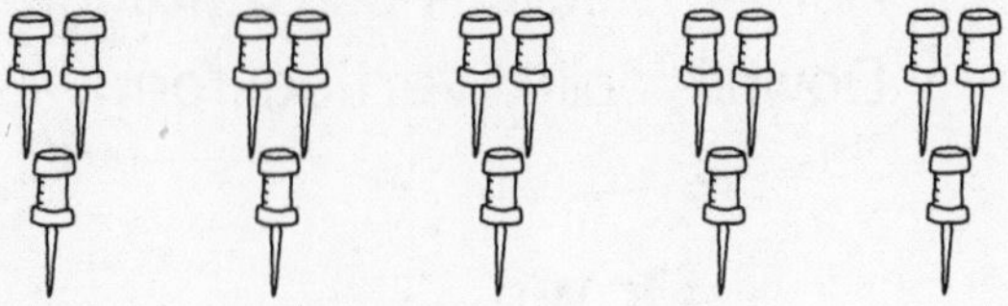

_____ in each group

× _____ groups

$5 \times 3 =$ 15

_____ in all

---

2. There are 2 boxes. 4 markers are in each box.
Which problem shows how many markers in all?

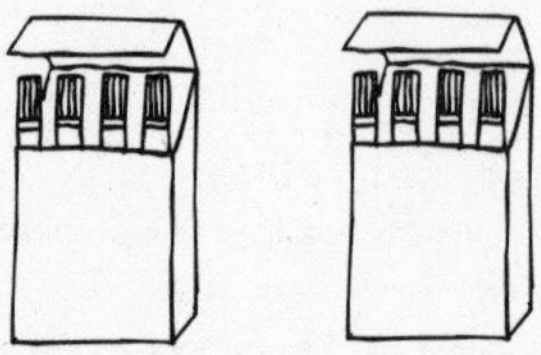

$$\begin{array}{r} 4 \\ +\ 2 \\ \hline 6 \end{array} \qquad \begin{array}{r} 8 \\ \times\ 1 \\ \hline 8 \end{array} \qquad \begin{array}{r} 4 \\ \times\ 2 \\ \hline 8 \end{array} \qquad \begin{array}{r} 2 \\ +\ 2 \\ \hline 4 \end{array}$$

○ ○ ○ ○

---

3. Algebra Write the missing numbers.

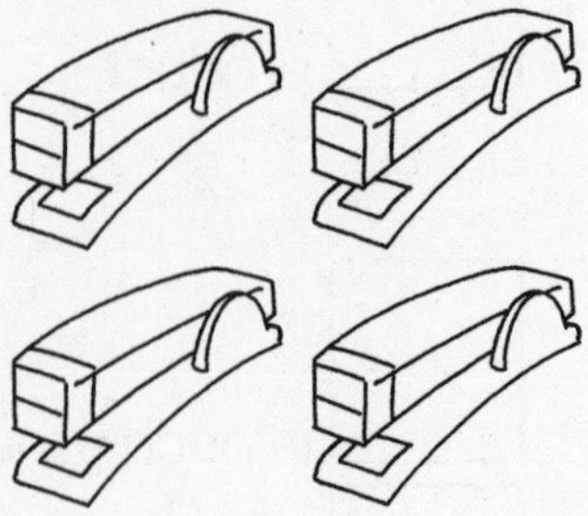

$$\begin{array}{r} \square \\ \times\ 1 \\ \hline \square \end{array}$$

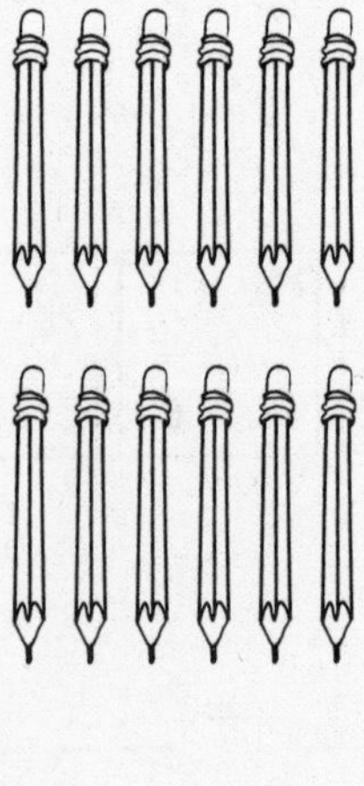

$$\begin{array}{r} 6 \\ \times\ \square \\ \hline \square \end{array}$$

Name ______________________________

Reteaching **18-5**

Multiplying in Any Order

You can multiply numbers in any order and get the same product.

Use counters to make 3 rows with 2 counters in each row.

2 and 3 are factors.
3×2 is the same as 2×3.

$3 \times$ 2 = 6

rows | in each row | product

Rearrange your counters. Make 2 rows with 3 counters in each row.

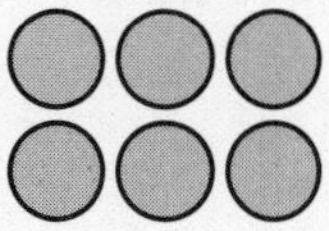

$2 \times$ 3 = 6

rows | in each row | product

Use counters to make the arrays.
Write the multiplication sentence for each array.

1.

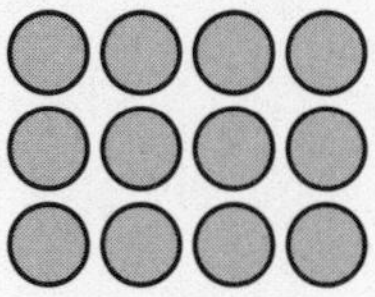

_____ × _____ = _____

rows | in each row | product

_____ × _____ = _____

rows | in each row | product

2.

_____ × _____ = _____

rows | in each row | product

_____ × _____ = _____

rows | in each row | product

3. Journal Draw a picture to show that the product of 5 x 2 and 2 x 5 is the same.

Name ____________________

Multiplying in Any Order

Complete the sentence for each grid.

1. 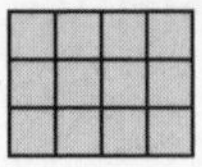

3 × 4 = 12
rows × in each row = product

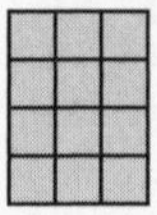

____ × ____ = ____
rows × in each row = product

2. 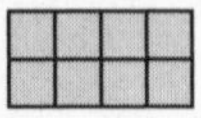

____ × ____ = ____
rows × in each row = product

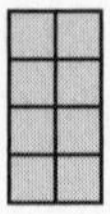

____ × ____ = ____
rows × in each row = product

Which number sentence fits the grid?

3. 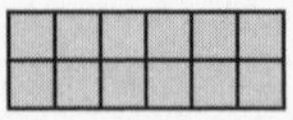

- ○ 2 × 5 = 10
- ○ 2 × 7 = 14
- ○ 2 × 6 = 12
- ○ 3 × 6 = 18

4. Reasonableness Write multiplication sentences.

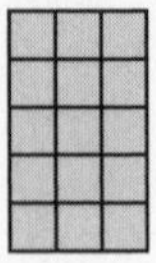

____ × ____ = ____

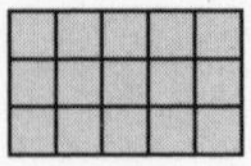

____ × ____ = ____

Do both grids show the same number? ________

Name ____________________

Reteaching 18-6

Problem Solving: Draw a Picture and Write a Number Sentence

You can draw a picture to solve a problem.
First, read the problem.

Fran knits 4 mittens.
Each mitten has 5 buttons.
How many buttons are there in all?

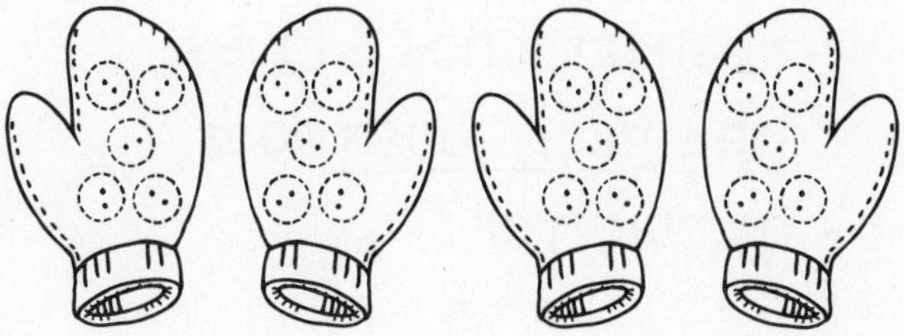

Next, draw 5 buttons on each mitten.

Then, write a number sentence.

4 × 5 = 20

mittens × buttons on each mitten buttons in all

Draw a picture to solve.
Then write a number sentence.

1. There are 6 vases.
Each vase has 3 flowers.
How many flowers are there in all?

____ × ____ = ____ flowers in all.

Name ______________________________

Problem Solving: Draw a Picture and Write a Number Sentence

Write number sentences to solve the problem.
Make part-part-whole drawings to help.

1. Zach buys 3 packs of tapes. Each pack has 3 tapes. How many tapes does he buy in all?

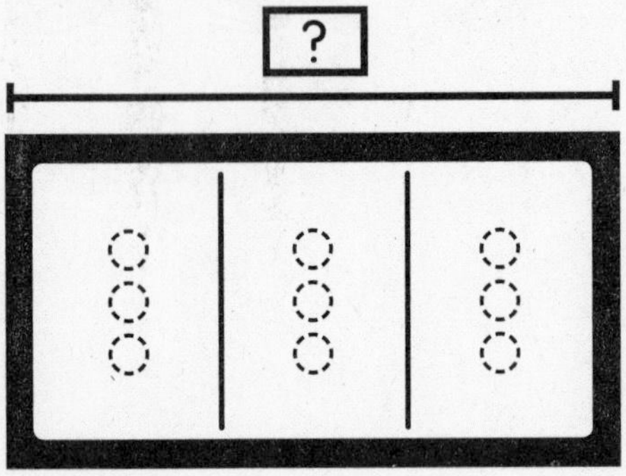

3 × 3 = 9 tapes

2. Carlos makes 2 books. Each book has 6 pages. How many pages did Carlos make in all?

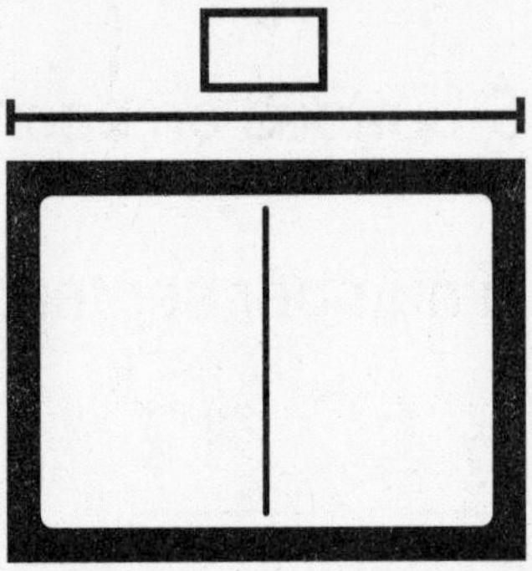

_____ × _____ = _____ tapes

3. Nell has 2 baskets. She has 9 toys in each basket. How many toys does she have in all?

- ○ 16 toys
- ○ 18 toys
- ○ 17 toys
- ○ 19 toys

4. **Reasoning** Which number sentence will solve the problem?

The flute section of a marching band has 4 rows. It has 5 players in each row. How many people are in the flute section?

- ○ $4 \times 4 = 16$
- ○ $4 \times 6 = 24$
- ○ $4 \times 5 = 20$
- ○ $5 \times 5 = 25$

Name ______________________

Reteaching
19-1

2 and 5 as Factors

Here are two ways to multiply by 2.

Skip count by 2s to show 3 × 2.

3 groups of 2 birds makes 6 birds in all.

3 × 2 = 6

Show 3 × 2 in an array.
Use connecting cubes.

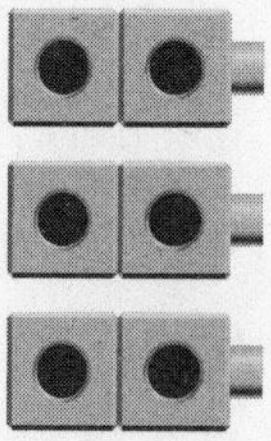

3 rows of 2 cubes makes 6 cubes in all.

3 × 2 = 6

Use skip counting and arrays to multiply by 5.
Write the multiplication sentence.

1. Skip count by 5s.
How many flowers?

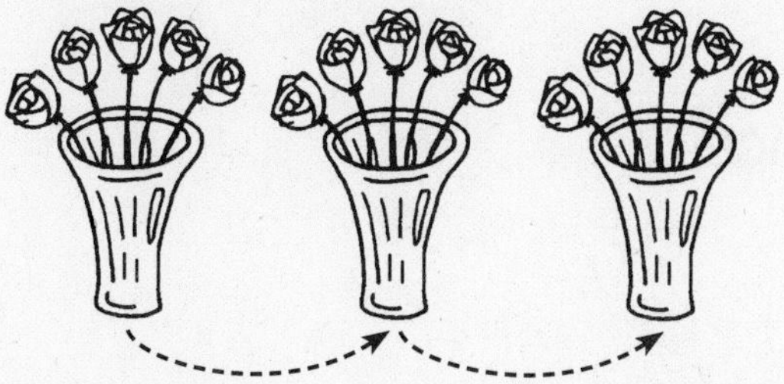

_____ × _____ = _____

2. Use connecting cubes to make this array.
How many cubes?

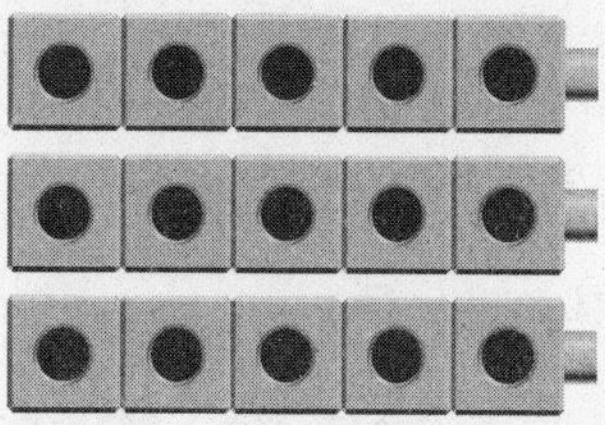

_____ × _____ = _____

Name ____________________

Practice
19-1

2 and 5 as Factors

Use the array to write a multiplication sentence.

1. 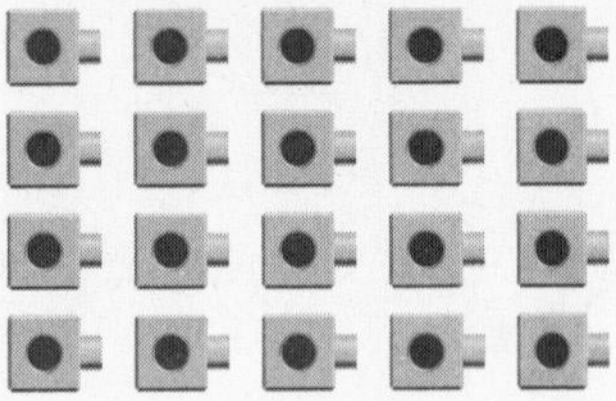

4 × 5 = 20

2. 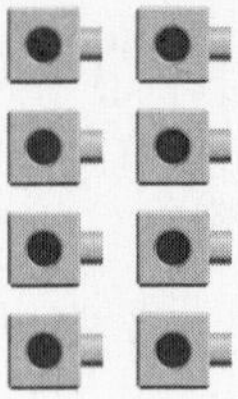

____ × ____ = ____

3. 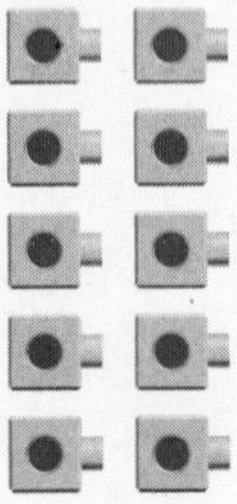

____ × ____ = ____

4. 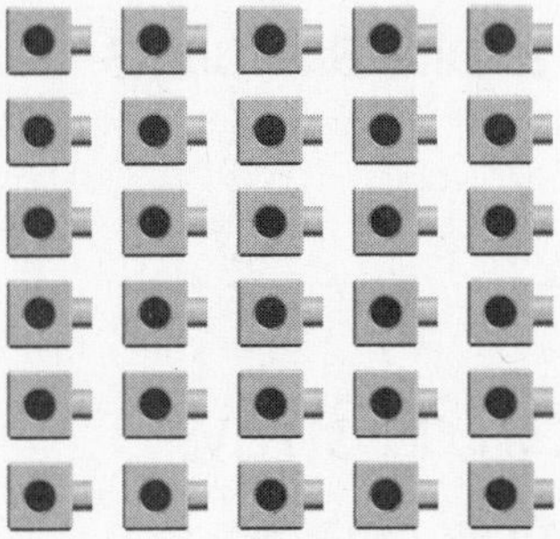

____ × ____ = ____

5. Danielle made this array of buttons. Which shows how many buttons she has in all?

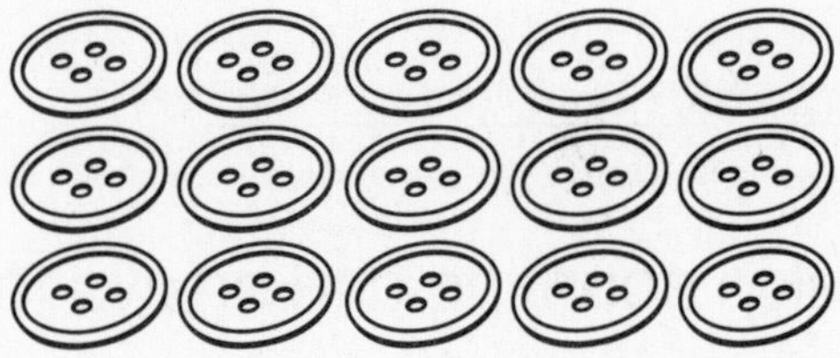

13 ○ 14 ○ 15 ○ 16 ○

6. **Journal** Draw a picture.
Then write a multiplication sentence.
Ramona has 7 dolls.
Each doll has 2 bows.
How many bows are there in all?

____ × ____ = ____ bows

Name ______________________________

10 as a Factor

4 × 10 = ?

There are different ways you can multiply by 10.

Skip count by 10s.

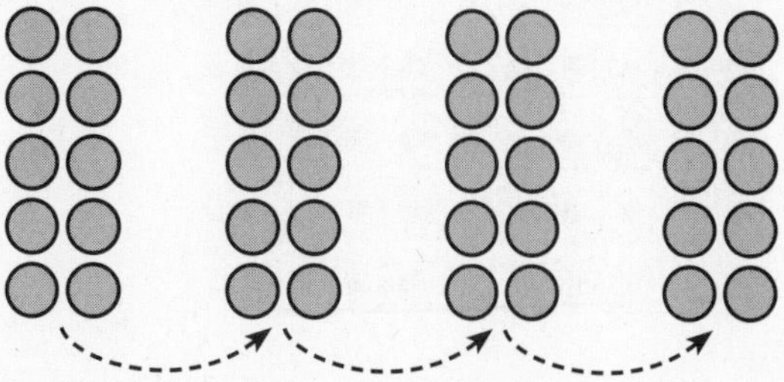

10, 20, 30, 40

Use repeated addition.

10 + 10 + 10 + 10 = 40 counters in all

Show 4 × 10 in an array.

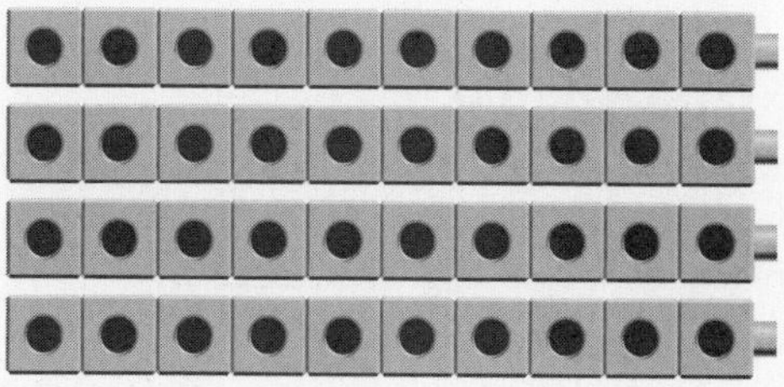

4 rows of 10 cubes = 40 cubes in all.

4 × 10 = 40

Multiply by 10.

Write the multiplication sentence.

1. Skip count by 10s.
How many dots in all?

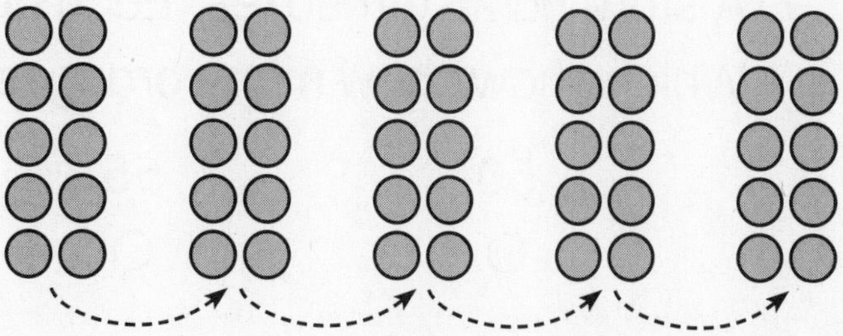

____ × ____ = ____

2. Use repeated addition.
How many dots in all?

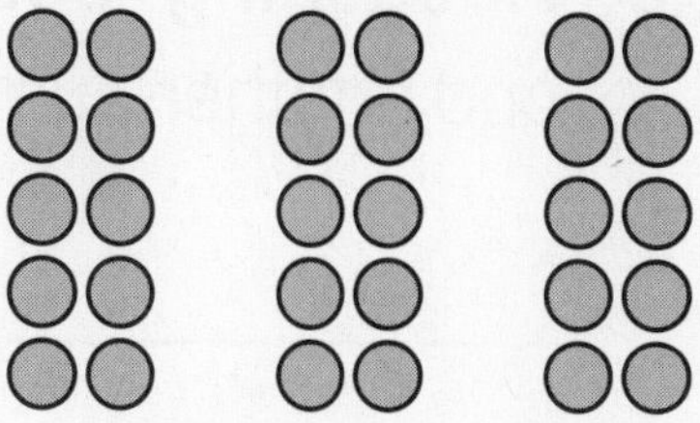

____ + ____ + ____ = ____

Name ______________________

Practice
19-2

10 as a Factor

Skip count or use repeated addition.
Write the multiplication sentence.

1. 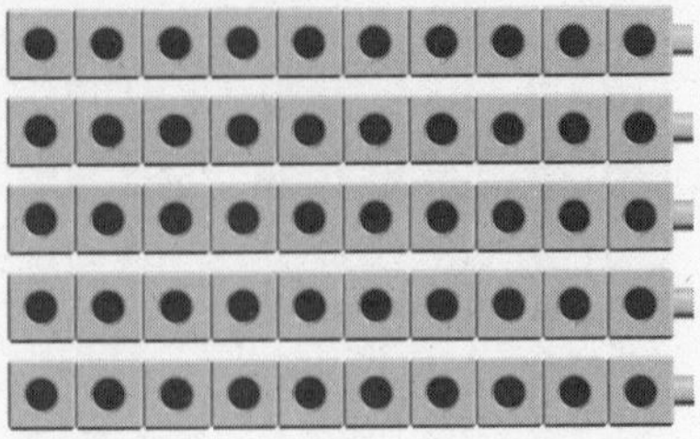

5 × 10 = 50

2. 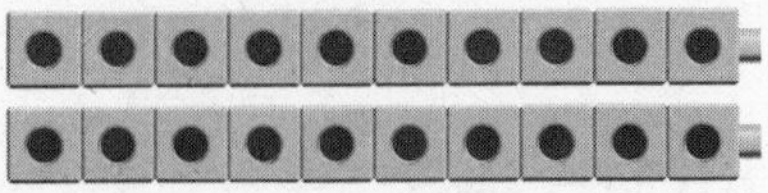

____ × ____ = ____

Find each product. Use connecting cubes if you need to.

3. 6 × 10 = ____

4. 5 × 10 = ____

5. 3 × 10 = ____

○ 13 ○ 15

○ 30 ○ 35

6. 7 × 10 = ____

○ 10 ○ 70

○ 17 ○ 72

7. A store has 5 gift boxes. Each box has 10 oranges.
Which shows how many oranges in all?

50	55	60	65
○	○	○	○

8. **Reasoning** Could 35 ever be the product of 10 and another number? Explain.

____

____

Name ____________________

Reteaching
19-3

Practicing with 2s, 5s, and 10s

You can solve $4 \times 5 = ?$ in different ways.

Skip count by 5s.

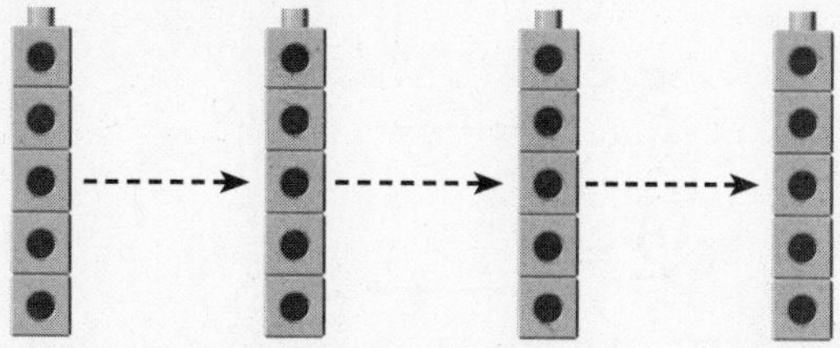

5 10 15 20

Use repeated addition.

$5 + 5 + 5 + 5 = 20$

Make an array.

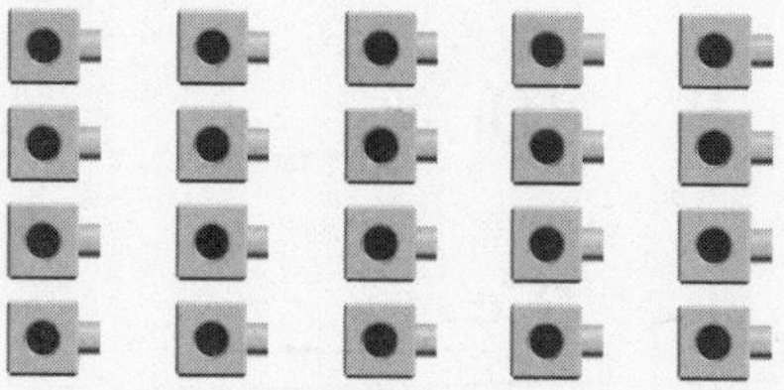

$4 \times 5 = 20$

Remember the multiplication fact: $4 \times 5 = 20$

Multiply. Choose a way to solve.

1. $5 \times 2 =$ ____

2. $3 \times 10 =$ ____

3. $6 \times 2 =$ ____

4. $4 \times 10 =$ ____

5. $7 \times 2 =$ ____

6. $5 \times 10 =$ ____

7. $2 \times 10 =$ ____

8. $6 \times 10 =$ ____

9. Number Sense Tell how you know that the multiplication fact $4 \times 5 = 20$ is correct.

____

____

Name ______________________________

Practice
19-3

Practicing with 2s, 5s, and 10s

Multiply. Use cubes if you need to.

1. $6 \times 5 =$ _____
2. $5 \times 10 =$ _____
3. $6 \times 10 =$ _____
4. $7 \times 5 =$ _____
5. $1 \times 2 =$ _____
6. $2 \times 2 =$ _____
7. $3 \times 2 =$ _____
8. $4 \times 2 =$ _____
9. $5 \times 2 =$ _____
10. $6 \times 2 =$ _____
11. $7 \times 2 =$ _____
12. $8 \times 2 =$ _____
13. $9 \times 2 =$ _____
14. $10 \times 2 =$ _____

15. Maura placed dimes in 2 rows of 10 dimes each. Which multiplication fact shows how many dimes she has?

○ $2 \times 2 = 4$ ○ $2 \times 5 = 10$

○ $2 \times 10 = 20$ ○ $10 \times 10 = 100$

16. **Estimation** Trent makes 3 rows. Each row has 5 toy cars. Does he use more or less than 18 toy cars? Explain.

____

____

Name ____________________

Reteaching
19-4

Problem Solving: Look for a Pattern

You can use the table to multiply.

1 × 10 = 10

2 × 10 = 20

3 × 10 = 30

	0	1	2	3	4	5	6	7	8	9	10
0	0	0	0	0	0	0	0	0	0	0	0
1	0	1	2	3	4	5	6	7	8	9	10
2	0	2	4	6	8	10	12	14	16	18	20
3	0	3	6	9	12	15	18	21	24	27	30
4	0	4	8	12	16	20	24	28	32	36	40
5	0	5	10	15	20	25	30	35	40	45	50
6	0	6	12	18	24	30	36	42	48	54	60
7	0	7	14	21	28	35	42	49	56	63	70
8	0	8	16	24	32	40	48	56	64	72	80
9	0	9	18	27	36	45	54	63	72	81	90
10	0	10	20	30	40	50	60	70	80	90	100

What pattern do you see?

The products increase by 10.

Use the table to find the missing numbers.

1. 5 × 2 = 10
6 × 2 = 12

7 × 2 = ____

8 × 2 = ____

9 × 2 = ____

2. 5 × 5 = 25
6 × 5 = 30

7 × 5 = ____

8 × 5 = ____

9 × 5 = ____

3. Number Sense Describe the pattern that you see when you multiply by 5.

____

Name ______________________

Practice **19-4**

Problem Solving: Look for a Pattern

Find the missing numbers.

Multiply by 2.

1. $1 \times 2 =$ 2

$2 \times 2 =$ _____

$3 \times 2 =$ _____

$4 \times 2 =$ _____

$5 \times 2 =$ _____

2. $6 \times 2 =$ _____

$7 \times 2 =$ _____

$8 \times 2 =$ _____

$9 \times 2 =$ _____

$10 \times 2 =$ _____

Multiply by 10.

3. $1 \times 10 =$ _______

$2 \times 20 =$ _______

$3 \times 30 =$ _______

$4 \times 40 =$ _______

$5 \times 50 =$ _______

4. $6 \times 10 =$ _______

$7 \times 10 =$ _______

$8 \times 10 =$ _______

$9 \times 10 =$ _______

$10 \times 10 =$ _______

5. Algebra Linda made this table.
She did not finish it.
What number is missing?

$2 \times 5 = 10$
$3 \times 5 = 15$
$4 \times 5 = 20$
$5 \times 5 = ?$

○ 21 ○ 25 ○ 30 ○ 55

Name ____________________

Reteaching
20-1

Division as Sharing

5 children want to share 10 counters equally. Draw 1 counter for each child. Keep drawing 1 counter for each child until you have drawn 10 counters in all.

If each child gets the same number of counters, each gets an **equal share.**

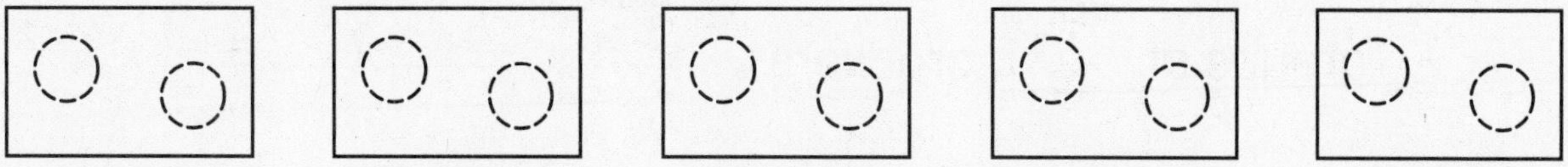

Brandon   Melissa   Joaquin   Dorothea   Janet

There are 10 counters to share equally.

There are 5 groups of counters.

There are 2 counters in each group.

Each child gets 2 counters.

Draw to show equal groups.
Write how many each child gets.

1. 4 children want to share 12 counters.

Gabriel   Talia   Shane   Natanya

Each child gets _____ counters.

Name ______________________

Practice
20-1

Division as Sharing

Make equal groups. Write the numbers.

1. 15 crackers shared by 3 friends

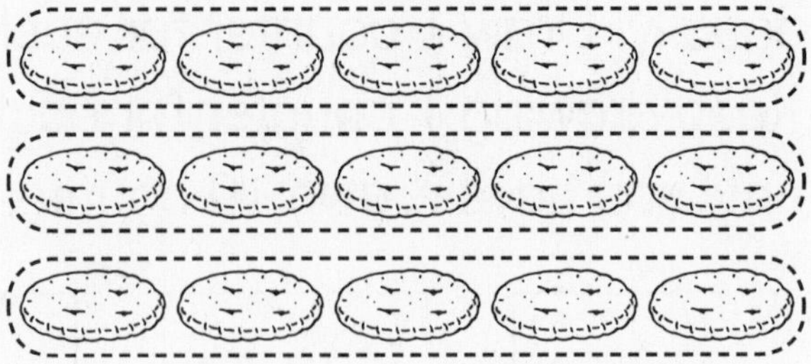

15 in all

3 groups of 5 crackers

2. 12 books shared by 4 friends

_____ in all

_____ groups of _____ books

3. 21 fish are shared equally by 7 bear cubs.
How many fish does each bear cub get?

○ 1 ○ 2 ○ 3 ○ 4

4. **Number Sense** You have 18 plums. Can you find 6 different ways to show equal groups?

_____ group of _____ _____ groups of _____

_____ groups of _____ _____ groups of _____

_____ groups of _____ _____ groups of _____

Name ____________________

Reteaching
20-2

Division as Repeated Subtraction

Subtract over and over to solve.

Erin has 15 blueberries. She puts 5 blueberries in each pancake. How many pancakes can she make?

15 − 5 = 10
10 − 5 = 5
5 − 5 = 0

How many times did you subtract to get to 0? 3

How many pancakes can Erin make?

3 pancakes

Subtract over and over to solve.
Use counters to help you.

1. Gina has 12 carrots. If she puts 4 carrots in each plastic bag, how many bags will she fill?

   ____ bags

12 − 4 = ____
____ − ____ = ____
____ − ____ = ____

2. Kofi has 20 grapes. If he gives grapes to 5 friends, how many grapes will each friend get?

   ____ grapes

____ − ____ = ____
____ − ____ = ____
____ − ____ = ____
____ − ____ = ____

Name ______________________________

Practice
20-2

Division as Repeated Subtraction

Use counters. Subtract over and over. Write the numbers.

1. Moira has 12 postcards.
She writes 4 postcards each day.
How many days until the postcards are gone?

3 days

12 − 4 = 8
8 − 4 = 4
4 − 4 = 0

2. Jesse has 20 quarters. He spends 5 quarters each day for lunch.
How many days until the quarters are gone?

_____ days

_____ − _____ = _____
_____ − _____ = _____
_____ − _____ = _____
_____ − _____ = _____

Subtract over and over to solve. Use counters if you need to.

3. Imani has 16 straws. He gives 4 straws to each friend.
How many friends get straws?

2	3	4	5
○	○	○	○

4. Reasoning Anita has 14 apples.
She puts 2 apples on each plate.
How many plates does Anita need?

2	4	6	7
○	○	○	○

Name ______________________________

Writing Division Stories

Look at the picture.
Read the story.
Then write a division sentence.

There are 15 pilots.
There are an equal number of pilots in 5 planes.
How many pilots are in each plane?

15 ÷ 5 = 3
pilots ÷ planes = pilots in each plane

15 divided by 5 is 3.

Look at the picture. Complete the story.
Use the picture to solve the division sentence.

1. A plane has 24 seats in one section.

   There are 3 seats in each row.
   How many rows of seats are there?

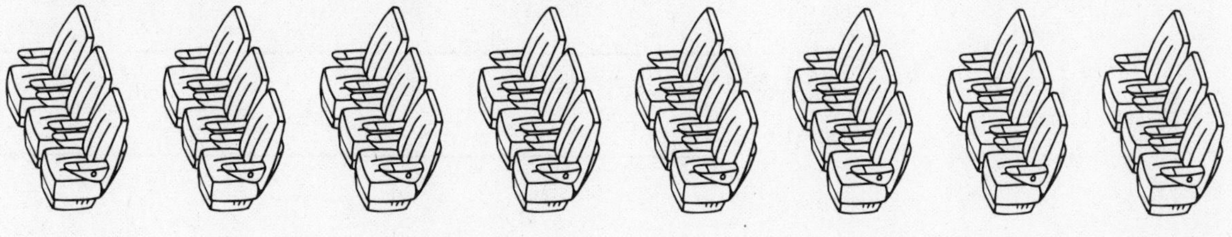

   24 ÷ 3 = _____ rows of seats

2. **Journal** Write a division story for the number sentence 16 ÷ 4 = _____. Solve the division sentence.

Name ______________________

Practice
20-3

Writing Division Stories

Draw a picture for the problem.
Then write a division sentence.

1. Alma has 9 shirts. She has 3 drawers. She puts the same number of shirts in each drawer. How many shirts does she put in each drawer?

   9 ÷ 3 = 3

   3 shirts

2. Felix divides 14 comic books into 2 piles. Which shows how many comic books are in each pile?

   ○ 2   ○ 4   ○ 7   ○ 9

3. **Journal** Draw a picture. Write a story. Use the picture to solve the problem.

   ____

   ____

   ____

   ____

   ____

   18 ÷ 3 = ____

Name ______________________

Reteaching
20-4

Relating Multiplication and Division

Zoe put 12 apples in baskets.
She put 3 apples in each.
How many baskets did she use?

12 ÷ 3 = ___?___

Multiplication can help you solve the problem.
Zoe has 12 apples in 4 groups of 3.

So, ___3___ × ___4___ = ___12___

There are 3 apples in ___4___ baskets. 12 ÷ 3 = ___4___

Draw a picture to solve. Write the multiplication sentence that helps you solve. Then write the division sentence.

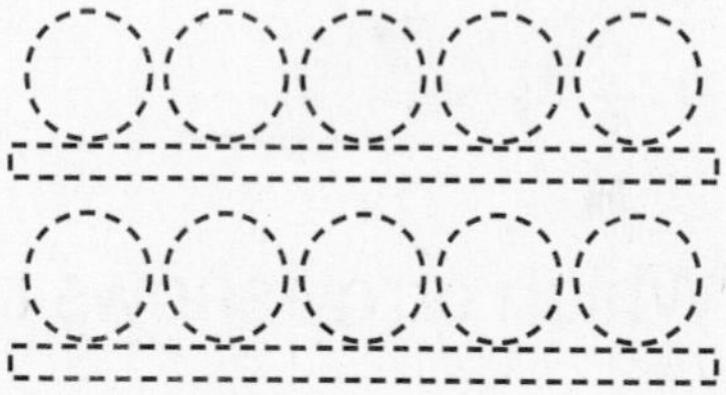

1. Karl puts 10 balls on shelves.
   There are 5 balls on each shelf.
   How many shelves does Karl fill?

   5 × ___2___ = 10

   10 ÷ 5 = ___?___

   _____ ÷ _____ = _____

2. Julio has 16 cards.
   He puts 4 cards in each row.
   How many rows are there?

   4 × _____ = _____

   16 ÷ 4 = ___?___

   _____ ÷ _____ = _____

Name ____________________

Relating Multiplication and Division

Complete each sentence. Use counters if you need to.

1. 2 × __8__ = 16

   16 ÷ 2 = __8__

2. 4 × _____ = 20

   20 ÷ 4 = _____

3. 4 × _____ = 12

   12 ÷ 4 = _____

4. 7 × _____ = 21

   21 ÷ 7 = _____

5. 5 × _____ = 25

   25 ÷ 5 = _____

6. 9 × _____ = 18

   18 ÷ 9 = _____

7. 4 × _____ = 8

   8 ÷ 4 = _____

8. 5 × _____ = 15

   15 ÷ 5 = _____

9. Which array shows both 2 × 3 = 6 and 6 ÷ 2 = 3?

○ 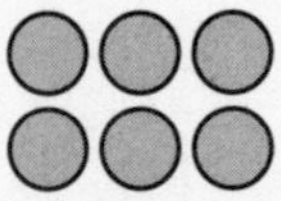

○ 

○ 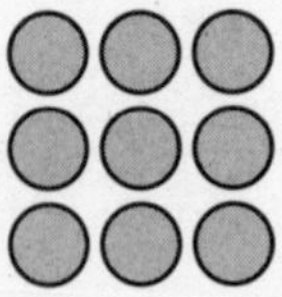

○ 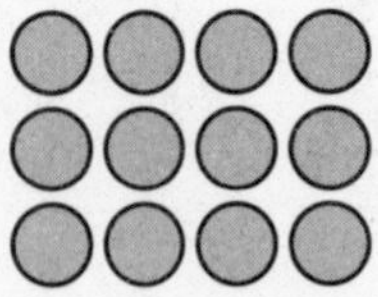

10. **Algebra** Which multiplication sentence will help you complete 24 ÷ 8 = _____?

○ 4 × 4 = 8

○ 8 × 4 = 32

○ 8 × 3 = 24

○ 8 × 8 = 64

Name ______________________________

Fact Families for 2 and 5

This fact family tells about the soccer balls.

There are **2** rows of **4** soccer balls. There are **8** balls in all.

The multiplication facts have the numbers 2, 4, and 8.

2 × 4 = 8   4 × 2 = 8

The division facts have the numbers 2, 4, and 8.

8 ÷ 4 = 2   8 ÷ 2 = 4

Complete the fact families.
Use the pictures to help you.

1. 2 × 3 = 6

____ × ____ = ____

____ ÷ ____ = ____

____ ÷ ____ = ____

2. 5 × 3 = 15

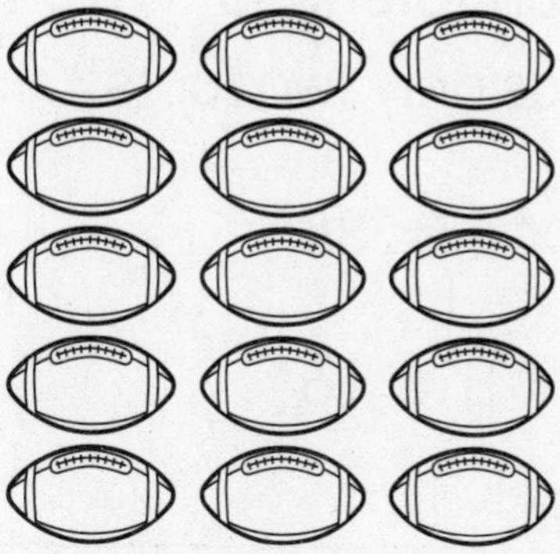

____ × ____ = ____

____ ÷ ____ = ____

____ ÷ ____ = ____

Name ____________________

Practice **20-5**

Fact Families for 2 and 5

Complete each fact family. Use counters if you need to.

1. $4 \times 5 = 20$

$5 \times 4 = 20$

$20 \div 4 = 5$

$20 \div 5 = 4$

2. ___ $\times$ ___ $=$ ___

___ $\times$ ___ $=$ ___

$14 \div 2 = 7$

___ $\div$ ___ $=$ ___

3. $2 \times 5 = 10$

___ $\times$ ___ $=$ ___

___ $\div$ ___ $=$ ___

___ $\div$ ___ $=$ ___

Write a multiplication fact or division fact from the same fact family to solve these problems.

4. Karina has 15 buttons and 5 dolls. She wants to sew the same number of buttons on each doll. How many buttons does each doll get?

___ $\div$ ___ $=$ ___

5. Karina gives 5 dolls with 3 buttons each to her sister. How many buttons do these dolls have altogether?

___ $\times$ ___ $=$ ___

6. Reasonableness Which fact is from a fact family that has only two facts?

○ $7 \times 5 = 35$

○ $2 \times 2 = 4$

○ $2 \times 8 = 16$

○ $5 \times 6 = 30$

Explain. ____________________

Name ______________________________

Fact Families for 10

Use the grid to complete the fact family.

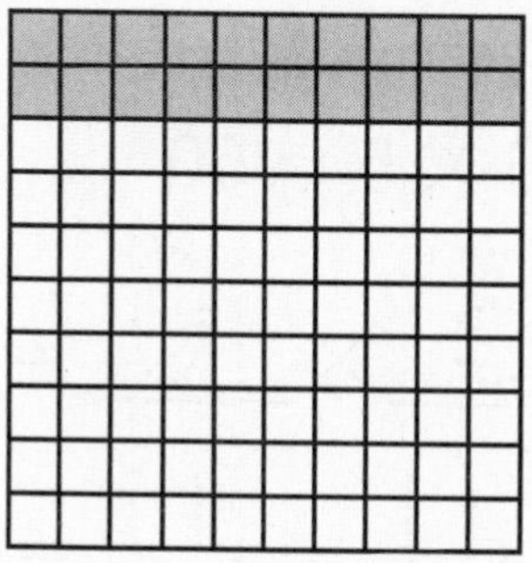

Each row has 10 boxes, so 2 rows make 20:
$2 \times 10 = 20$.

The fact family for 2, 10, and 20:

$2 \times 10 = 20$ $\quad$ $10 \times 2 = 20$

$20 \div 2 = 10$ $\quad$ $20 \div 10 = 2$

Complete the fact families. Use the grid to help you.

1. $10 \times 5 = 50$

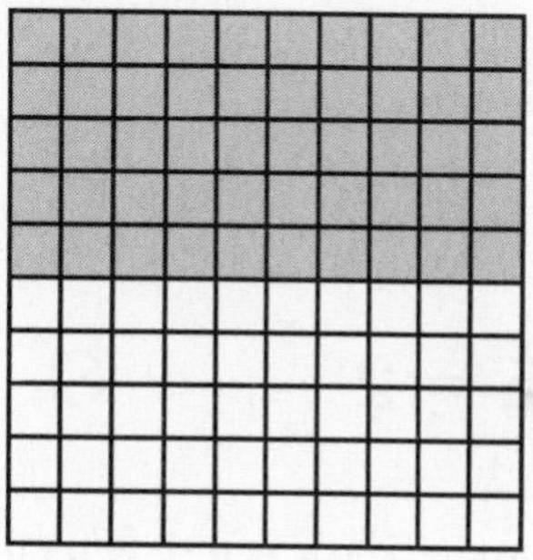

____ × ____ = ____

____ ÷ ____ = ____

____ ÷ ____ = ____

2. $4 \times 10 = 40$

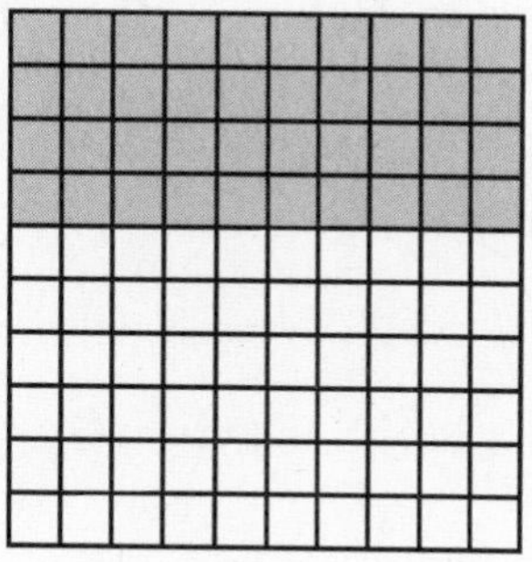

____ × ____ = ____

____ ÷ ____ = ____

____ ÷ ____ = ____

3. **Journal** Use counters and a grid to help you write the fact family for 3, 10, and 30.

Name ____________________

Practice
20-6

Fact Families for 10

Complete each fact family.

1. $10 \times 5 = 50$

$\underline{5} \times \underline{10} = \underline{50}$

$\underline{50} \div \underline{10} = \underline{5}$

$\underline{50} \div \underline{5} = \underline{10}$

2. ____ × ____ = ____

____ × ____ = ____

$70 \div 10 = 7$

____ ÷ ____ = ____

3. Algebra Kevin made this grid and wrote the division sentence. Which other division sentence could he write?

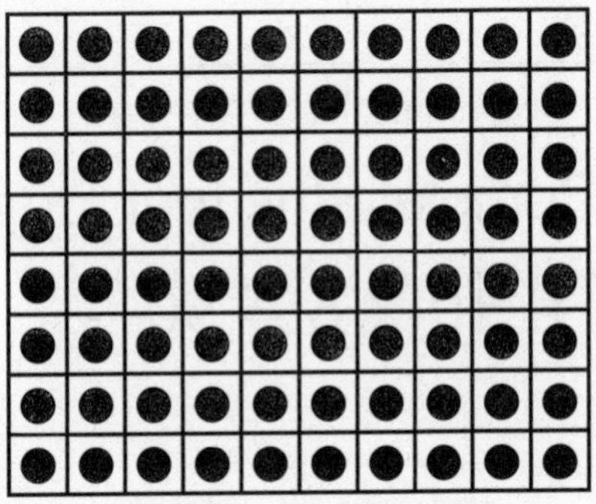

$80 \div 8 = 10$

○ $80 \div 10 = 8$　　○ $8 \div 8 = 1$

○ $10 \div 5 = 2$　　○ $70 \div 7 = 10$

4. Which shows the fact family for this grid?

$80 \times 10 = 800$	$80 \times 1 = 80$	$8 \times 8 = 64$	$10 \times 8 = 80$
$80 \times 8 = 160$	$80 + 8 = 88$	$8 \times 10 = 80$	$8 \times 10 = 80$
$80 \div 1 = 80$	$80 - 8 = 72$	$80 \div 10 = 8$	$80 \div 8 = 10$
$80 \div 8 = 10$	$80 \div 8 = 10$	$80 \div 8 = 10$	$80 \div 10 = 8$
○	○	○	○

Name ____________________

Reteaching
20-7

Division and Remainders

How many groups of 2 counters can you make? 3

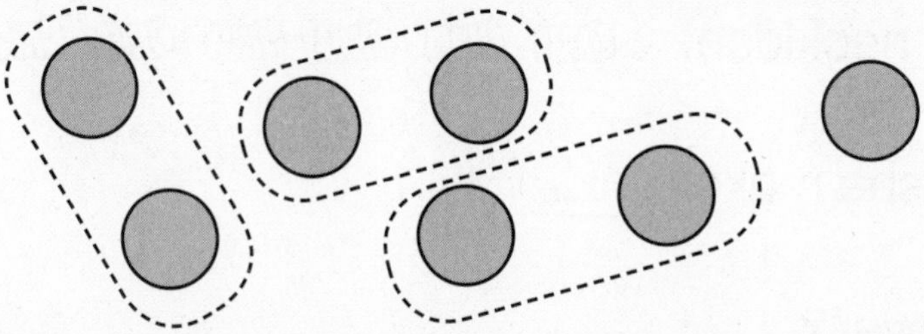

The number left over is called the **remainder.**

The remainder is 1.

Use counters to make equal groups.
Write the remainder.

1. There are 10 counters.
How many groups of 3 counters can you make?

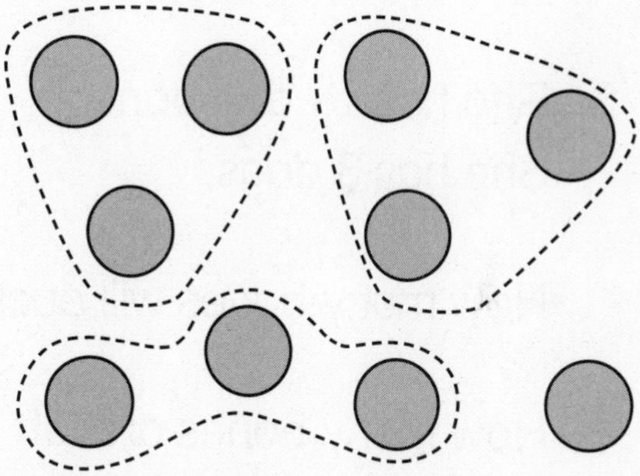

_____

The remainder is _____.

2. There are 14 counters.
How many groups of 4 counters can you make?

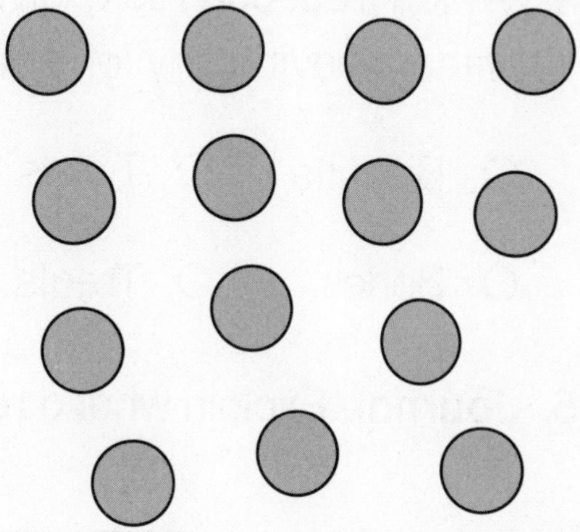

_____

The remainder is _____.

Name ______________________

Practice
20-7

Division and Remainders

Circle groups to solve.

1. Sami has 11 beads.
She puts 4 beads on each necklace.

How many necklaces can she make? 2

How many beads are left over? 3

2. Tommy has 10 balls.
He puts 3 balls in each bag.

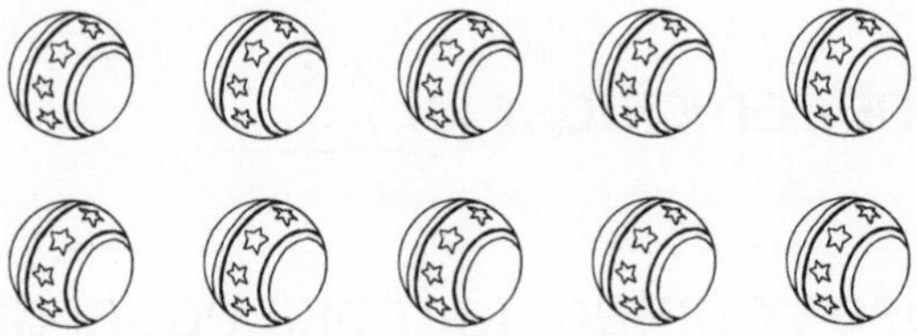

How many bags can he fill? _____

How many balls are left over? _____

3. Rita has 14 dog bones.
She has 3 dogs.

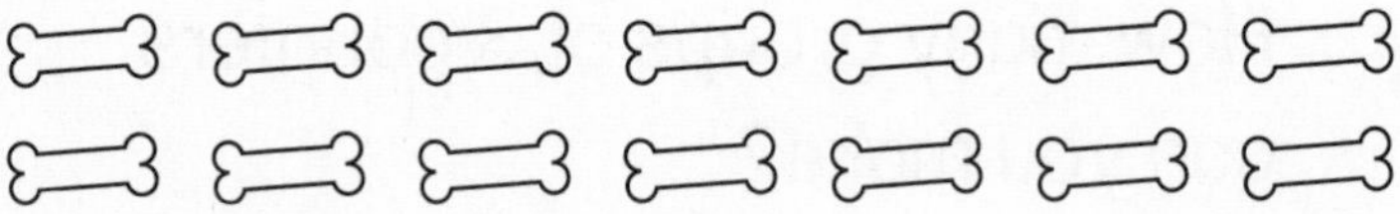

How many bones will each dog get? _____

How many bones are left over? _____

4. Which treat can Ricky give to 3 dogs without having any left over?

○ Biscuits ○ Twists

○ Bones ○ Treats

Dog Treats	
Biscuits	18
Bones	7
Twists	20

5. Journal Explain what a remainder is.

____

Name ______________________

Reteaching
20-8

Problem Solving: Make a Table and Look for a Pattern

Matt is making sandwiches. The number of slices of bread he uses is the **input.** The number of sandwiches he makes is the **output.**

Input	2	4	6	8
Output	1	2	3	?

Matt uses 2 slices of bread for each sandwich.
How many sandwiches can Matt make from 8 slices of bread?

Look for a pattern in the table to help you.
The pattern, or rule, is to divide the **input** by 2.
So, if Matt uses 8 slices of bread,

$8 \div 2 =$ 4.

Look for a pattern and complete the table.
Use the table to solve the problem.

Ira buys bunches of bananas. There are 5 bananas in each bunch.

Input (bunches)	1	2	3	4	5
Output (bananas)	5	10	15		

1. What is the rule? multiply by 5

2. How many bananas are there in 1 bunch? _____

3. How many bananas are there in 4 bunches? _____

Name ______________________________

Problem Solving: Make a Table and Look for a Pattern

1. Complete the table and look for a pattern.
   Then use the table to solve the problems.

Input	1	2	3	4	5
Output	5	10	15		

2. Ling cuts 3 stars out of paper. Each star has 5 points. How many points are there in all?

   _____ points

3. What is the rule?

   ____

4. How many points are there in 5 stars? _____

5. **Spatial Thinking** Complete the table.

Input	1	2			
Output	3	6			

What is the rule for the table?

○ Add 3.
○ Multiply by 3.
○ Multiply by 6.
○ Divide by 15.

Step Up to Grade 3

Name ______________________________

Equal Parts of a Whole

Materials rectangular sheets of paper, 3 for each student; crayons or markers

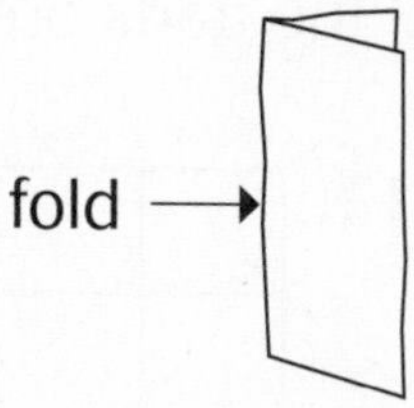

1. Fold a sheet of paper so the two shorter edges are on top of each other, as shown at the right.

2. Open up the piece of paper. Draw a line down the fold. Color each part a different color.

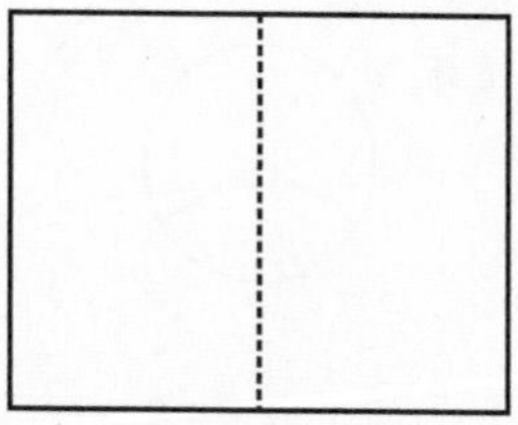

The table below shows special names for the equal parts. All parts must be **equal** before you can use these special names.

3. Are the parts you colored equal in size?

4. How many equal parts are there?

5. What is the name for the parts you colored?

Number of Equal Parts	Name of Equal Parts
2	halves
3	thirds
4	fourths
5	fifths
6	sixths
8	eighths
10	tenths
12	twelfths

6. Fold another sheet of paper like above. Then fold it again so that it makes a long slender rectangle as shown below.

7. Open up the piece of paper. Draw lines down the folds. Color each part a different color.

8. Are the parts you colored equal in size?

9. How many equal parts are there?

10. What is the name for the parts you colored?

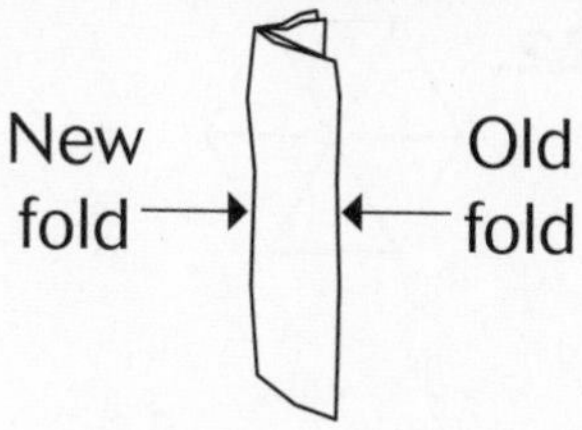

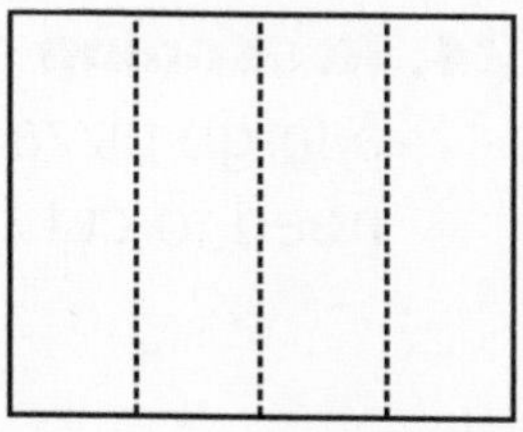

11. Fold another sheet of paper into 3 parts that are *not* equal. Open it and draw lines down the folds. In the space below, draw your rectangle and color each part a different color.

© Pearson Education, Inc.

Name ______________________________

Equal Parts of a Whole (continued)

Tell if each shows parts that are equal or parts that are not equal. If the parts are equal, name them.

12. 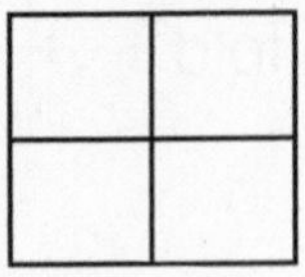

13. 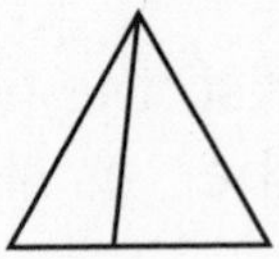

____

14. 

15. 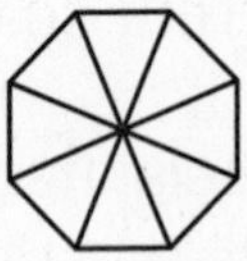

____

16. 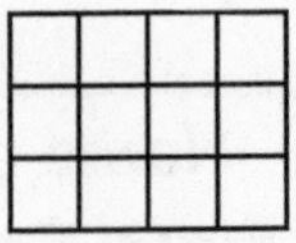

17. 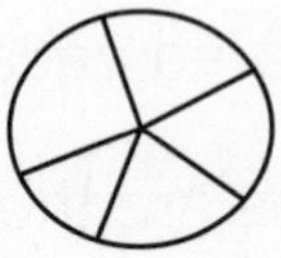

____

18. 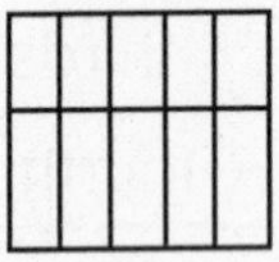

19. 

____

20. 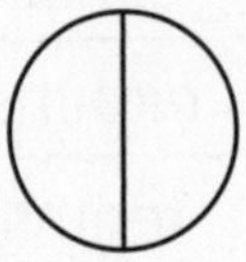

21. 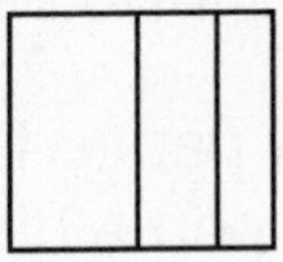

____

22. 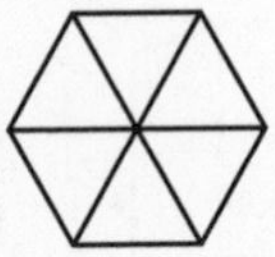

23. 

____

24. Reasoning If 5 children want to equally share a large pizza and each gets 2 pieces, will they need to cut the pizza into fifths, eighths, or tenths?

© Pearson Education, Inc.

Name ______________________

Parts of a Region

Materials crayons or markers

1. In the circle at the right, color 2 of the equal parts blue and 4 of the equal parts red.

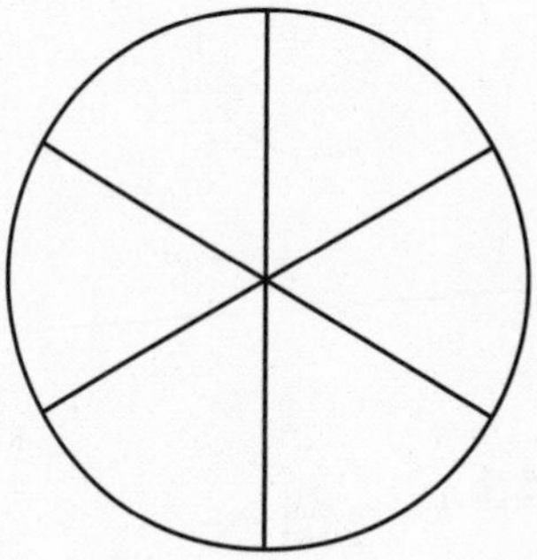

Write fractions to name the parts by answering 2 to 6.

2. How many total equal parts does the circle have?

3. How many of the equal parts of the circle are blue?

4. What fraction of the circle is blue?

$$\frac{\square}{\square} = \frac{\text{number of equal parts that are blue}}{\text{total number of equal parts}} = \frac{\text{(numerator)}}{\text{(denominator)}}$$

Two sixths of the circle is blue.

5. How many of the equal parts of the circle are red?

6. What fraction of the circle is red?

$$\frac{\square}{\square} = \frac{\text{number of equal parts that are red}}{\text{total number of equal parts}} = \frac{\text{(numerator)}}{\text{(denominator)}}$$

Four sixths of the circle is red.

Show the fraction $\frac{3}{8}$ by answering 7 to 9.

7. Color $\frac{3}{8}$ of the rectangle at the right.

8. How many equal parts does the rectangle have?

9. How many parts did you color?

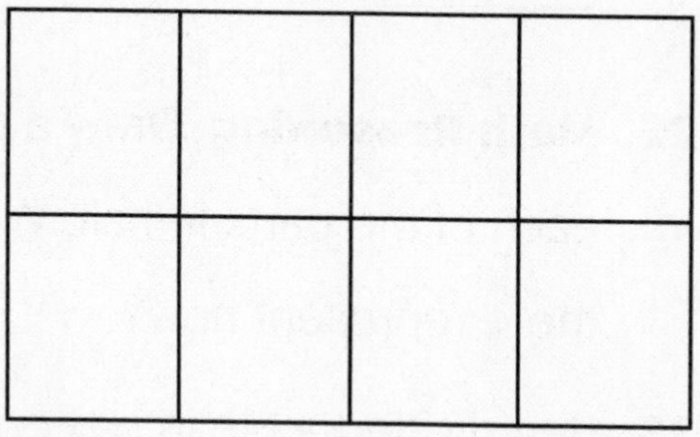

© Pearson Education, Inc.

Name ____________________

Parts of a Region (continued)

Write the fraction for the shaded part of each region.

10. 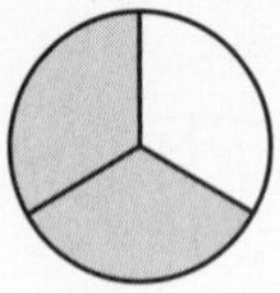 ______

11. 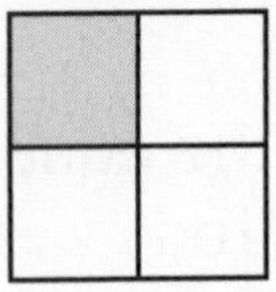 ______

12. 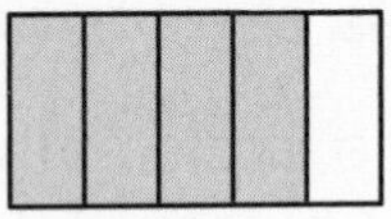 ______

13. 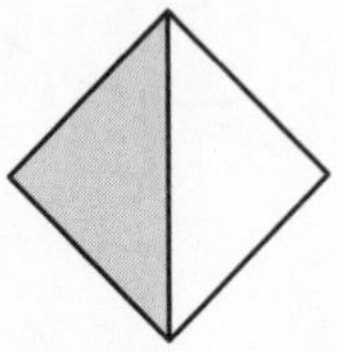 ______

14. 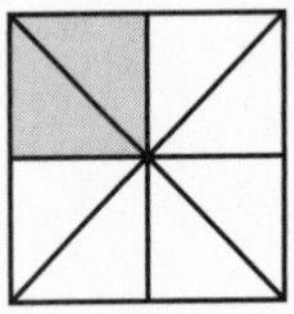 ______

15. 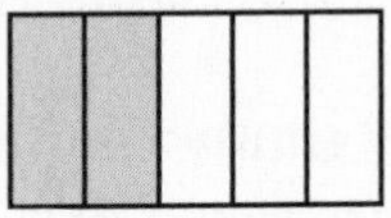 ______

16. 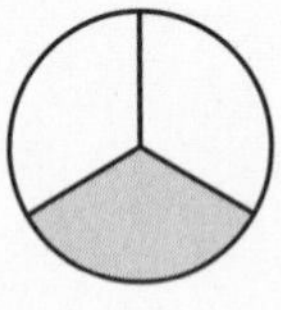 ______

17. 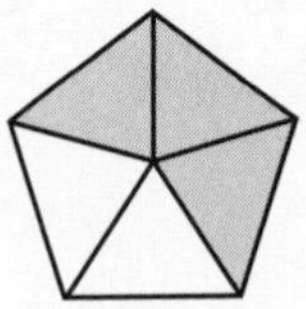 ______

18. 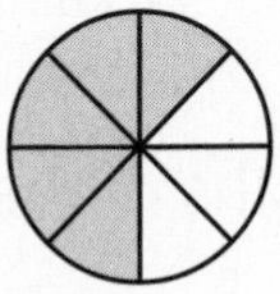 ______

Color to show each fraction.

19. $\frac{3}{4}$

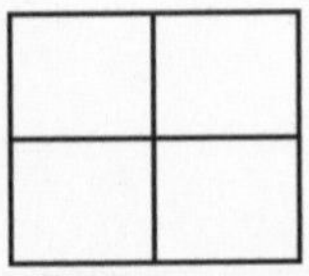

20. $\frac{5}{6}$

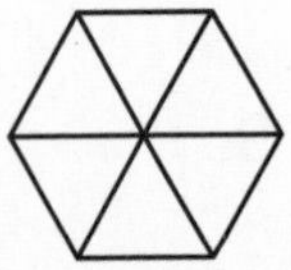

21. $\frac{7}{10}$

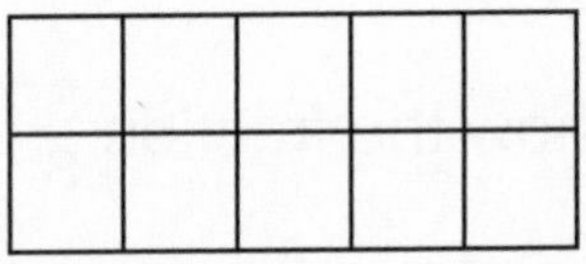

22. Math Reasoning Draw a picture to show $\frac{1}{3}$. Then divide each of the parts in half. What fraction of the parts does the $\frac{1}{3}$ represent now? ______

23. Ben divided a pie into 8 equal pieces and ate 3 of them. How much of the pie remains? ______

© Pearson Education, Inc.

Name ______________________________

Using Models to Compare Fractions

Materials fraction strips

Use >, <, or = to compare $\frac{4}{5}$ and $\frac{2}{3}$ by answering 1 to 3.

1. Show 1, $\frac{4}{5}$, and $\frac{2}{3}$ with fraction strips.

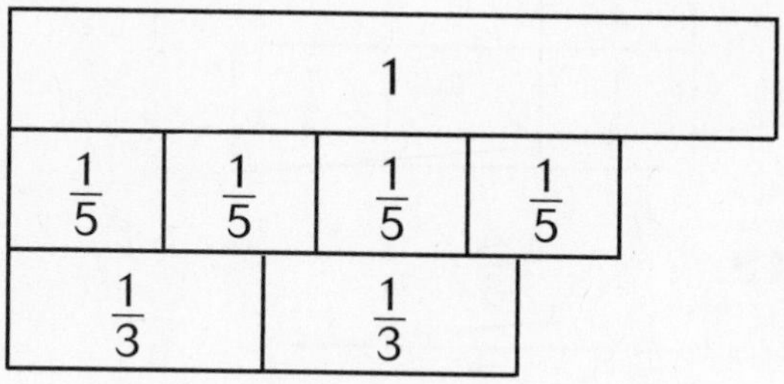

2. Compare. Which is greater in total length, $\frac{4}{5}$ or $\frac{2}{3}$? ________

3. Since $\frac{4}{5}$ is longer than $\frac{2}{3}$, $\frac{4}{5}$ is **greater than** $\frac{2}{3}$. Write >, <, or =.

$\frac{4}{5}$ ◯ $\frac{2}{3}$

Compare $\frac{1}{10}$ and $\frac{1}{4}$ by answering 4 to 6.

4. Show 1, $\frac{1}{10}$, and $\frac{1}{4}$ with fraction strips.

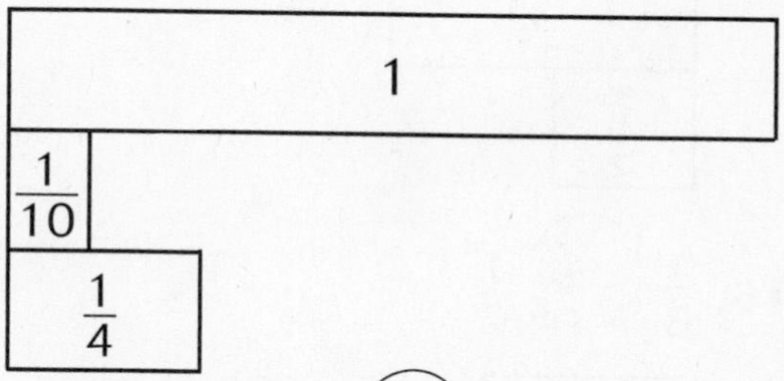

5. Compare. Which is greater in total length, $\frac{1}{10}$ or $\frac{1}{4}$? ________

6. Since $\frac{1}{10}$ is shorter than $\frac{1}{4}$, $\frac{1}{10}$ is **less than** $\frac{1}{4}$. Write >, <, or =.

$\frac{1}{10}$ ◯ $\frac{1}{4}$

Compare $\frac{2}{5}$ and $\frac{4}{10}$ by answering 7 to 9.

7. Show 1, $\frac{2}{5}$, and $\frac{4}{10}$ with fraction strips.

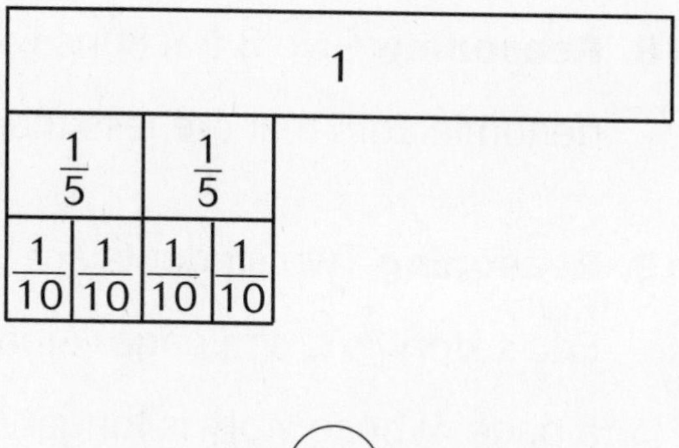

8. Compare. Which is greater in total length, $\frac{2}{5}$ or $\frac{4}{10}$?

____

9. Since $\frac{2}{5}$ and $\frac{4}{10}$ are the same length, $\frac{2}{5}$ is **equal to** $\frac{4}{10}$. Write >, <, or =.

$\frac{2}{5}$ ◯ $\frac{4}{10}$

© Pearson Education, Inc.

Name ______________________________

Using Models to Compare Fractions (continued)

Compare. Write <, >, or =.

10. $\frac{1}{4}$ ◯ $\frac{3}{4}$

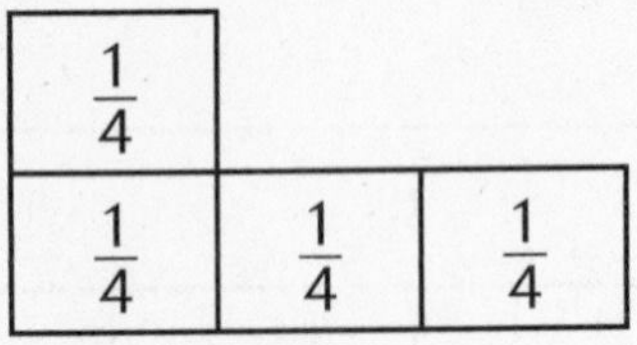

11. $\frac{3}{4}$ ◯ $\frac{2}{8}$

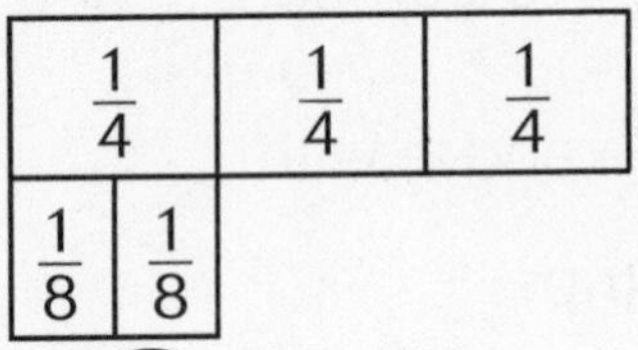

12. $\frac{2}{3}$ ◯ $\frac{4}{6}$

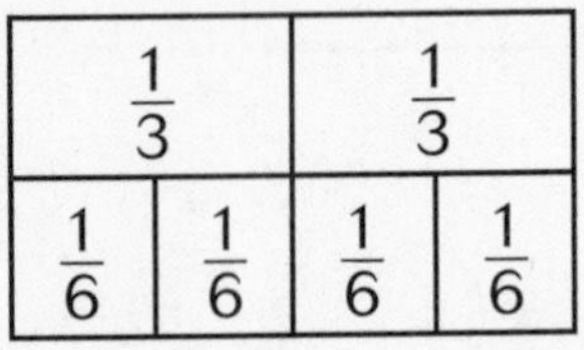

13. $\frac{1}{5}$ ◯ $\frac{5}{10}$

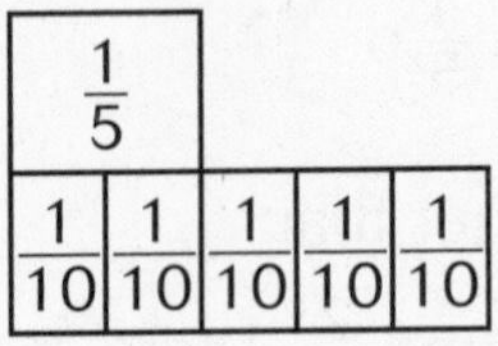

14. $\frac{1}{2}$ ◯ $\frac{1}{5}$

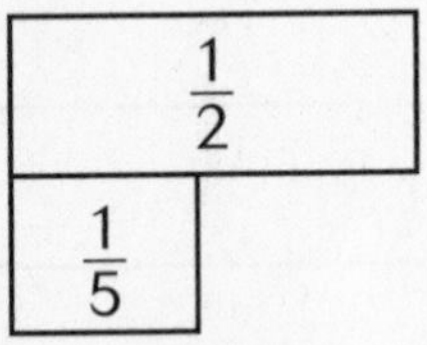

15. $\frac{7}{8}$ ◯ $\frac{3}{4}$

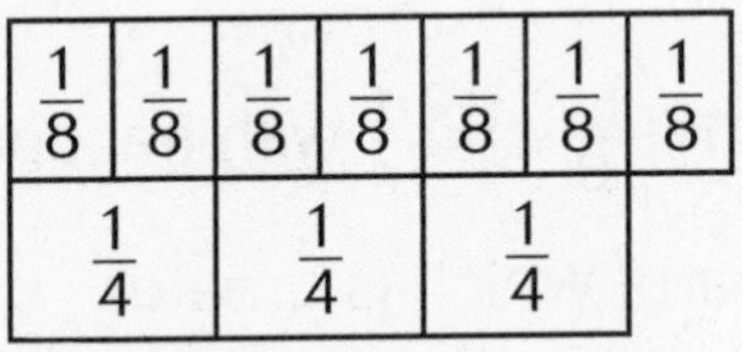

16. $\frac{2}{6}$ ◯ $\frac{1}{2}$

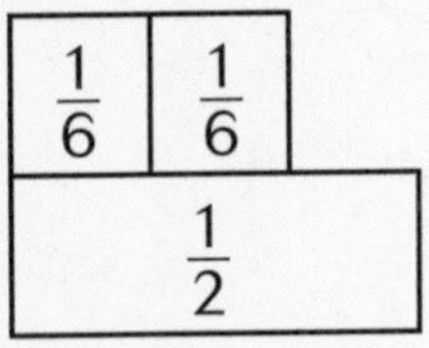

17. $\frac{3}{5}$ ◯ $\frac{1}{4}$

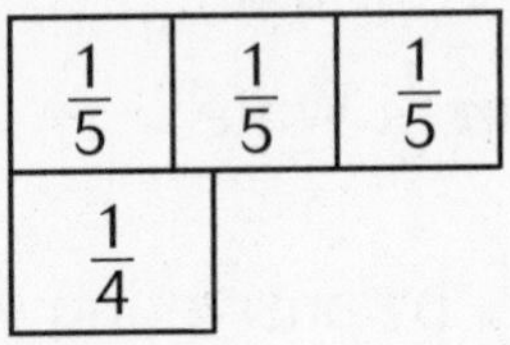

18. Reasoning Give 3 fractions with different denominators that are less than $\frac{4}{6}$. ______________________

19. Reasoning Two students are writing stories. Eric's story is $\frac{2}{3}$ of a page. Alba's story is $\frac{4}{6}$ of a page. Whose story is longer? ______________________

© Pearson Education, Inc.

Name ______________________________

Using Models to Find Equivalent Fractions

Materials fraction strips

Find a fraction equivalent to $\frac{3}{4}$ by answering 1 to 3.

1. Show a 1 and $\frac{3}{4}$ with fraction strips.

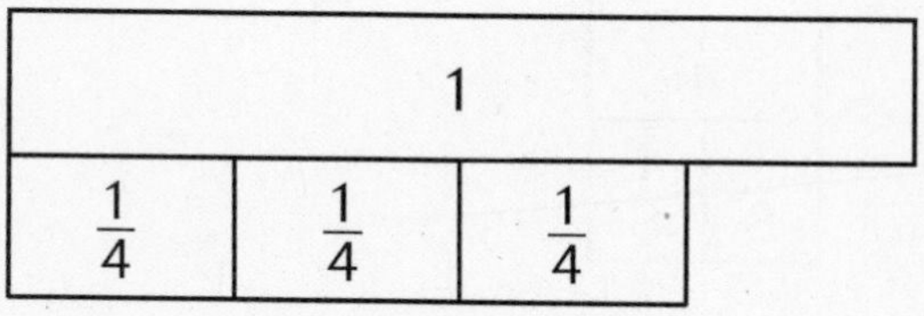

2. How many $\frac{1}{8}$ strips does it take to equal $\frac{3}{4}$? ______

$\frac{3}{4} = \frac{\square}{8}$

3. So, $\frac{3}{4}$ is equal to six $\frac{1}{8}$ strips.

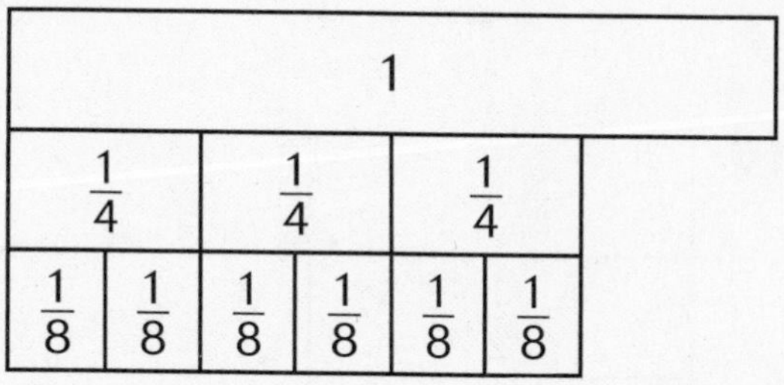

Find the missing number in $\frac{1}{2} = \frac{?}{10}$, by answering 4 to 7.

The denominators of the fractions tell which fraction strips to use.

4. Show 1 and $\frac{1}{2}$ with fraction strips.

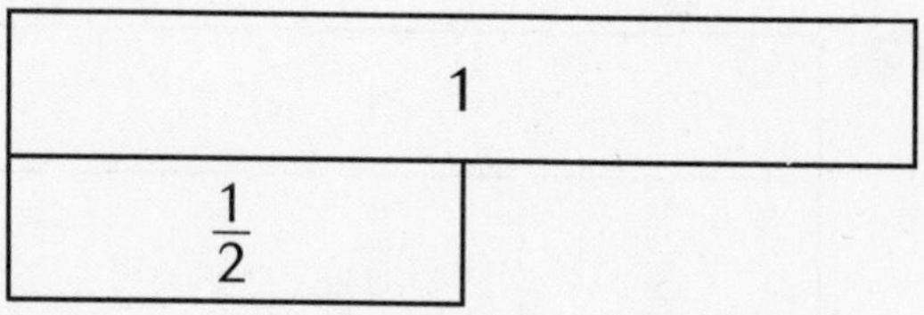

5. What is the denominator of the second fraction? ______

6. Since the denominator of the second fraction is 10, find the number of $\frac{1}{10}$ strips equal to $\frac{1}{2}$. ______

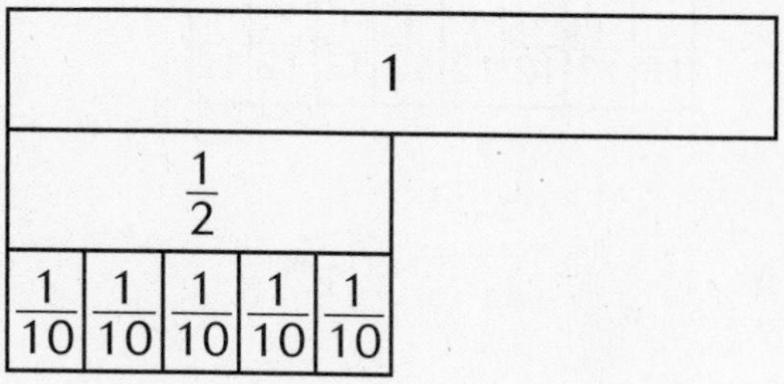

7. So, $\frac{1}{2}$ is equal to five $\frac{1}{10}$ strips.

$\frac{1}{2} = \frac{\square}{10}$

© Pearson Education, Inc.

Name ______________________________

Using Models to Find Equivalent Fractions (continued)

Complete each number sentence.

8.

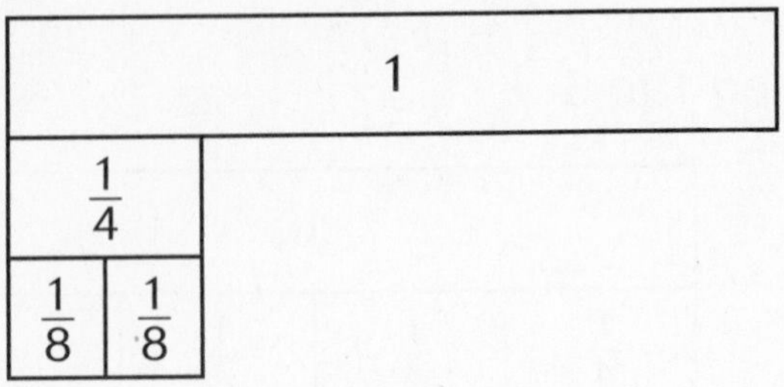

$\frac{1}{4} = \frac{\_\_\_}{8}$

9.

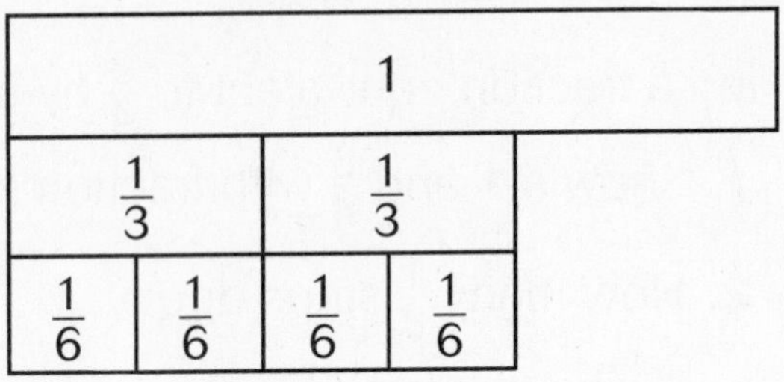

$\frac{2}{3} = \frac{\_\_\_}{6}$

10.

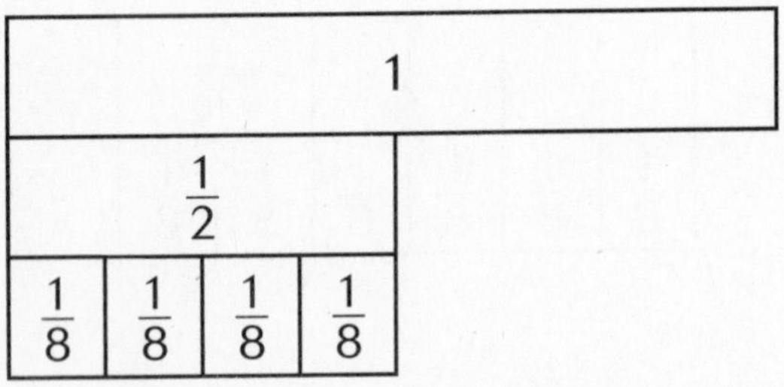

$\frac{1}{2} = \frac{\_\_\_}{8}$

11.

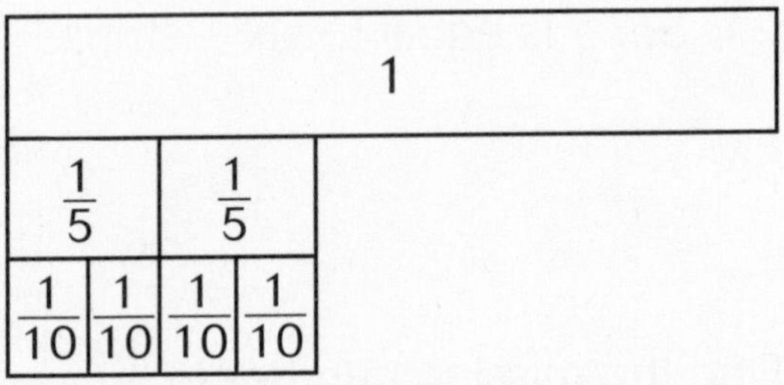

$\frac{2}{5} = \frac{\_\_\_}{10}$

12.

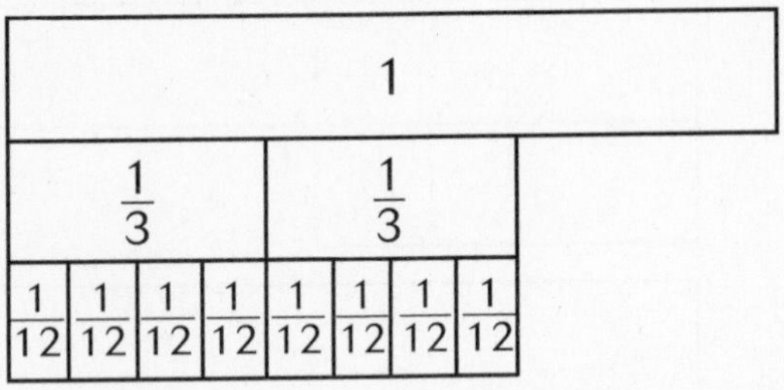

$\frac{2}{3} = \frac{\_\_\_}{12}$

13.

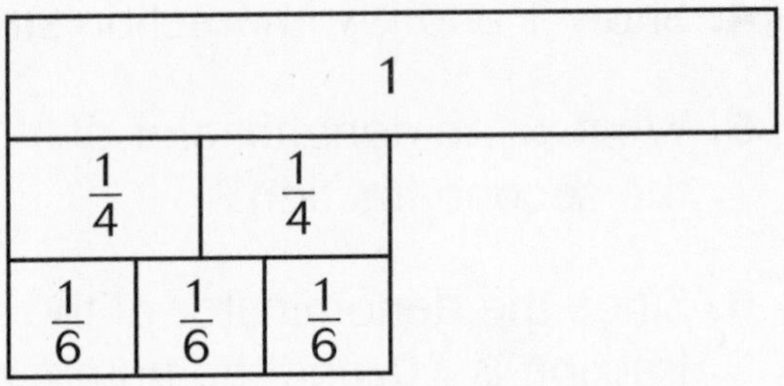

$\frac{2}{4} = \frac{\_\_\_}{6}$

14. Reasoning On Tuesday, $\frac{2}{3}$ of the class time was spent on math projects. How many *sixths* of the class time was spent on math projects? ________

© Pearson Education, Inc.

Name ______________________

Repeating Patterns

Materials pattern blocks or shapes cut out of colored paper (10 orange squares, 10 green triangles, 10 red trapezoids) for each pair of students; 24 index cards (eight labeled 2, eight labeled 3, and eight labeled 4) for each pair of students

Look at the pattern of shapes.

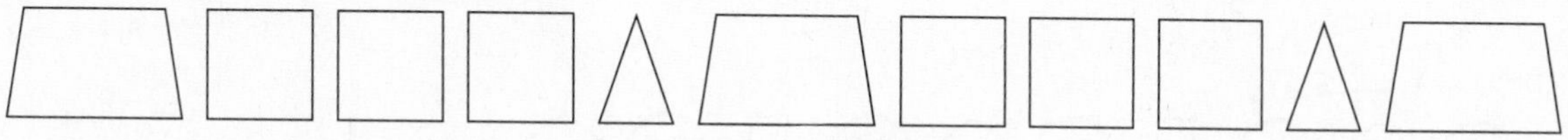

1. Work with your partner to show the pattern. What is the next shape? ______

2. Continue the pattern. What is the 14th shape? ______

3. What is the 16th shape? ______

4. Work with your partner and use the shapes to make a new pattern. Draw the pattern below. Draw the next four shapes.

Look at the pattern of numbers.

3	3	2	4	3	3	2	4	3

5. Work with your partner to show the pattern. What is the next number? ______

6. Continue the pattern. What is the 12th number? ______

7. What is the 15th number? ______

8. Work with your partner and use the numbers to make a new pattern. Write the pattern below. Write the next four numbers.

© Pearson Education, Inc.

Name ______________________________

Repeating Patterns (continued)

Draw the next three shapes to continue each pattern.

9. 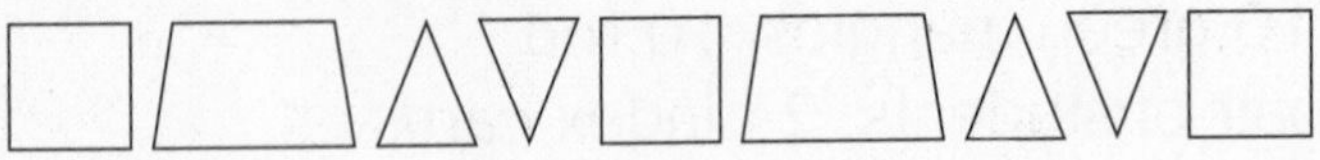 _____ _____ _____

10.  _____ _____ _____

11.  _____ _____ _____

Write the next three numbers to continue each pattern.

12. 1, 4, 6, 7, 1, 4, 6, 7, 1, 4, _____, _____, _____

13. 8, 8, 9, 8, 8, 9, 8, 8, 9, 8, _____, _____, _____

14. 3, 2, 0, 0, 3, 2, 0, 0, 3, 2, 0, _____, _____, _____

15. 4, 4, 6, 6, 8, 8, 4, 4, 6, 6, 8, 8, 4, _____, _____, _____

16. Create a pattern using all the shapes shown below.

_____ _____ _____ _____ _____ _____ _____ _____

17. Create a pattern using all the letters shown below.

T T T L L W W L W

© Pearson Education, Inc.

Name ______________________________

Using Multiplication to Compare

Materials 12 counters per student

Alicia has 2 stickers. Pedro has 3 times as many stickers as Alicia. How many stickers does Pedro have?

1. Show Alicia's stickers with counters.

2. Show Pedro's stickers with counters.

3. Write a multiplication sentence.

3	times	as many as Alicia has	equals	number Pedro has
↓	↓	↓	↓	↓
______	×	______	=	______

4. How many stickers does Pedro have? ______

Mia has 4 yo-yos. Flo has twice as many as Mia. How many yo-yos does Flo have?

The word **twice** in a word problem means 2 times as many.

5. Show Mia's yo-yos with counters.

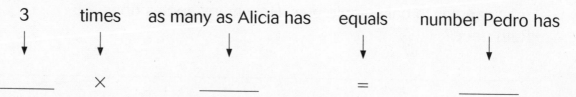

6. Show Flo's yo-yos with counters.

7. Write a multiplication sentence.

2	times	as many as Mia has	equals	number Flo has
↓	↓	↓	↓	↓
______	×	______	=	______

8. How many yo-yos does Flo have? ______

© Pearson Education, Inc.

Name ____________________

Using Multiplication to Compare (continued)

Solve. You may use drawings or counters to help.

9. Janos has 3 stickers. Lucy has twice as many stickers as Janos. How many stickers does Lucy have?

____

10. Rob has 4 model airplanes. Julio has 3 times as many model airplanes as Rob. How many model airplanes does Julio have?

____

11. Mr. King has 5 apples left in his store. Ruth needs twice as many apples to bake apple pies. How many apples does Ruth need?

____

Use the recipe to answer Exercises 12–15.

Fruit Smoothie

3 large bananas
2 cups strawberries
1 cup orange juice
1 cup cranberry juice
1 cup ice cubes

Blend until smooth.
Makes 5 servings.

12. The recipe serves 5 people. Joan wants to make the recipe for 15 people. How many times more is this?

____

13. How many bananas will Joan need to make the recipe for 15 people?

____

14. How many cups of strawberries will Joan need to make the recipe for 15 people?

____

15. Reasoning If Joan wants to make twice as much as the recipe in the chart, what will she need to do to all of the ingredients?

© Pearson Education, Inc.

Name ______________________________

Multiplying by 9

Learn how to multiply by 9 by answering 1 to 5.

1. Complete the table.

Fact	Product	Two Digits in the Product	Sum of the Two Digits in the Product
0 × 9 =	0	0 and 0	0 + 0 = 0
1 × 9 =	9	0 and 9	0 + 9 = 9
2 × 9 =	18		
3 × 9 =	27	2 and 7	2 + 7 = 9
4 × 9 =	36		
5 × 9 =	45	4 and 5	
6 × 9 =	54		
7 × 9 =	63		
8 × 9 =	72		
9 × 9 =	81		8 + 1 = 9

2. Reasoning Besides the product of 0 × 9, what pattern do you see in the sums of the digits of each product?

3. Look at the number being multiplied by 9 in each product and the tens digit of that product.

When 3 is multiplied by 9, what is the tens digit of the product? ________.

When 6 is multiplied by 9, what is the tens digit of the product? ________.

© Pearson Education, Inc.

Name ______________________

Multiplying by 9 (continued)

4. **Reasoning** Complete to describe the pattern you see in the tens digits of the products when a factor is multiplied by 9.

The tens digit of the product is ______ less than the other factor.

5. Complete the following to find 7×9.

The tens digit is $7 - 1 =$ ______.

The ones digit is $9 - 6 =$ ______.

So, $7 \times 9 =$ ______ and $9 \times 7 =$ ______.

Find each product.

6. 1×9

7. 9×2

8. 9×4

9. 9×0

10. 6×9

11. 9×9

12. 8×9

13. 5×9

14. 9×7

15. 3×9

16. 2×9

17. 9×6

18. **Reasoning** Joshua and his sister have each saved $9. They wish to buy a new game that costs $20. If they put their savings together, do they have enough money to buy the game?

19. **Reasoning** Jane said that $7 \times 9 = 62$. Explain how you know this is incorrect.

© Pearson Education, Inc.

Name ______________________________

Multiplying Three Numbers

Does it matter how you multiply 5 × 2 × 3? Answer 1–8 to find out.

To show the factors you are multiplying first, use parentheses as grouping symbols.

1. Group the first two factors together. (______ × ______) × 3
2. Multiply what is in the parentheses first. 5 × 2 = ______
3. Then, multiply the product of what is in parentheses by the third factor. 10 × 3 = ______
4. So, (5 × 2) × 3 = ______.
5. Start again and group the last two factors together. 5 × (______ × ______)
6. Multiply what is in the parentheses first. 2 × 3 = ______
7. Then, multiply 5 by the product of what is in parentheses. 5 × 6 = ______
8. So, 5 × (2 × 3) = ______.

It does not matter how the factors are grouped; the product will be the same.

9. 5 × (2 × 3) = (5 × ______) × 3

Find 3 × 2 × 4 two different ways.

10. Do the 3 × 2 first.

    3 × 2 = ______ 6 × 4 = ______ So, (3 × 2) × 4 = ______.

11. Do the 2 × 4 first.

    2 × 4 = ______ 3 × 8 = ______ So, 3 × (2 × 4) = ______.

© Pearson Education, Inc.

Name ________________________________

Multiplying Three Numbers (continued)

Find each product two different ways.

12. (1 × 3) × 6 = _____

1 × (3 × 6) = _____

13. (5 × 2) × 4 = _____

5 × (2 × 4) = _____

14. (2 × 4) × 1 = _____

2 × (4 × 1) = _____

15. (2 × 2) × 5 = _____

2 × (2 × 5) = _____

Find each product.

16. 2 × 4 × 3 = _____ **17.** 7 × 1 × 3 = _____ **18.** 3 × 3 × 2 = _____

19. 3 × 2 × 6 = _____ **20.** (4 × 2) × 2 = _____ **21.** 3 × (0 × 7) = _____

22. 1 × 7 × 9 = _____ **23.** 8 × (2 × 3) = _____ **24.** (2 × 5) × 6 = _____

25. 9 × 0 × 3 = _____ **26.** 4 × 5 × 1 = _____ **27.** (3 × 6) × 1 = _____

28. Reasoning When multiplying three numbers, if one of the factors is zero, what will the answer be? __________

29. A classroom of students is getting ready to take a test. There are 5 rows of desks in the room and 4 students are in each row. Each student is required to have 2 pencils. How many pencils are needed? __________

© Pearson Education, Inc.

Name ______________________________

Dividing by 8 and 9

Materials Have counters available for students to use.

You can use multiplication facts to help you divide.

At the museum, 32 students are divided into 8 equal groups. How many students are in each group?

Find 32 ÷ 8.

1. To find 32 ÷ 8, think about the related multiplication problem.

8 times what number equals 32? 8 × ______ = 32

2. Since you know 8 × 4 = 32, then you know 32 ÷ 8 = ______.

3. How many students are in each group at the museum? ______ students

Find 36 ÷ 9.

4. To find 36 ÷ 9, think about the related multiplication problem.

9 times what number equals 36? 9 × ______ = 36

5. Since you know 9 × 4 = 36, then you know 36 ÷ 9 = ______.

Find $8\overline{)80}$.

6. To find $8\overline{)80}$, think about the related multiplication problem.

8 times what number equals 80? 8 × ______ = 80

7. Since you know 8 × 10 = 80, then you know $8\overline{)80}$ = ______.

8. Reasoning Explain how to find 56 ÷ 8.

© Pearson Education, Inc.

Name ____________________

Dividing by 8 and 9 (continued)

Use the multiplication fact to find each quotient.

9. $8 \times 2 = 16$

$16 \div 8 =$ ______

10. $9 \times 5 = 45$

$45 \div 9 =$ ______

11. $8 \times 3 = 24$

$24 \div 8 =$ ______

12. $9 \times 6 = 54$

$54 \div 9 =$ ______

13. $8 \times$ ______ $= 32$

$32 \div 8 =$ ______

14. $8 \times$ ______ $= 48$

$48 \div 8 =$ ______

15. $9 \times$ ______ $= 27$

$27 \div 9 =$ ______

16. $9 \times$ ______ $= 90$

$90 \div 9 =$ ______

17. $8 \times$ ______ $= 72$

$72 \div 8 =$ ______

Find each quotient.

18. $9\overline{)63}$

19. $8\overline{)32}$

20. $9\overline{)36}$

21. $8\overline{)64}$

22. $9\overline{)81}$

23. $8\overline{)16}$

24. $9\overline{)45}$

25. $8\overline{)56}$

26. $8\overline{)40}$

27. Reasoning If you know that $8 \times 12 = 96$, then what is $96 \div 8$? ______

28. Nine friends go to lunch and split the $54 ticket evenly. How much does each friend pay? ______

© Pearson Education, Inc.

Name ______________________________

0 and 1 in Division

Think about related multiplication facts to help you divide.

Find 5 ÷ 1.

1. Think: 1 times what number equals 5? $1 \times$ _______ $= 5$

2. Since you know $1 \times 5 = 5$, then you know $5 \div 1 =$ _______.

3. If Karina had 5 oranges to put equally in 1 basket, how many oranges would go in each basket? _______ oranges

Find 9 ÷ 1.

4. $1 \times$ _______ $= 9$ So, $9 \div 1 =$ _______.

5. What is the result when any number is divided by 1? ____________

Find 0 ÷ 7.

6. Think: 7 times what number equals 0? $7 \times$ _______ $= 0$

7. Since you know $7 \times 0 = 0$, then you know $0 \div 7 =$ _______.

8. If Karina had 0 oranges to put equally in 7 baskets, how many oranges would go in each basket? _______ oranges

Find 0 ÷ 2.

9. $2 \times$ _______ $= 0$ So, $0 \div 2 =$ _______.

10. What is the result when zero is divided by any number (except 0)? _______

Find 5 ÷ 0.

11. **Reasoning** If Karina had 5 oranges to put equally in 0 baskets, how many oranges would go in each basket? Explain.

You cannot divide a number by 0.

© Pearson Education, Inc.

Name ______________________________

0 and 1 in Division (continued)

Find 4 ÷ 4.

12. Think: 4 times what number equals 4? 4 × _______ = 4

13. Since you know 4 × 1 = 4, then you know 4 ÷ 4 = _______.

14. If Karina had 4 oranges to put equally in 4 baskets, how many oranges would go in each basket? _______ orange

Find 8 ÷ 8.

15. 8 × _______ = 8 So, 8 ÷ 8 = _______.

16. What is the result when any number (except 0) is divided by itself? _______

Find each quotient.

17. 4 ÷ 1 = _______ **18.** 0 ÷ 5 = _______ **19.** 6 ÷ 6 = _______

20. $3\overline{)0}$ **21.** $9\overline{)9}$ **22.** $5\overline{)5}$

23. $1\overline{)6}$ **24.** $1\overline{)1}$ **25.** $8\overline{)0}$

26. Reasoning Use the rule for division by 1 to find 247 ÷ 1. Explain.

27. Larry has 3 friends who would like some cookies but he has no cookies to give them. How many cookies can Larry give each friend?

© Pearson Education, Inc.

Name ______________________________

Using Mental Math to Add

Materials place-value blocks: 6 tens and 12 ones per pair

Find the sum of 26 and 42 by breaking apart each addend.

1. Show 26 with place value blocks.

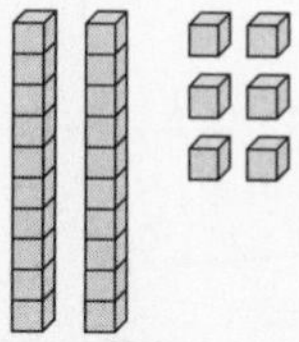

2 tens = ________ 6 ones = ________

2. Show 42 with place value blocks.

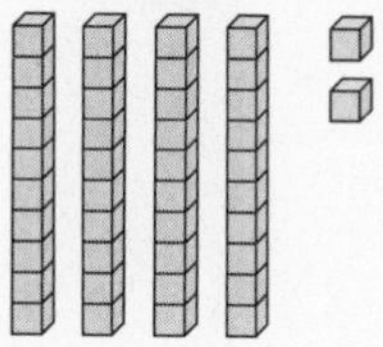

4 tens = ________ 2 ones = ________

3. Add the tens. 20 + ________ = ________

Add the ones. 6 + ________ = ________

4. Add the tens and the ones together. ________ + 8 = ________

So, 26 + 42 = ________.

Find the sum of 18 and 34 by breaking apart the second addend.

5. Show 18 with place value blocks.

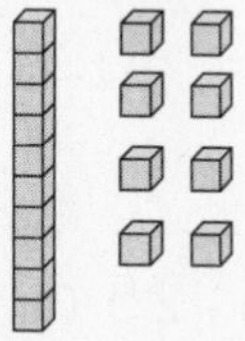

1 ten = ________ 8 ones = ________

6. Show 34 with place value blocks.

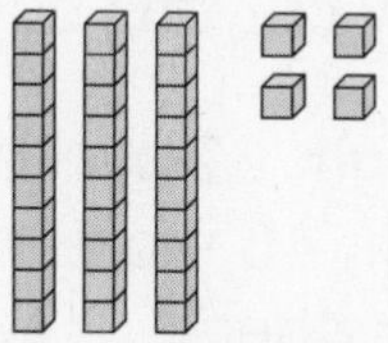

3 tens = ________ 4 ones = ________

7. Take 2 ones from the 34 and add them to 18. What sum do you have now?

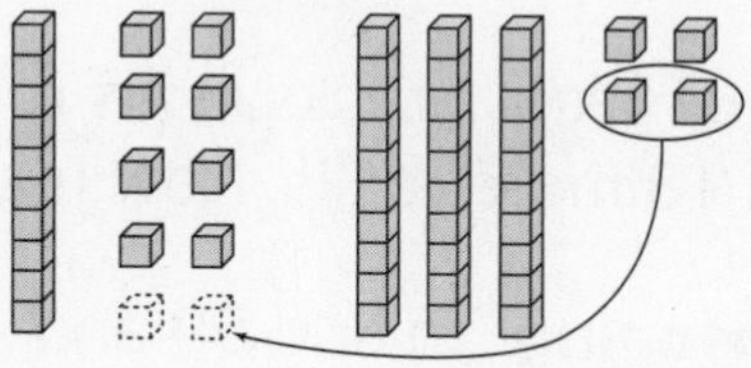

18 + 34 = ________ + ________

8. Add. 20 + 32 = ________

So, 18 + 34 = ________.

© Pearson Education, Inc.

Name ______________________________

Using Mental Math to Add (continued)

Find each sum using mental math.

9. 22 + 56 = ______ **10.** 37 + 24 = ______ **11.** 43 + 36 = ______

12. 55 + 32 = ______ **13.** 23 + 21 = ______ **14.** 43 + 44 = ______

15. 44 + 34 = ______ **16.** 52 + 32 = ______ **17.** 45 + 4 = ______

18. 45 + 34 = ______ **19.** 37 + 51 = ______ **20.** 23 + 46 = ______

21. 64 + 23 = ______ **22.** 26 + 73 = ______ **23.** 35 + 63 = ______

24. 88 + 26 = ______ **25.** 39 + 45 = ______ **26.** 57 + 16 = ______

Fill in the blanks to show how to add mentally.

27. 35 + 12 = 40 + _____ = _____ **28.** 83 + 46 = _____ + 9 = _____

29. 49 + 16 = 50 + _____ = _____ **30.** 78 + 24 = 80 + _____ = _____

31. Reggie has 25 crayons. Brett gives him 14 more. How many crayons does he have now? ______

32. Darla bought 32 stickers on Monday. Two days later she bought 46 more. How many stickers does she have altogether? ______

33. Rafael has 41 rocks in his rock collection. His friend gave him 18 more rocks. How many rocks did he have then? ______

34. Reasoning To add 59 and 16, Juan took one from the 16 to make the 59 a 60. What number should he add to 60? ______

35. Reasoning To add 24 and 52, Ashley first added 24 and 50. What numbers should she add next? ______

© Pearson Education, Inc.

Name ______________________________

Using Mental Math to Subtract

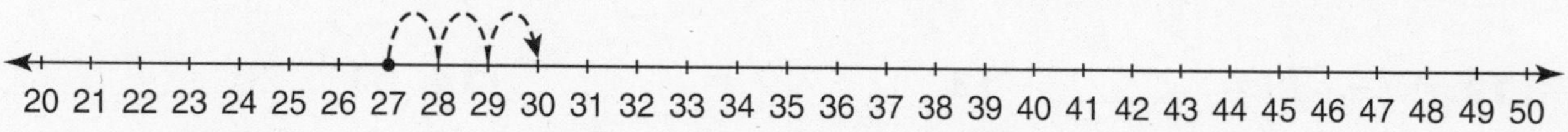

Find the difference of 46 − 27 one way, by doing the following.

1. Round the number being subtracted.

27 rounded to the nearest ten is ________.

2. Solve the new problem.

46 − 30 = ________

3. Since you rounded 27 to 30, did you subtract too much or too little from 46? ____________

4. How much more is 30 than 27? ________

5. Since 30 is 3 **more than** 27, you subtracted too much. You must now add 3 to the difference in Question 2.

16 + 3 = ________

6. So, 46 − 27 = ________.

Find the difference of 46 − 27 another way, by doing the following.

7. How much needs to be added to the 27 so that it forms a ten? 27 + ________ = 30

8. Since you added 3 to 27, you need to add 3 to 46. 46 + 3 = ________

9. Solve the new problem. 49 − 30 = ________

10. So, 46 − 27 = ________.

11. How can you change 52 − 18 to make it easier to subtract mentally?

52 − 18 = ________ − 20 = ________

© Pearson Education, Inc.

Name ________________________________

Using Mental Math to Subtract (continued)

Find each difference using mental math.

12. 57 − 38 = ______ **13.** 32 − 17 = ______ **14.** 61 − 26 = ______

15. 85 − 29 = ______ **16.** 43 − 28 = ______ **17.** 67 − 42 = ______

18. 32 − 18 = ______ **19.** 52 − 46 = ______ **20.** 41 − 18 = ______

21. 28 − 16 = ______ **22.** 55 − 33 = ______ **23.** 86 − 23 = ______

24. 39 − 26 = ______ **25.** 57 − 28 = ______ **26.** 93 − 34 = ______

27. 62 − 47 = ______ **28.** 33 − 16 = ______ **29.** 84 − 35 = ______

30. Reasoning To find 56 − 48, add the same amount to both numbers to make it easier to subtract. Explain what you did to solve the problem.

56 − 48

31. Lupe has $32. She buys a present for her mother and gets $9 in change. How much money did she spend on the present? ______

32. Reasoning Becca subtracts 73 − 26 mentally by thinking: "73 − 30 = 43, and 43 − 4 = 39. The answer is 39." What did she do wrong? Explain.

© Pearson Education, Inc.

Name ______________________________

Adding Two-Digit Numbers

Materials place-value blocks: 6 tens and 13 ones per pair

There are 25 boys and 38 girls at the library. How many children total?

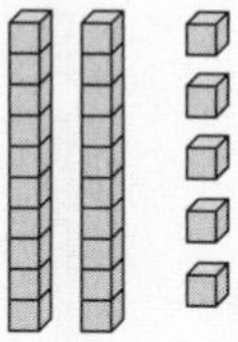

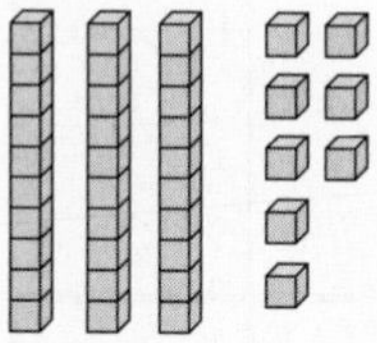

1. Show 25 using place-value blocks.

2. Show 38 using place-value blocks.

3. Add 25 + 38 to find the total children.

Add the ones. 5 + 8 = ________

4. Do you have more then 10 ones? ________

5. Since you have 13 ones, regroup them into tens and ones

13 ones = ________ ten and ________ ones

	Tens	Ones
	☐	☐
	2	5
+	3	8

6. Record the 3 ones at the bottom of the ones column of the Tens and Ones chart. Record the 1 ten at the top of the tens column.

7. Add the tens. Add the 1 ten that you regrouped, the 2 tens from the 25, and the 3 tens from the 38.

1 ten + 2 tens + 3 tens = ________ tens

8. Record the tens at the bottom of the tens column of the Tens and Ones chart.

9. So, 25 + 38 = ________

How many children are at the library? ________.

10. Use place value-blocks and the Tens and Ones chart to add 46 + 29.

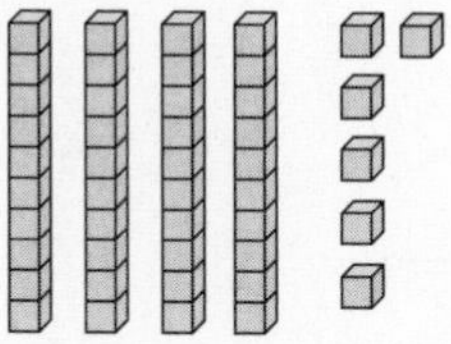

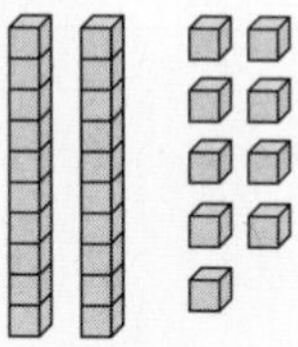

	Tens	Ones
	☐	☐
	4	6
+	2	9

© Pearson Education, Inc.

Name ______________________________

Add.

11.

	Tens	Ones
	1	3
+	2	8

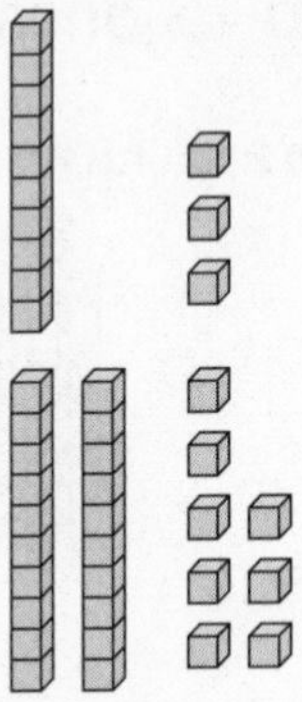

12.

	Tens	Ones
	2	4
+	2	9

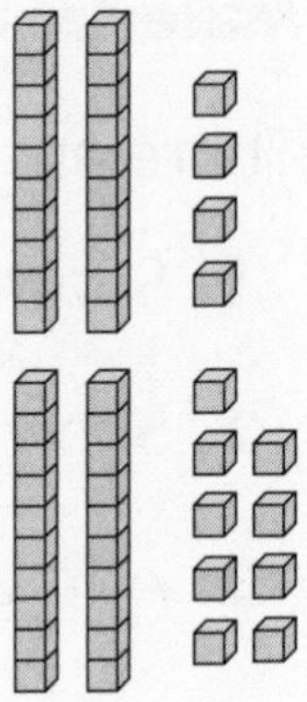

Add. Use a tens and ones chart if you like.

13. 58 + 17 = 75

14. 56 + 11

15. 18 + 19

16. 20 + 28

17. 46 + 45

18. 36 + 17

19. 17 + 49

20. 45 + 14

21. 32 + 66

22. 26 + 37

23. 22 + 65

24. 33 + 33

25. 21 + 39

26. 17 + 29

27. 36 + 16

28. 64 + 27

29. A puppy weighs 15 pounds. His mother weighs 65 pounds. How much do the puppy and his mother weigh together? ______________

30. Reasoning What number do you add to 19 to get 30? ________

© Pearson Education, Inc.

Name ______________________________

Subtracting Two-Digit Numbers

Materials place-value blocks: 3 tens and 20 ones per pair

There are 34 kittens and 16 puppies. How many more kittens than puppies?

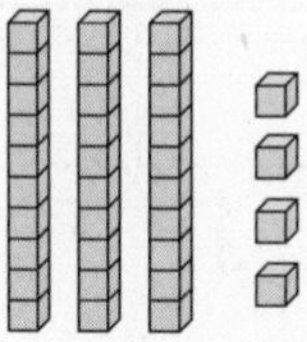

1. Show 34 with place-value blocks.

2. Do you have enough ones to take away 6 ones? ________

3. Regroup 1 ten into 10 ones. Show this with your place-value blocks.

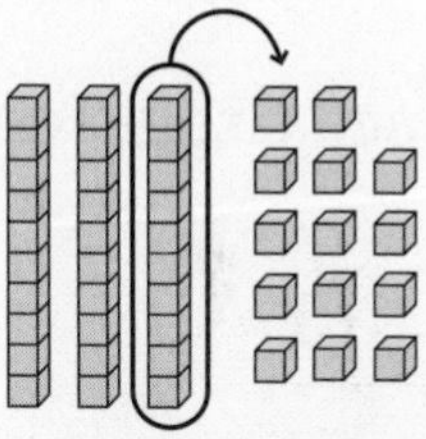

3 tens and 4 ones = ________ tens and 14 ones.

4. Cross out the 3 tens in the Tens and Ones chart and write 2 above it. Cross out the 4 ones and write 14 above it.

	Tens	Ones
	☐	☐
	~~3~~	~~4~~
−	1	6

5. Now, take away 6 ones and write the difference at the bottom of the ones column.

14 ones − 6 ones = ________ ones

6. Subtract the tens and write the difference at the bottom of the tens column.

2 tens − 1 ten = ________ ten

7. So, 34 − 16 = ________

How many more kittens than puppies are there? ________

8. Use place-value blocks and the Tens and Ones chart to subtract 56 − 27.

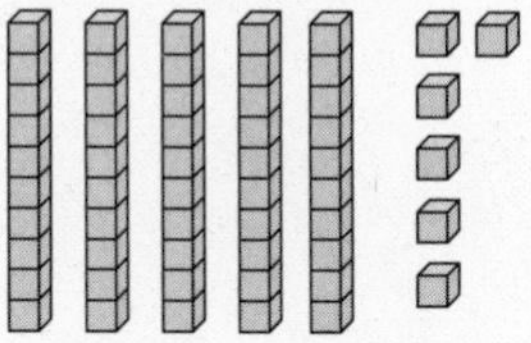

	Tens	Ones
	☐	☐
	~~5~~	~~6~~
−	2	7

© Pearson Education, Inc.

Name ______________________

Subtracting Two-Digit Numbers (continued)

Subtract.

9.

	Tens	Ones
	☐	☐
	4	2
−	1	9

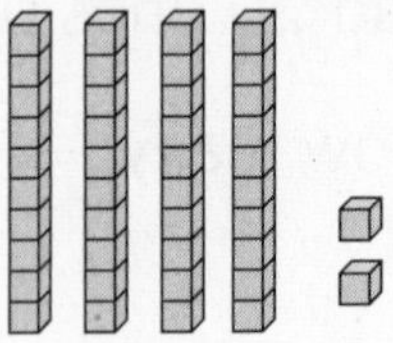

10.

	Tens	Ones
	☐	☐
	5	0
−	2	4

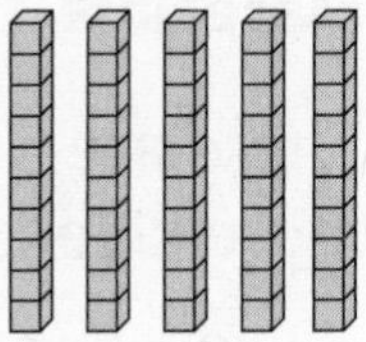

Subtract. Use a Tens and Ones chart if you like.

11. 35 − 17 = ____

12. 80 − 38 = ____

13. 45 − 39 = ____

14. 61 − 13 = ____

15. 74 − 45 = ____

16. 22 − 18 = ____

17. 50 − 32 = ____

18. 48 − 20 = ____

19. 95 − 69 = ____

20. 34 − 7 = ____

21. 61 − 26 = ____

22. 90 − 74 = ____

23. Thompson has 32 flowers. If he plants 18 flowers in the front yard, how many will he have left? ____________

24. Reasoning In which problem do you need to regroup to subtract, 53 − 28 or 58 − 23? Explain.

© Pearson Education, Inc.

Name ______________________________

Adding Three Numbers

Materials place-value blocks: 2 hundreds, 6 tens, and 14 ones per pair or group

How many total pieces of fruit are in a box containing 45 apples, 107 oranges, and 112 bananas?

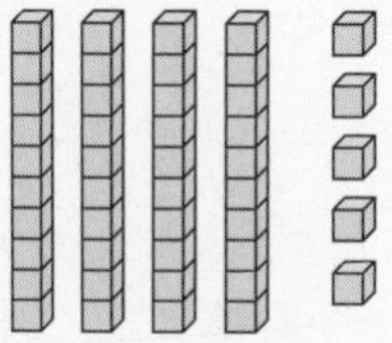

1. Show 45, 107, and 112 using place-value blocks.

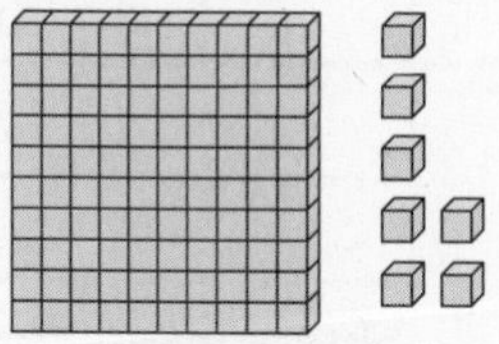

2. Add 45 + 107 + 112 to find the total pieces of fruit in the box.

3. Do you have more then 10 ones? ________
Add the ones.

5 ones + 7 ones + 2 ones = ________ ones

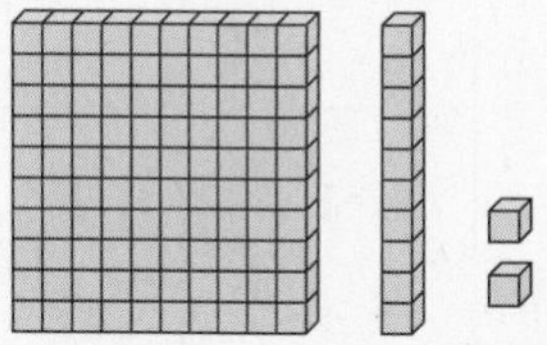

4. Since you have 14 ones, regroup them into tens and ones.

14 ones = ________ ten and ________ ones

5. Record the 4 ones at the bottom of the ones column of the Hundreds, Tens, and Ones chart. Record the 1 ten at the top of the tens column.

	Hundreds	Tens	Ones
	☐	☐	☐
		4	5
	1	0	7
+	1	1	2

6. Add the tens.

1 ten + 4 tens + 1 ten = ________ tens

7. Do you have more than 10 tens? ________

8. Record the tens at the bottom of the tens column of the chart.

9. Add the hundreds and record the value at the bottom of the hundreds column.

1 hundred + 1 hundred = ________ hundreds

10. So, 45 + 107 + 112 = ________

How many total pieces of fruit are in the box? ________

© Pearson Education, Inc.

Name ________________________________

Adding Three Numbers (continued)

Add.

11.

	Hundreds	Tens	Ones
	☐	☐	☐
	2	5	4
	1	2	9
+		6	2

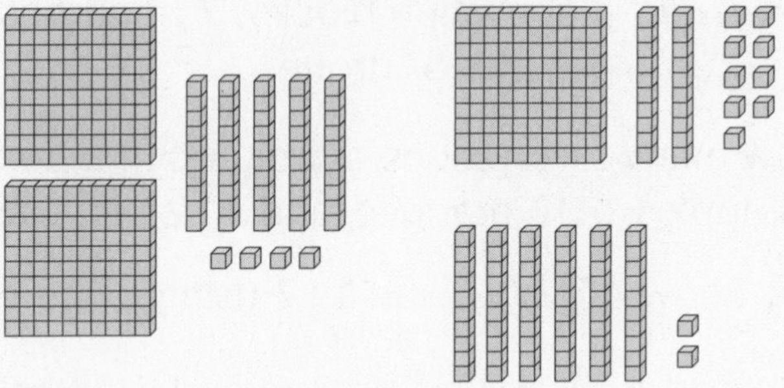

12.

	Hundreds	Tens	Ones
	☐	☐	☐
	1	1	7
	1	0	6
+		7	4

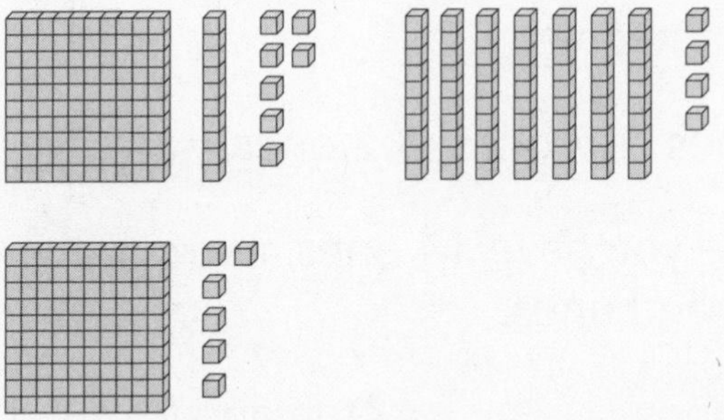

13. 123 + 365 + 50

14. 211 + 423 + 23

15. 23 + 45 + 14

16. 322 + 43 + 16

17. 335 + 125 + 32

18. 543 + 144 + 46

19. 613 + 205 + 64

20. 851 + 32 + 40

21. There were 234 books returned to the library on Monday, 109 books returned on Tuesday, and 41 books returned on Wednesday. How many books were retuned to the library in the three days? ________

22. Reasoning Write the smallest 2-digit number that when added to 345 and 133 would require regrouping of both the ones and the tens. ________

© Pearson Education, Inc.

Name ______________________________

Solid Figures

Materials power solids arranged in stations around the room

Find each solid to complete the tables below.

	Solid	Number of Faces	Number of Edges	Number of Vertices	Shapes of Faces
1.	Pyramid 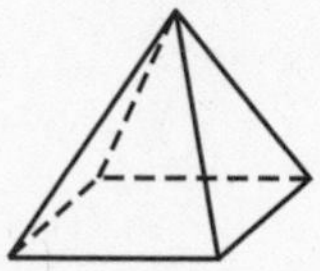	5	8	5	1 square 4 triangles
2.	Rectangular Prism 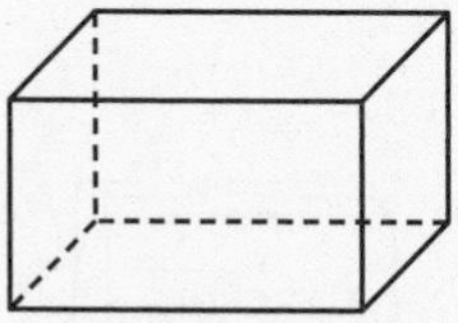				
3.	Cube 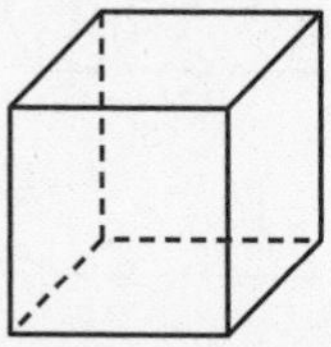				

Objects that roll do not have faces, edges, or vertices.

	Solid	Number of Flat Surfaces	Shape of Flat Surfaces
4.	Cone 	1	1 circle

© Pearson Education, Inc.

Name ______________________

Solid Figures (continued)

	Solid	Number of Flat Surfaces	Shape of Flat Surfaces
5.	Cylinder 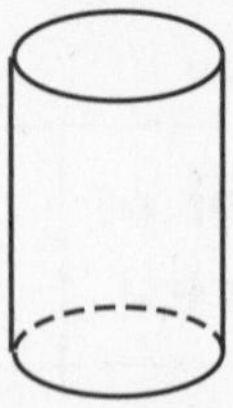		
6.	Sphere 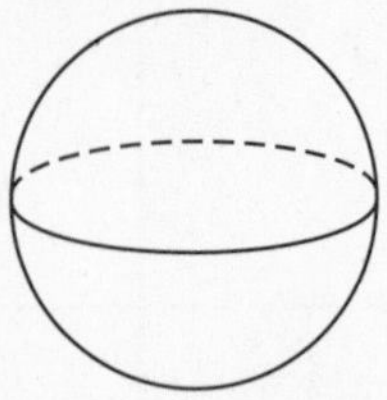		

Name the solid figure that each object looks like.

7. 

8. 

9. 

Use the solids in the table above to answer Exercises 10–12.

10. Which solid figure has 2 flat surfaces that are circles?

11. Which of the 6 solid figures has 6 rectangular faces?

12. Which 3 figures have no vertices?

13. Reasoning How are the sphere and cone alike?

© Pearson Education, Inc.

Name ______________________________

Acute, Right, and Obtuse Angles

Materials 1 inch square piece of paper for each student, crayons or markers

A *ray* is part of a line. The endpoint is the beginning of the ray, and the arrow shows it goes on forever.

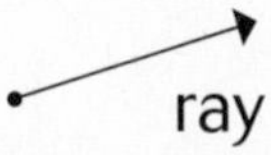

An *angle* is made by two rays that have the same endpoint. That endpoint is called the *vertex*.

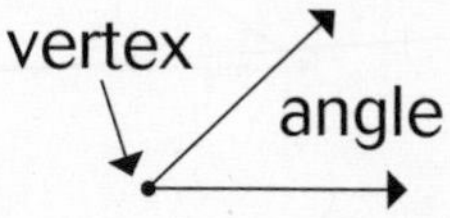

1. Color each ray of the angle at the right, a different color.

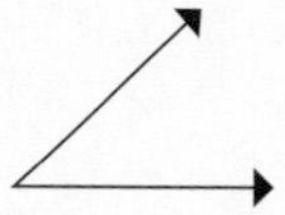

Place a side of your square on one ray, and the corner on the vertex for each angle in 2 to 4.

2. Reasoning *Right angles* are shown below. What do you notice about the openings of right angles?

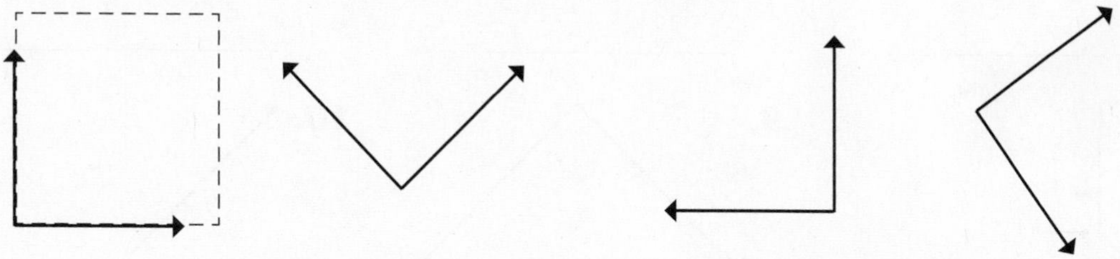

3. Reasoning *Obtuse angles* are shown below. What do you notice about the openings of obtuse angles?

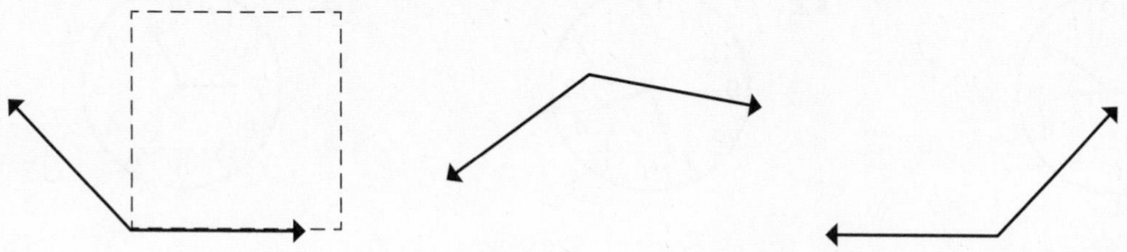

© Pearson Education, Inc.

Name ______________________________

Acute, Right, and Obtuse Angles (continued)

4. Reasoning *Acute angles* are shown below. What do you notice about the openings of acute angles?

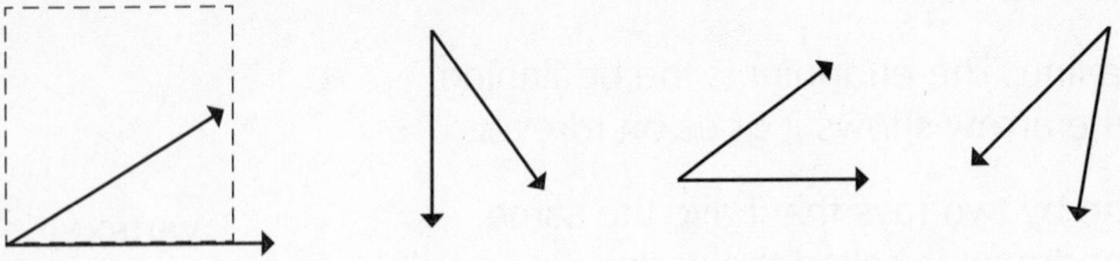

Write *ray, vertex, right angle, acute angle,* or *obtuse angle* to name each.

5. 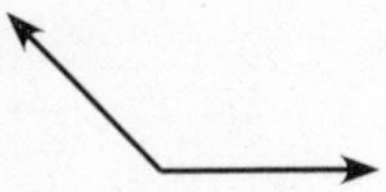 ______________

6. 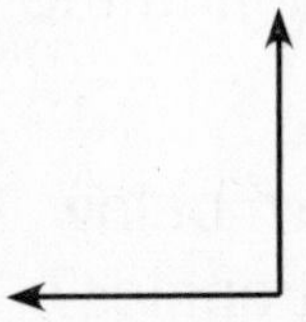 ______________

7. 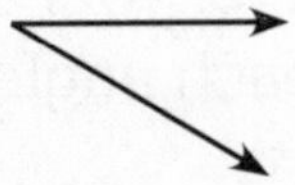 ______________

8. 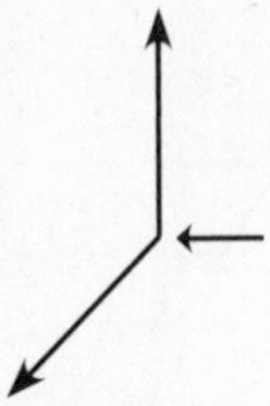 ______________

9. 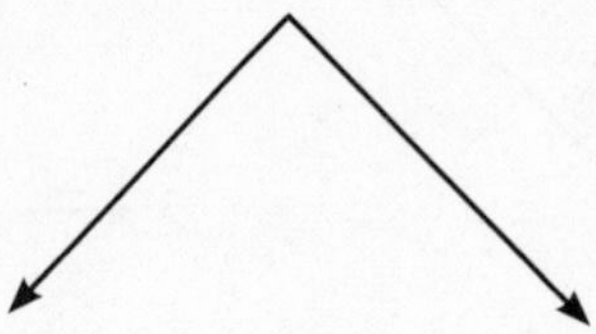 ______________

10. 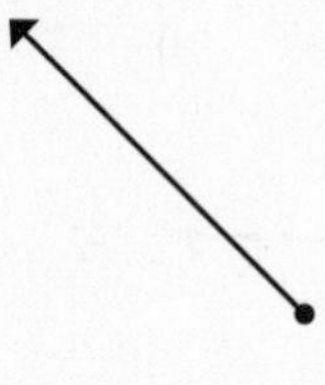 ______________

What kind of angle do the hands of each clock show?

11. 

____

12. 

____

13. 

____

© Pearson Education, Inc.

Name ______________________________

Polygons

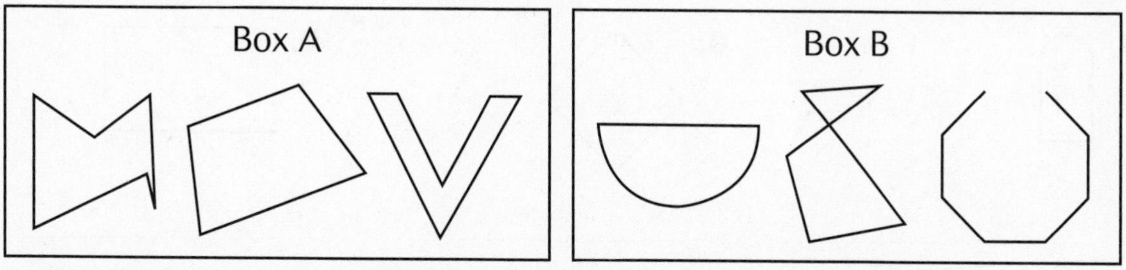

1. The figures in Box A are polygons. The figures in Box B are not. How are the figures in Box A different from those in Box B?

To be a polygon:

- All sides must be made of straight line segments.
- Line segments must only intersect at a vertex.
- The figure must be closed.

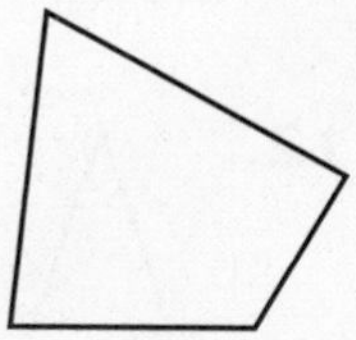

Polygons are named by the number of sides each has. Complete the table.

	Shape	Number of Sides	Number of Vertices	Name
2.	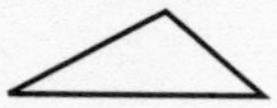			Triangle
3.				Quadrilateral
4.	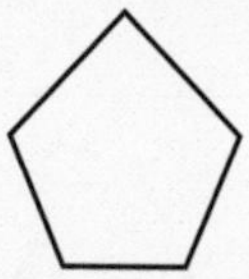			Pentagon
5.	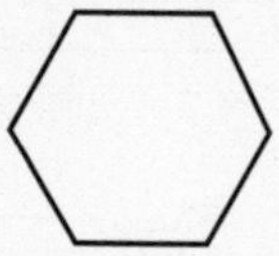			Hexagon
6.	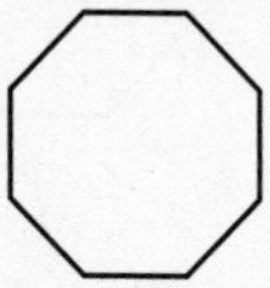			Octagon

© Pearson Education, Inc.

Name ______________________________

Polygons (continued)

Tell if each figure is a polygon. Write *yes* or *no*.

7. 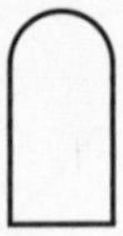

____

8. 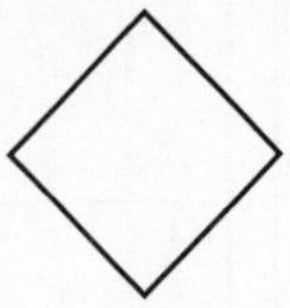

____

9. 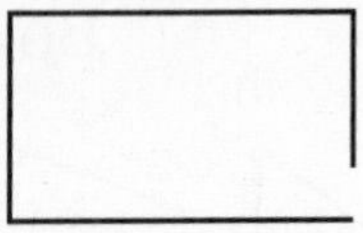

____

Name each polygon. Then tell the number of sides and the number of vertices each polygon has.

10. 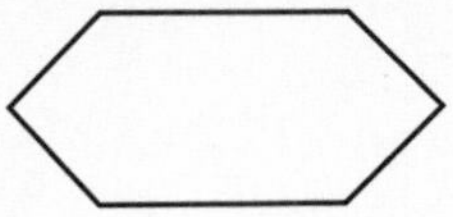

____

11. 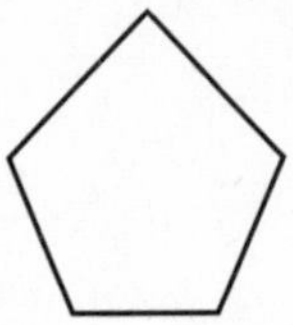

____

12. 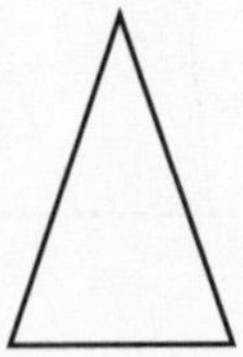

____

13. 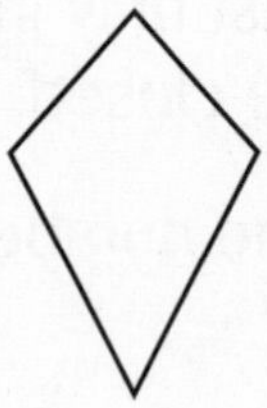

____

14. 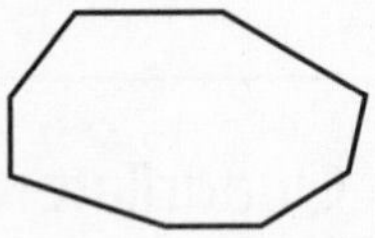

____

15. 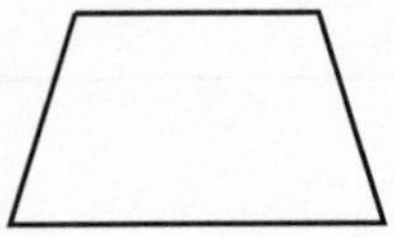

____

16. Reasoning What is the least number of sides a polygon can have? ______________

17. Reasoning A regular polygon is a polygon with all sides the same length. Circle the figure on the right that is a regular polygon.

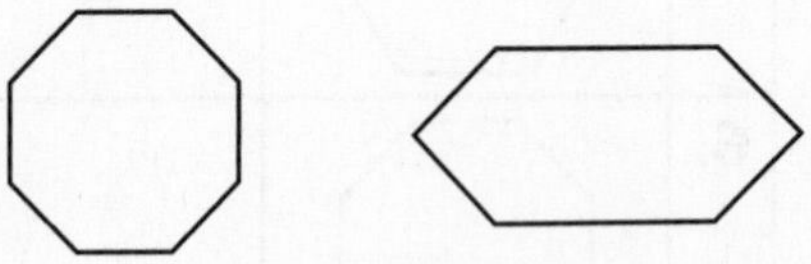

© Pearson Education, Inc.

Name ______________________________

Classifying Triangles Using Sides and Angles

Materials 2 yards of yarn, scissors, 6 sheets of construction paper, markers for each student and glue

Create a book about triangles by following 1 to 7.

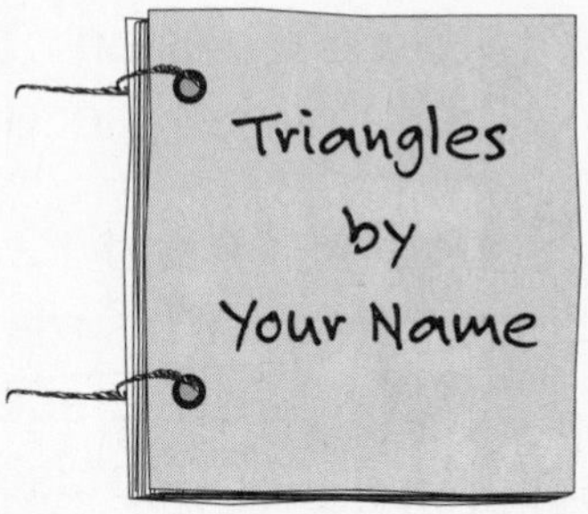

1. Put the pieces of construction paper together and fold them in half to form a book. Punch two holes in the side and use yarn to tie the book together. Write "Triangles" and your name on the cover.

Each two-page spread will be about one type of triangle. For each two page spread:

- Write the definition on the left page.
- Write the name of the triangle near the top of the right page.
- Create a triangle with yarn pieces and glue the yarn pieces under the name of the triangle to illustrate the triangle.

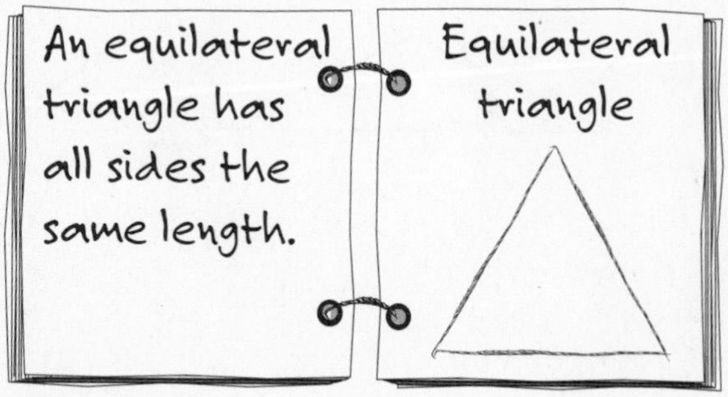

2. Pages 1 and 2 should be about an **equilateral triangle.** This triangle has 3 sides of equal length. So, your 3 yarn pieces should be cut to the same length.

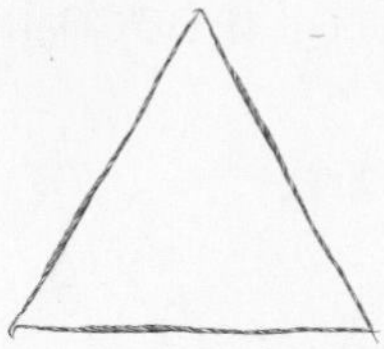

3. Pages 3 and 4 should be about an **isosceles triangle.** This triangles has at least two sides the same length. Cut 2 pieces of yarn the same length and glue them on the page at an angle. Cut and glue a third piece to complete the triangle.

4. Pages 5 and 6 should be about a **scalene triangle.** This triangle has no sides the same length. So your 3 yarn pieces can be cut to different lengths.

5. Pages 7 and 8 should be about a **right triangle.** This triangle has exactly one right angle. Two of your yarn pieces should be placed so that they form a right angle. Cut and glue a third piece to complete the triangle.

© Pearson Education, Inc.

Name ______________________________

Classifying Triangles Using Sides and Angles (continued)

6. Pages 9 and 10 should be about an **obtuse triangle.** This triangle has exactly one obtuse angle. Two pieces of yarn should be placed so that it forms an obtuse angle. Cut and glue down a third yarn piece to complete the triangle.

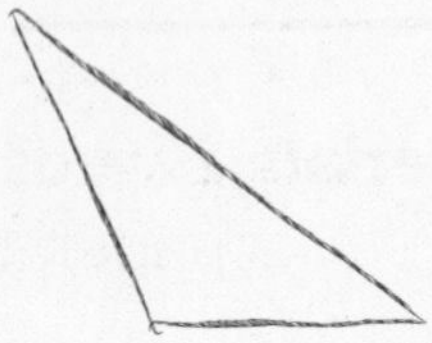

7. Pages 11 and 12 should be about an **acute triangle.** This triangle has three acute angles. Your 3 yarn pieces should be placed so that no right or obtuse angles are formed.

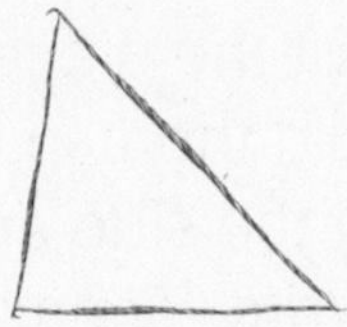

Tell if each triangle is equilateral, isosceles, or scalene.

8. 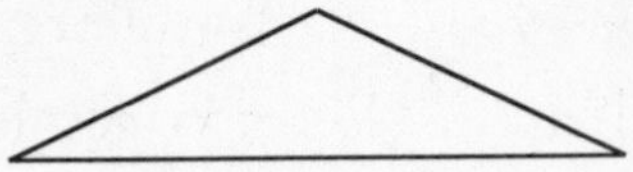

____

9. 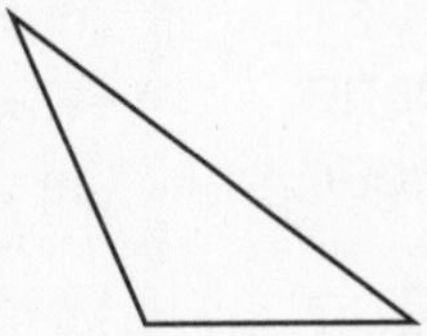

____

10. 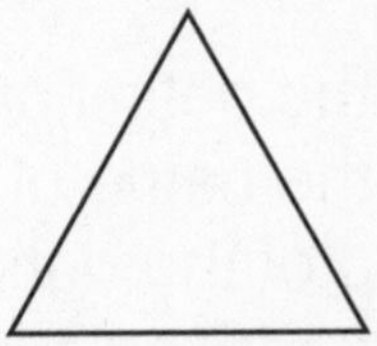

____

Tell if each triangle is right, acute, or obtuse.

11. 

____

12. 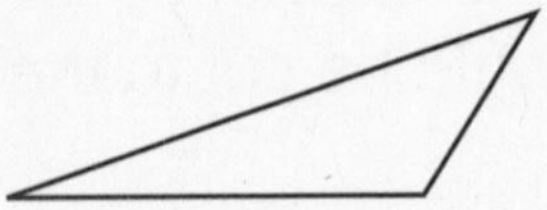

____

13. 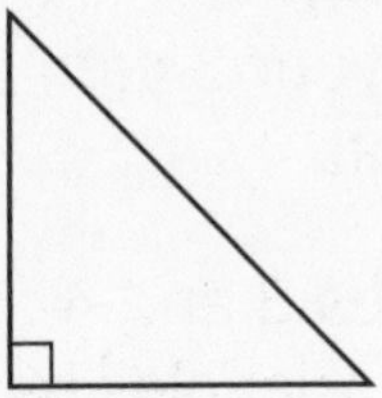

____

14 How many acute angles does an acute triangle have? ______________

15. Reasoning How many acute angles does a right triangle have? ______________

16. Describe this triangle by its sides and by its angles. (Hint: Give it two names.)

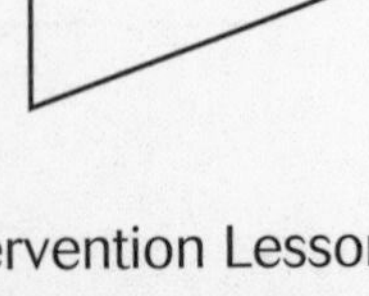

______________ ______________

© Pearson Education, Inc.

Name ______________________________

Quadrilaterals

Materials Have quadrilateral power shapes available for students who want to use them.

For 1 to 5 study each quadrilateral with your partner. Identify the types of angles. Compare the lengths of the sides. Then draw a line to match the quadrilateral with the best description. Descriptions can be used only once.

1. Trapezoid

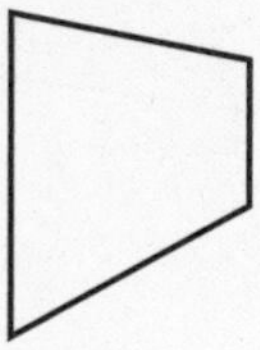

2. Parallelogram

3. Rectangle

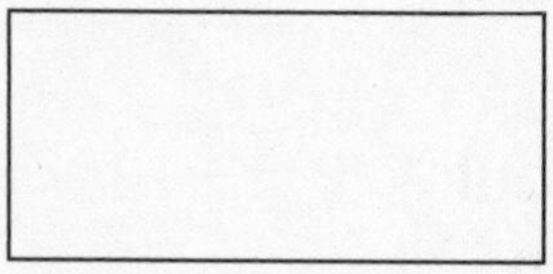

4. Square

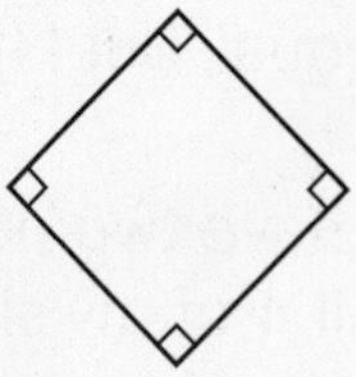

5. Rhombus

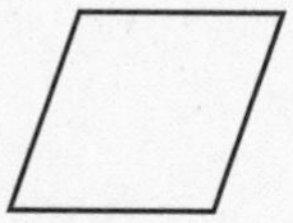

- Four right angles and all four sides the same length
- All sides are the same length
- Exactly one pair of parallel sides
- Two pairs of parallel sides
- Four right angles and opposite sides the same length

6. Reasoning What quadrilateral has four right angles and opposite sides the same length, and can also be called a rectangle? ______________

7. Reasoning What quadrilaterals have two pairs of parallel sides, and can also be called parallelograms?

____

© Pearson Education, Inc.

Name ______________________________

Quadrilaterals (continued)

For Exercises 8–13, circle squares red, rectangles blue, parallelograms green, rhombuses orange and trapezoids purple. Some quadrilaterals may be circled more than once.

8.

9.

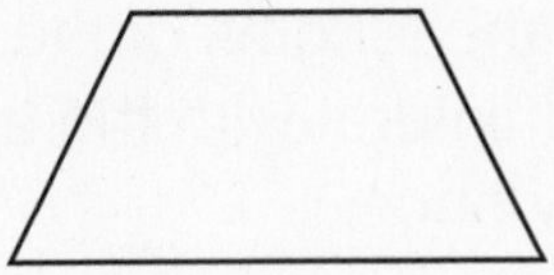

10.

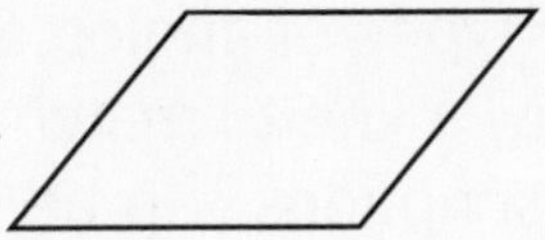

11.

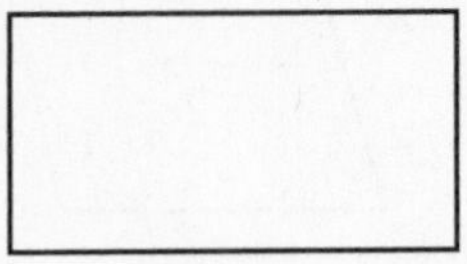

12.

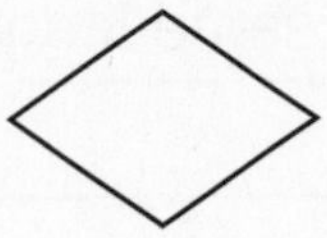

13.

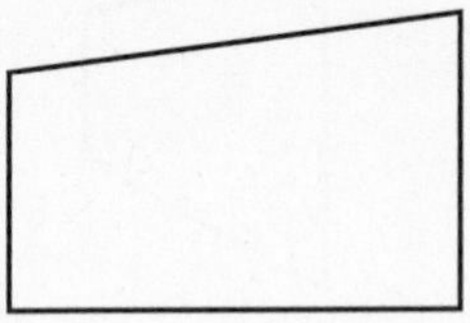

14. I have two pairs of parallel sides, and all of my sides are equal, but I have no right angles. What quadrilateral am I? ____________

15. I have two pairs of parallel sides and 4 right angles, but all 4 of my sides are not equal. What quadrilateral am I? ____________

16. Name all of the quadrilaterals in the picture at the right.

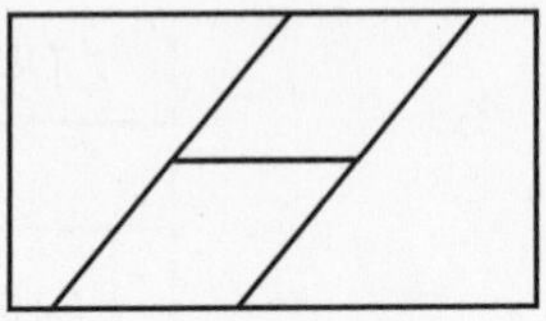

17. Reasoning Why is the quadrilateral on the right a parallelogram, but not a rectangle?

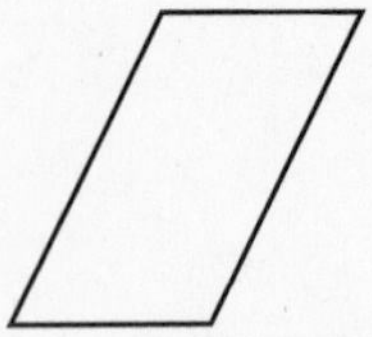

© Pearson Education, Inc.